THE
BUSINESS
OF
INNOVATION

THE
BUSINESS
OF
INNOVATION

MANAGING THE CORPORATE
IMAGINATION FOR MAXIMUM RESULTS

ROGER BEAN AND RUSSELL RADFORD

AMACOM
AMERICAN MANAGEMENT ASSOCIATION
NEW YORK • ATLANTA • CHICAGO • KANSAS CITY • SAN FRANCISCO • WASHINGTON, D. C.
BRUSSELS • MEXICO CITY • TOKYO • TORONTO

This publication is designed to provide accurate and authoritative information in regard to the subject matter covered. It is sold with the understanding that the publisher is not engaged in rendering legal, accounting, or other professional service. If legal advice or other expert assistance is required, the services of a competent professional person should be sought.

Library of Congress Cataloging-in-Publication Data

Bean, Roger
    The business of innovation : managing the corporate imagination for maximum results / Roger Bean, Russell Radford.
        p. cm.
        Includes bibliographical references and index.
        ISBN 0-8144-0631-9
        1. Knowledge management. 2. Organizational change. 3. Intellectual capital. I. Radford, Russell W. II. Title.

HD30.2 .B43 2001
658.4'06—dc21   *2001027948*

Printing number

10 9 8 7 6 5 4 3 2 1

CONTENTS

PREFACE

THE CAPACITY TO INNOVATE IS the source of a company's enduring strength. Ultimately, innovation is a company's source of value. This aptitude for innovation and improvement is nothing less than a direct reflection of the organization's ability to change, to adapt to new and competent competitors, to skillfully fit its products and services to the ever-evolving needs of customers. The innovative organization, by its wits, frequently survives, continues, and succeeds. It's hard to imagine a witless organization as being innovative.

Innovation is nothing less than the wellspring of a company's future. The organization bereft of innovation, creativity, and ingenuity is an organization on the way down. It may take a long time to exit the stage of commerce completely, but surely it forfeits any claim to a bright and vibrant future.

Why then is the quality of innovation so elusive? Why do managers find commercially successful innovation so difficult? Why, as consumers, are we so delighted when we find the occasional spark emerging from that well-designed product, from an efficiently proffered service or skillfully crafted structure, but then unthinkingly accept mediocrity each day? Why aren't all companies innovative or at least actively developing their creative competence?

SEEKING ANSWERS TO OUR QUESTIONS

OVER THE PAST twenty-five years, we have been working with many companies and have been separately drawn to these same questions. It comes down to the following: Why do some companies find it so difficult to achieve an acceptable level of innovation? A corollary question also asserts itself: Why do those companies that do generate a high degree of innovation often find it difficult to profit from their creativity? Why do many innovations fail to become commercially successful? More to the point, how do organizations stimulate high levels of useful creative activity and realize the market rewards from their own creativity? How any company can be more innovative, more creative, and ultimately more successful is the focus of this book.

There is a genre of business books that seeks to encourage us to greater innovation through the anecdotal recitation of how company after company supposedly achieved success. They basically say, "Just look at these companies. Don't you wish you had thought of that?" The message is: "Be like them, and your problems will be solved." These books seem to be in constant demand, some achieving remarkable heights. Yet if one were to track the companies featured in these books ten years later, one would find that invariably, many have fallen on hard times. If these organizations really had so much to teach us, wouldn't they still be leading their industries?

Surely, aping another's success begs the issue. Were these companies' success the result of luck or skill? Were they brilliant or just in the right place at the right time? If their success was truly because of skill or proprietary insights, would these companies not still be setting the pace? We think they would. One good decision or lucky guess does not make for a successful company over time. We have never met a CEO who was able to turn his company around by reading an anecdotal account of another company. It takes more than mindless imitation to innovate successfully and repeat that success time after time. But then, in humans, hope springs eternal. The appeal of the magic sword is strong, so we continually search for the new Excalibur.

Magic swords are not the answer to business success. Instead, this book examines commercial innovation, its creation, and most important, its management. We will introduce you to a model to guide that management of creative innovation. The model flows throughout the book as we explore the various elements of managing innovation, since we rely heavily on a systems approach to managing this fragile and powerful organizational asset.

Our approach to managing innovation is driven by three beliefs:

1. Innovation matters.

2. Management matters.

3. Strategy is the key enabler.

THE LEARNING ACHIEVED

WHAT HAVE WE learned over the past twenty-five years, and what conclusions have we reached? We arrived at the inescapable conclusion that failure to achieve innovation and then bring that innovation to the marketplace is the direct result of not one but several factors. The causes of these failures span the breadth and depth of the organization and cry out for more than piecemeal fads to remedy them. Replacing one broken brick in a 40-foot wall does little to improve the wall's overall stability. We will demonstrate why unexpected, random innovation can only occasionally be exploited and why such random innovation often just wastes resources that could be better used elsewhere. It is heartening to have employees and management alike contributing ideas, but unfocused innovation can be a costly distraction. Corporate focus can become the unintended casualty—the collateral damage of random innovation in an environment of poor strategic alignment.

We postulate that focused and directed innovation is not only possible but produces results consistently superior to any other method. (Despite our belief, it is obvious that many companies find it arduous to focus their innovation investment successfully—their strikeouts far exceed their home runs.) We apply our combined experience in product development, operations management, corporate strategy, and managing innovation-intense projects to show how the interaction of these elements works to either stimulate or repress a general level of useful innovation.

Whether or not an innovation goes on to produce market success depends on multiple factors. The situation is most often described in a linear fashion, but real life is more circular than linear. The different factors involved each affect the other in ways that cannot be understood in a linear way. It's one of the most common reasons things don't work out the way we think they should. It is, in essence, a systems problem. The discipline of systems thinking was developed to explain and describe precisely the kind of situation found in managing innovation. It is a circular situation where one element feeds another, which in turn loops back to influence the first. Linear thinking usually misses important relationships by oversimplifying central issues. We will seek to unravel at least a little of this apparent enigma and make it clear how your company can more effectively manage innovation.

In doing so, we will travel some territory previously visited by authorities in the fields of natural science, systems thinking, psychology, and history to bring you the key background elements that influence innovation. We will introduce an integrated view of innovation, the management of innovation, and the commercialization of innovation. We combine key elements in ways you have probably not seen before to make the management of innovation more intelligible and hence more successful.

In our earlier book, *Powerful Products* (AMACOM, 2000), we proposed an integrated approach for the development of successful new products. We showed how the three elements of customer selection (through market segmentation), strategy, and the development process interact synergistically to produce successful new products time after time. Obviously, innovation is an important part of new product development, and we touched on the subject there. But innovation is a larger topic than we felt we could do justice to in that volume. Innovation plays (or should play) a role in all areas of a company, not just product development. Thus, we chose to address innovation separately, in a volume devoted to the subject. This is that book.

The title of this book—*The Business of Innovation: Managing the Corporate Imagination for Maximum Results*—implies that innovation is serious business, and indeed it is. Any organization seeking to prosper must be capable of innovation. Frequently, innovation is thought of as "research" or R&D, and certainly innovation is central to success in these areas. Applied research, however, is directed research. It is research targeted at a specific application. Managed innovation is innovation directed by corporate strategy, by corporate intent. It is directed to achieving a specific market result. Yes, it is easier said than done, but it is indeed achievable, and without extreme sacrifice either. It is a different perspective, a different way of seeing the innovation process and investment. But it works, time and again.

ORGANIZATION OF THE BOOK

THIS BOOK FOLLOWS the general process of innovation. The first two chapters set the stage for developing the model. Chapter 1 states the strategic impetus for innovation and the basic creative process on which the innovation process builds. Chapter 2 builds a systems foundation, important as the basic means of understanding and modeling the dynamic system—which describes any innovative business.

Chapter 3 introduces the model for managing innovation, and the next four chapters look at elements of the first cluster of activities in the model: nurturing innovation. Chapter 4's focus is nurturing innovation in general. Chapter 5 discusses purposive innovation, on which any company intent on being innovative should be focused. Chapter 6 is concerned with developing the capacity to innovate and the many forms of capacity the innovative company needs if innovations are to be successful. Structuring the innovative organization is the focus of Chapter 7.

The next four chapters deal with focusing and supporting market-focused innovation. Chapter 8 looks at organizational policies and innovation, noting how easy it is for policies to thwart the innovative drive of individuals and the organization itself. In Chapter 9 we think about leveraging logic, noting in particular how errors in logic can sidetrack innovation. Serendipity is the focus of Chapter 10, and we see that there is a real need to effectively manage what we stumble upon. And in Chapter 11 the topic is measuring and evaluating innovations and the innovation process. In any system, feedback loops are important, and carefully selected evaluation processes and measures provide us with effective feedback.

In the last major section of the book, we spend three chapters looking at the physical innovation process. Chapter 12 examines developing and launching innovations, and Chapter 13 concentrates on exploiting innovations after launch. The Internet has played a major role in commerce and competition in recent years, and Chapter 14 looks at how innovation and the management of innovation may be changing right now as a result of the Internet and the dot-com phenomenon.

Chapter 15 is the last chapter, and in it we look forward. We don't see anything clearly, but we do see a couple of trends that might shape where we are going. First, we see a lot of instability, and where there is instability there is opportunity. But you have to be nimble to take advantage, so we consider how to be nimble and manage in this transition period. The other trend we see is toward smallness and understanding fundamental elements of systems. This draws us to thinking about that most fundamental element of social organizations: the individual. Any developments in the practice of innovation are going to take place in systems in which the individual is the focus. This turns earlier thoughts on purposive innovation on its head and seems to offer a whole new and exciting focus for this strategically important pursuit: crafting the organization of tomorrow.

Acknowledgments

W E WOULD LIKE TO EXTEND our very special thanks to the many people who gave generously of their time and expertise. Of the many folks who contributed to our understanding of the management of innovation, several deserve special recognition. Steve James, Joey Klappman, Ed McMahon, Mike O'Sullivan, Jane Reardon, George Simons, Tim Stern, Peter Watson, and Terry West deserve our gratitude for sharing their experience and wisdom. A posthumous thanks goes to Bruce Finlayson, who sadly passed away shortly after our interview. He was a friend, a thinker, an industrial designer, and much more. He will be missed. Thanks again to Frank Bacon and Jerry McCarthy for inspiration that innovation can indeed be planned and managed.

We also owe thanks to Adrienne Hickey of AMACOM for her guidance and assistance. Mike Sivilli is the magician who guided the book through the production labyrinth. Mike is always cheerful, helpful, capable, and on top of all the details. Thank you, Mike. Thanks also to our copy editor, Jacqueline Laks Gorman, and to our proofreader, Judy Lopatin.

The team that supported the writing of our earlier book, *Powerful Products*, was in place again for this achievement. Wiser and more experienced, but still tolerant, supportive—and bemused. This was again the work of the Gang of Four. Lynnette and Debra, we owe you the greatest debt of all.

THE
BUSINESS
OF
INNOVATION

CHAPTER ONE

THE STRATEGIC IMPETUS FOR INNOVATION

SOME 59 MILLION YEARS AGO, a solitary triceratops pushed slowly through the heavy foliage of what is now southern Montana. She was beautiful—or she would have been to a male triceratops. At 26 feet long, with three prominent horns and weighing in at a svelte 20 tons, she was as desirable as a triceratops could be. But there were no male triceratops left. She was the last dinosaur, the very last of a great multitude of similar species that had roamed the earth for 140 million years. We don't know whether she died of old age, disease, or loneliness. But she died nevertheless, and there were no more.

Paleontologists tell us that dinosaurs vanished because their environment changed. They are not sure exactly what changed, but something changed, and these seemingly invincible animals were unable to adapt and perished. There were, however, some exceptions. Many paleontologists believe that birds were almost certainly evolved from the small bipedal dinosaurs of the Jurassic era. These creatures did change. They were able to adapt. They were able to evolve.

In the natural world, evolution is a continuous process. There are currently 2 million species sharing our fragile blue sphere, but over the past 600 million years, some 2 billion species have lived and evolved. Of all the species that have ever lived, today, 99.9 percent are extinct.

The natural environment changes, and business organizations share an environment of similar continuous change. The economy, political and legislative requirements, competition (both domestic and global), and technology are all advancing at an uncomfortable pace. The organization is itself also changing. It evolves each day through changes in personnel, knowledge, customer base, and stockholder value. And as with the natural world, many businesses also become extinct. The companies that survive and prosper are the ones that are continually changing in ways that favor their continued survival.

Every business will adapt, or it will disappear. The key to survival and vitality is innovation. The way to premium profits is innovation. Peter Drucker once wrote that innovation is the only thing that will support a premium price. We agree. The stairway to a successful future is a continuing series of creative improvements.

THE BUSINESS OF INNOVATION

OVER THE PAST quarter-century, we have worked with a variety of companies. Some were innovative, successful, and vibrant. More were innovative only when necessity demanded it, though most were able to "get along" okay. A few found innovation difficult, troublesome, and expensive. But none had found a way to successfully and consistently manage the innovation gremlin that determines their ultimate survival and prosperity. Perhaps it is more accurate to say that none were content with "their way" for the management of innovation. Even the best—particularly the best—were sure they could do better and in fact were actively seek that better way.

This book is about stimulating, creating, and directing innovation. It's about selecting the best area in which to focus innovation. It's about exploiting unexpected innovations and implementing innovation in ways that result in competitive advantage. It is about the excitement, the confidence, and the vibrant environment that comes with being an innovative organization. In short, it's about managing the ever-evolving successful business.

THREE BIG IDEAS

IN OUR DISCUSSIONS with organizations great and small, we hear three recurring themes, three big ideas that surface again and again. These ideas are omnipresent and powerful beyond their humble countenance. If neglected, these ideas will reduce even the most profitable opportunities to just another mundane day at the office. The ideas are:

1. Innovation matters.

2. Management matters.

3. Strategy is the key enabler.

Let's look at the three big ideas.

INNOVATION MATTERS

IN VIRTUALLY EVERY case, our discussions with managers and employees alike identify innovation as an essential ingredient to future success. After all, every organization innovates to some degree. For some, innovation takes the form of creative and successful new products. Others rely on innovative solutions for achieving cost reduction and higher quality service. Still others see innovation as the source of competitive advantage to secure greater market share. At every level, conscientious members of the corporate family see innovative ways to help the organization prosper. Innovation matters—and it matters to everyone.

Why does innovation matter? It matters because when organisms fail to adapt, they die out—corporate organisms included. In the natural world of the triceratops and the bird, evolution helps each organism to survive by producing alternatives and mutations, some of which are better suited to their environment, and thus they go on. Innovation is the organizational equivalent of evolution. Without a continuous flow of innovative energy, the organization is sluggish, if it can change at all. It is vulnerable to changes in its environment, usually from competition but maybe from legislation or technology. The organization does not shape events. Instead, events act upon the organization. It is at the mercy of outside elements, and it is vulnerable. A vulnerable organization may not survive. It surely will not prosper. It is ripe to become a dinosaur.

Management fads of the past several decades, whether or not they satisfied the promises made for them, all depended upon innovation for success. Reengineering asked us for radical redesign of our business processes to achieve dramatic improvements. Was this not a call for innovation? In fact, to the extent that reengineering succeeded, it was because of the innovation it inspired. Total quality management asked everyone in the enterprise to take an active role in continuous-process improvement. TQM is an enterprisewide application of kaizen, the Japanese idea of "everybody improving everything all the time." How does this come about if not by innovation, by everybody?

Another recent management fad, quality function deployment (QFD), is a technique used for analyzing customer needs and relating them to specific actions that will satisfy those needs. It is certainly a useful methodology, but aren't the specific actions that will satisfy those needs the product of someone's innovation?

When an organization adopts a strategy of value stream reinvention (VSR), it seeks to identify current and potential "value streams." The purpose of each value stream is to provide specific results for a customer (either internal or external), thus making that customer as satisfied as possible. The goal of VSR is to reinvent the value stream to meet those customer needs in the most simple and direct manner. How would one go about doing so in the absence of innovation?

Innovation matters because it is all around us. Every enterprise depends on innovation to a much greater degree than it may recognize. Success without innovation is almost inconceivable. Success over an extended period becomes impossible. The reality is that it is not enough just to survive. The vibrant organization must *prosper*. For this organization, innovation is not negotiable.

WHAT IS INNOVATION?

Webster's New Unabridged Dictionary defines the noun *innovation* as the "introduction of new things or methods." The same dictionary defines the verb *to innovate* as "to make something new or to make changes in anything established." While this is a concise and accurate definition, it certainly fails to capture the flavor and energy of innovation as normally envisaged in business. The official definition may be bland and neutral, but when innovation is mentioned in business circles, it often takes on a reverence approaching piety and virtue.

There are many ways of defining innovation. For most people, though, innovation is something good. But is innovation *always* good? Are there—just maybe—some situations when innovation is counter-productive, or at least not particularly helpful? We find that occasionally innovation can be a two-edged sword, a kind of commercial version of the sword of Damocles, signifying impending disaster. For instance, take the case when implementation of an important new program is nearly complete, and someone proposes an innovative new way to achieve still better results. What if this improvement would delay implementation of the program another six months? Is this new proposal helpful? It may be innovative, but it may not be appropriate.

In every sizable organization, there are many folks who are unaware of the goals or strategies being pursued. When the goals are unclear, these folks are the first to find themselves out on a limb and out of the mainstream of directed activity. Would it not be preferable to communicate clearly as to when innovation is useful so every one of us can recognize when our ideas support corporate goals and when such ideas are most helpful? The word *appropriate* is a good fit here. When is an innovation appropriate and when is it inappropriate?

Introducing the concept of commercial relevance (think of it as appropriate innovation) fits our concept of applied strategy—that is, strategy harnessed to the task of focusing innovation. Frank Bacon defines *invention* as the solution to a problem.[1] He defines *innovation* as the commercially successful use of the invention. It's an important and useful distinction, pointing out that invention is not, by itself, necessarily commercially important. Take the case at Xerox. Xerox's Palo Alto Research Center (PARC) has been responsible for some of the most significant inventions of the past thirty years. For example, UNIX came from the PARC laboratories, as did the graphic user interface (GUI) that skyrocketed the Apple Lisa and Macintosh computers to stardom. The mouse, now a standard fixture on Windows computers as well as Macintoshes, is also a PARC invention. But it was Apple that brought it to market and put one on every desk. Xerox had the inventions, but it did not commercially and successfully make use of them. It invented, but it did not innovate.

As this is being written, in early 2001, there is considerable comment in the press on Xerox's performance and future. The company has failed to impress Wall Street that it can innovate in ways that will prove sufficient to guarantee a healthy and profitable future, and its stock price is taking a beating. This icon of corporate success finds itself at an important and challenging crossroads.

The Xerox case shows that invention in itself, even brilliant invention, does not ensure commercial success. It is not enough. In the examples given above of Xerox's inventions, none were commercialized or exploited by Xerox. Innovation, on the other hand (as Frank Bacon defines it, as the "commercially successful use of the invention"), can produce monumental commercial gain.

Because of its more humble origins, innovation can seem deceptively simple. Jacques Barzun puts it this way:

> Technology, or more exactly *techne*, the practical arts . . . came earlier and was for a long time the foster mother of science. The working inventions of the mechanic, who fiddles to improve his tools, accumulate into large aids to science. We are not used to the reverse effect: so-called pure science finds some new principle and applied science—engineering—embodies it in a device for industry or domestic use. That is why industry devotes part of its profits to research and development, an innovation that dates only from 1890.[2]

As Barzun points out, organized R&D (innovaton) is relatively recent. Even what today passes for organized research still relies heavily on the tinkering and fiddling of talented individuals. With the skyrocketing costs of research today, we can and we must find ways to ensure that our efforts are relevant.

MAKING INNOVATION RELEVANT

Innovation can take place in the product, obviously, but there can be equally significant gains from innovation in promotion, sales, pricing, support services, or distribution. Developing a better way to get the product to the user can be an enormous innovation. Amazon.

com began as an electronic bookstore, but Jeff Bezos saw it as an electronic bookstore with a vision and a strategy. Hence, Amazon today is much more than just an online bookstore.

Commercial relevance is realized most visibly in the direct support of the strategic goals of the organization. If it's this simple, why do so many companies find innovation—relevant innovation—so difficult to achieve? Having a strategy to guide what is appropriate is a big help. Exactly what is appropriate is determined by three factors: (1) whether the idea supports the strategic direction, (2) the company's current structure, and (3) whether the innovation is within the company's capacity. Let's look at the three factors.

The first, of course, is whether the innovative idea supports the company's strategic direction outlined in the corporate vision. Alignment begins here. Effort that does not directly support the chosen strategic direction is wasted.

The second factor is equally important: How is your company currently structured? What are its prevailing cultural beliefs, values, and behaviors, which all determine its ability to innovate successfully? Culture is central to capabilities. Some companies (like 3M or DuPont) are organized specifically to take maximum advantage of a continuous stream of inventions. Such companies conjure the image of a marketing department perched like a hungry hawk atop the corporate fence post overlooking the mouse hole of R&D—ready to pounce on innovations as they emerge. Not all companies are able to capitalize on every opportunity that may emerge—certainly not immediately, and maybe not at all. If your company has historically been a risk-averse, plodding leader in a gentlemanly and mannered industry, it will take more than publishing new slogans and exhorting employees to be creative, and it is unlikely to happen quickly.

A word of caution is needed for companies that historically have not had the freewheeling entrepreneurial verve to capitalize on diverse ideas. Appropriateness may have a very different meaning for a conservative, methodical, risk-averse company than it does for a company more willing to accept risk like Rubbermaid. We are certainly advocates of innovation. (After all, we're writing this book.) But just how companies find their way to innovation differs. Simply deciding to "become innovative" overnight as some pundits seem to advocate appears to us like a great way to waste money, create confusion, and probably fail miserably. Not all companies can afford the basic research approach of a DuPont. They lack the diverse and massive resources 3M can draw on. Not all companies are like 3M or Rubbermaid, geared to produce a continuous flow of new products. Not all organizations *want* to be like 3M or Rubbermaid—nor should they. All companies can certainly learn from these innovators, but ultimately they will have to create their own "best practices."

We need to learn how to identify commercially relevant innovation and how to achieve it consistently. Relevant innovation is specific to each organization and each situation, and appropriate innovation is always commercially relevant. Strategic alignment provides the clothesline from which innovators try to hang their ideas. Strategic alignment provides a focus, a point of departure. But when the truly exceptional breakthrough—the radical innovation—does appear, only genuinely misguided management would ignore it. Management will be at the center of the action, as it should be.

The third requirement for determining what is appropriate is that an innovation must be within the capacity of the organization's resources. If you can't afford it, it's not appropriate. (Note that alliances and joint ventures may well permit an organization to pursue innovation opportunities that may be outside the parties' individual resource limitations.) Creating the capacity for innovation, as we will see later, is a critical management responsibility.

MANAGEMENT MATTERS

MANAGERS AT ALL levels understand that new and effective products and processes are a key to future success. They know that management matters. But the importance of good management is also recognized at the factory workstation, at the reception desk at headquarters, and at the copy center in the basement. These operational folks seldom use the latest technical jargon of management. They don't ponder the next shareholder meeting or concern themselves with Franklin planners or stock options. But they know that management is important since they see the failures as well as the successes of management. Often, they demonstrate their feeling of disappointment by posting Dilbert cartoons on the walls or circulating humorous e-mail messages poking fun at some management faux pas. Management matters, and employees know it too.

There is a disturbing flow of material appearing today that takes a somewhat mean-spirited view of corporate management, at least where innovation is concerned. These pundits often exclaim that management is the problem. They say that management stifles innovation, and that if management would just let the people do what they already know how to do, innovation would flourish. In other words, they think that management should stop managing and that employee innovation is the answer. Can this be the proper view? Is this today's prescription for the innovative company?

We don't think so. A lot of faults can be placed at the doorstep of management, but we think this particular invective is unfair. Senior managers are no less human and seek no less to do a good job than any other employee. We never met a manager at any level who woke up in the morning with the thought, "I think I'll go into the office today and make some stupid decisions." But it's also true that their missteps are more visible and their mistakes more consequential than those of other employees. It's not overmanagement causing a lack of innovation. In most cases, it is the absence of any management at all. Lack of focus is a failure of management. Lack of focus causes lack of alignment, and lack of alignment surely does frustrate and inhibit innovation.

A STRATEGIC MANAGEMENT OBJECTIVE

Innovation should be a strategic objective of management. If it's so important, it should be on the list of objectives. As with any other goal, if there is no planning or priority effort devoted to achieving that objective, it's unlikely to happen. One could fairly argue that it's difficult if not impossible to "plan to be creative." It does sound like an oxymoron—precisely because *managing creativity is not the same thing as planning creativity.* Rather, managing creativity is *providing the capacity and environment for innovation.* The organization must have the capability to innovate, and this is well within the purview of management. Management is responsible for providing the resources and the environment necessary for success, and if innovation is one of those resources, then it's the job of management, because no one else can do it.

The substance of developing a capacity for innovation is discussed in Chapter 6. Suffice it to say here that corporate strategy should address the development of this capacity for innovation, and it most effectively does so when it focuses innovation on the market and on the competitive impact of innovation. When the capacity for innovation is provided, the organization can move to the actual work at hand. The capacity for innovation occurs along one or more of three trajectories:

1. Product innovations

2. Process innovations

3. Management or organizational innovations

The innovation-capable organization is prepared to innovate as and when the situation or opportunity requires and is simultaneously able to pursue routine, small innovations and to envision big or radical acts of creativity. The capacity to innovate in process and product goes far to producing sustainable competitive advantage. But it doesn't stop there.

Management must go on continuously, and organizational innovation must go on continuously. It is no less significant than product innovation or process innovation, and in some cases it is considerably more so. The strategically innovative organization is focused on satisfying the needs of a clearly defined and understood customer group. Thus, the strategically innovative organization is always looking to better serve its customers and actively seeks improvements in all three areas (product, process, and organization). It actively seeks to cultivate the capability to think on many levels at the same time. Make no mistake: It is focused on its goals. But like the bald eagle, it can hunt and fish equally well. Unlike the eagle, however, the truly innovative organization must do more than one thing—here, all three things—at the same time.

The great commanders of history are usually remembered for their battles and their victories. The victories ensured their place in history, but what made the victories possible was their attention to developing the capabilities necessary for victory. Training, logistics, strategy, and equipment are capabilities the commander must create *before* he can win—before he can fight. Given any choice at all, the great generals have always focused on developing the capacity for winning. The great manager, like the great general, is always training for the next battle. The capacity to win doesn't always mean you *will* win.

But without it, you are very likely destined to lose. The best executives follow the example of the great generals in continuously marshaling the necessary capabilities for success.

A ROLE FOR ALL LEVELS OF MANAGEMENT

However, innovation is not only an executive responsibility. All levels of management have an important role in achieving innovation. Individual roles differ, but all levels are necessary. Organizations that do not have alignment through the entire organization find innovation unintentionally stifled in the most unexpected places and for the most surprising reasons. Misalignment causes expensive failures and internal contention. At the very best, a lack of alignment causes frustration and distraction.

Figure 1-1 shows the cascading roles of various levels of management in achieving innovation. Each level is supportive of those above it but also exerts a specific emphasis unique to its own level. The levels shown are intended to be generic and represent the flow of roles rather than specific recommendations for organizing your company.

The challenge of managing innovation may be formidable, but for many organizations it is also urgent. Figure 1-1 reflects our strong feeling that management is an essential part of the "innovation team" and must be included—not pushed out of the way like an unused footstool. The idea of the generic manager who can manage anything in any business has proved disappointing. Managers need to know the specifics about the business they manage. Thus, executives who love their products have a distinct advantage over those who just "manage them" from a distance. Innovations are like children: They benefit from continual nurturing. Many of the key requirements for successful innovation can happen only with management assistance and ap-

FIGURE 1-1. THE ROLES OF ALL LEVELS OF MANAGEMENT IN ACHIEVING INNOVATION.

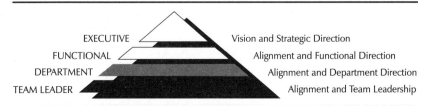

EXECUTIVE	Vision and Strategic Direction
FUNCTIONAL	Alignment and Functional Direction
DEPARTMENT	Alignment and Department Direction
TEAM LEADER	Alignment and Team Leadership

proval. The executive who is always dropping by the research and development department because she is really interested in what they're doing has a distinct advantage. And innovation will benefit because she cares.

STRATEGY IS THE KEY ENABLER

LESS OBVIOUS, PERHAPS, is the role of strategy in creating an environment of innovation. Strategy is the root structure supporting the tree of company action—all action. If the roots are strong, the organization can weather storms of competition and grow yet stronger. In the sturdy oak, nourishment rushes up from the roots, providing what is needed for survival and vitality. That's precisely what strategy is supposed to do for the organization. When the fundamental thinking, the essential business design, and the critical assumptions of the organization are faulty or fuzzy, meaningful activity is obscured by indecision and risk avoidance. And innovation, it seems, is one of the first casualties.

THREE KEY QUESTIONS

There are a number of fundamental questions that have a powerful impact on innovation. Three key questions top the list:

1. Developing the essential business design: *What* should it be?

2. Selection of target markets: *Whom* should we serve?

3. Selection of strategies: *How* should we compete?

What Should It Be?

The business design is nothing less than your vision, your perspective on the business you've chosen. How does the company generate revenue, create value, and provide profits? At its pithiest, most minimalist essence, this is your mission statement.

Whom Should We Serve?

Every business chooses its customers. It has that right—in fact, that obligation—to select those customer segments it wishes to serve. (We acknowledge that there are some legal limitations for some industries, particularly those pertaining to nondiscrimination, but in our view these do not detract from the point.) Why then do so many companies find it so difficult to define their precise target markets? We suggest that the answer lies generally in our instinctive inclination not to turn away any customer we think may want to buy our products or services. Some very large and sometimes successful companies are extremely vague about precisely what customers (market segments) they mean to serve. Down deep we'd all like to do everything for everybody. We would like to have everyone queuing up to pay us money.

But alas, this well-intentioned inclusiveness immediately begins to work against the clarity necessary for effective and efficient action across the organization. Somewhere, there may be a company that can do everything well for every potential customer, but we've yet to see one. Until we do, we'll continue to advocate that the selection of target markets is one of the most important strategic decisions management ever makes. When the remainder of the company is unclear about whom the company is supposed to be satisfying, people will make assumptions. They will look around for patterns, and they will find them (or create them). They will "fill in the blanks" so they can do their job. It is the inevitable result that many of the assumptions, many of the perceived patterns—though well-intentioned—will be wrong.

Innovation then becomes crippled because many ideas and products will be rejected. The proponent of the idea will not understand why it is being rejected. It sounded like a great idea to her, and she probably invested a lot of psychological capital in the idea. However, when formal guidance is weak, innovators are forced to guess at what will be an acceptable idea. Many may try, but with predictable results of guessing incorrectly.

How Should We Compete?

Selection of strategies revolves around the four "Ps" first popularized by E. J. McCarthy in the 1960s. According to McCarthy, the primary tools for the execution of corporate strategy are product, price, place (distribution), and promotion. When strategy is undefined, or when it's unclear how the company intends to compete in its target markets, people are again forced to guess at the daily decisions they need to make. One employee is competing on the basis of lowest price, the next on product availability, another on superior quality, and yet another on superior service. Each thinks he is doing the right thing, and each has some reasonable basis for thinking so. When the people making these inconsistent decisions are the sales department, the design department, or manufacturing, the outcome is always trouble.

THINKING AND DOING

Focus, alignment, clarity, purpose, and shared vision all flow directly from strategic thinking. When insufficient time is devoted to strategy, we invariably see the result in inconsistent day-to-day decisions that confuse, frustrate, and ultimately discourage even the most loyal members of the corporate family. Each of these three management decisions (business design, selection of target markets, and development of strategy) is in itself an innovative act. The executive group is creating something that was not there before. Their creativity becomes evident in the success and effectiveness of their decisions. Innovation is every bit as important in the boardroom as it is in the design department. Innovation is not just something everybody else does: It is what executives do too. At least, it is what the successful ones do.

Securing the alignment of the organization with its organizational goals and strategies is virtually impossible unless those goals and strategies are skillfully crafted. When goals and strategies are haphazard or unconvincing, or evidence shouts that they are not working in the marketplace, employees try to construct better guidelines to focus their personal work or that of their department, etc. Then, working at cross-purposes becomes the norm. There seems to be no apparent solution as people work harder, and longer, and to less effect.

As noted earlier, the process of managing innovation begins with the strategic plan. The overarching policies and strategies of the company, as indicated in the plan, establish and sustain the environment for innovation. Those few key strategic decisions will determine a great deal of whatever success is achieved by the organization. Some strategies are set out clearly in the official strategic plan and distributed for employees to see. Other strategies are only implied and thus are subtler (insofar as everyone thinks they understand what the boss wants done but may not know for sure). In either event, the official plan sets the tone for innovation within the company. Innovation always means changes in thinking and/or changes in methods. Whether the organization changes willingly or goes kicking and screaming is determined both by the stated strategies (of the company's strategic plan) and by the unstated but implicit strategies as people *think* they understand them.

The "mental models" held by management have a major influence on both the strategies and the environment for innovation. Mental models are basic assumptions or "mind maps" as owned and implemented by individuals. These models are extremely powerful and go a long way to explaining individual behavior, since we are very much a product of our beliefs and our assumptions. When the mental models of management presume employees to be lazy, stupid, dishonest, or otherwise less than managers see themselves, innovation will not come easily. Neither will it come easily to an organization conservatively managing to preserve the status quo. Timidity is another enemy of innovation. The lesson here? That the manager's strategic obligation is a serious one indeed.

THE CREATIVE PROCESS: WHO ARE THE INNOVATORS?

THE CREATIVE ORGANIZATION enjoys the contributions of many people, many times over, and in diverse situations. It is a healthy organization, an energized organization. It is exciting to watch such a company and even more exciting to be part of such a company. Such an organization develops an unstoppable momentum that competitors find unable to resist. These are the companies that make headlines. These companies often become the icons of Main Street and the darlings of Wall Street.

But where does the creativity come from? Those companies generally thought to be "creative" have somehow learned to attract and encourage creative people. Likewise, they've learned ways to focus their creative talent in productive and powerful directions. These are companies that value "good thinkers" and provide an environment for these treasures to contribute their unique skills. Creative people can be found anywhere in the organization. They are not by any means limited to design, engineering, advertising, or R&D. The organization realizes the greatest benefit when everyone is and feels free to contribute creative solutions to the company's most perplexing issues. Hence, the more candid management is about the real issues, the real goals, and the actual strategy, the more appropriate are the contributions.

The "creative department" is what comes to most people's minds when they think of successful innovation. For simplicity, the model we introduce later implies that this is a neat, compact entity. This is often not the case. Successful innovation—commercially successful innovation—is almost never the sole offspring of some creative department (whatever that may be). Certainly, ideas, concepts, and proposals emanate from the creative departments and individuals in the company, but on their own these talented folks can only dream, create, and propose. Their creative products and ideas must be implemented, and for any sizable product or process, implementation requires approval—and therein lies the rub. Approval requires management involvement.

The creative process is therefore only one key element. The process is, of course, central, but it cannot succeed apart from the strategic and implementing functions that make commercial success possible.

PLANNING TO BE CREATIVE

How does one "plan" to be creative? In a recent book, Robinson and Stern[3] report their findings that the most important creative contributions were usually the unplanned, unofficial, and unsolicited acts of individual employees. Our experience is much the same. Many of the best and most significant creative acts in corporate America are indeed unexpected. However, while it may be accurate that many powerful innovations are unexpected, it is necessary to be structured to exploit both planned and unplanned innovations. It is possible to manage creative acts by focusing effort in strategically important directions, while at the same time simultaneously permit the exploitation of those worthy unplanned and unexpected innovations as they infrequently occur.

Many companies pursue continuous improvement initiatives, including internal innovation. Is it possible that internal innovation (those creative acts that make up a good part of continuous improvement efforts) benefits most frequently from unplanned and unexpected innovation? Surely, these nonstrategic (loosely defined) innovations demand less attention from management. Certainly, they are less distracting than those exerting a powerful impact on product lines, customer selection, and corporate image. But these unexpected innovations in continuous improvement are also most powerful when the innovations support and augment well-conceived plans and strategies.

So, do companies get most of their good innovations from unsolicited and unplanned activities because that method is superior? Or do most innovations come from unplanned activities precisely *because* innovation is left unplanned, by a lapse of management or by default? The answer makes a big difference. Our experience seems to indicate that both propositions are true. The most creative and important ideas may well be unplanned—because no one is actively trying to plan for precisely those innovations the company needs the most.

A SYSTEM OF FOCUSED INNOVATION

WE ARE NOT prepared to abdicate control of the business to fortuitous events. It is because we're not prepared to relinquish guidance of the business or the innovative process that we envision a model of planned/unplanned innovation like the one in Figure 1-2.

In this view we can begin to envision the process as a system. (It's an important point, and it draws on the principles of systems thinking discussed later in Chapter 2.) Figure 1-2 includes a plan wherein management attempts to identify those competitive advantages that would provide the most desirable results—presumably, seeking a sustainable competitive advantage in the marketplace. Solving for this advantage requires creativity and innovation. But this innovation is focused effort directed at a specific goal. This activity is labeled in the figure as "creative project development."

This development activity (which can be any creative problem-solving activity) is sanctioned and funded with the express goal of obtaining some desired result. This is simple goal-directed activity. The concepts, ideas, products, or solutions that emerge from this process must then be implemented if they're to do any good. Once successfully implemented, the plan addresses itself to new issues. This is a planning/action loop.

But there is another loop in this seemingly organized activity. The outer loop acknowledges that good, productive ideas can arise either out of the project work, or separate (unplanned and unrelated) from it. In the figure, this unplanned activity is labeled "unexpected ideas or opportunities." Our system shows, via this feedback loop, how these unplanned ideas are inserted into the planning and sanctioning activity. If they do not get into the management environment, these ideas

FIGURE 1-2. A SYSTEMS VIEW OF FOCUSED INNOVATION.

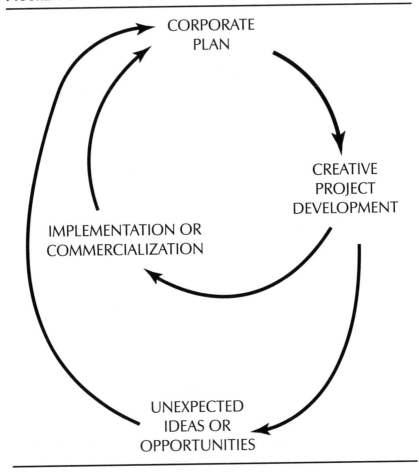

will never get implemented. To get the unplanned ideas into the system for development and implementation, they must eventually be sanctioned and funded (unless they are very small). This outer loop is really a communication loop. It is the vehicle for optimizing our unplanned ideas or opportunities. This loop is how unplanned innovations connect with management. It is how ideas or innovations connect with the implementation process.

As noted earlier, management must be "in the loop" if anything is to get done. Going around management is ultimately counterproductive (despite those occasional examples of someone "cheating the system" and getting away with it). It is infinitely better to fix the system and thus make the process work efficiently. Having everyone trying to cheat the system is seldom much better than pandemonium.

Systems thinking and the use of models like the one in Figure 1-2 are addressed at much greater length in Chapter 2. For the moment, though, we wish only to propose that corporate innovation not be limited to a proposition of either planned or unplanned. It must be both planned *and* unplanned at the same time, and managed via an efficient communication loop.

ALIGNMENT AND INNOVATION

IN THE JARGON of business, the term *alignment* is usually used to indicate the convergence of corporate goals and strategies with the actual efforts and activities of employees. Alignment is a central requirement for stimulating consistently productive innovation in any organization. The question is, though, alignment with what? Certainly not just any old strategy or goal. Aren't there some assumptions that must go along with effective alignment? We think so, and list four such assumptions:

1. That the goals are well founded

2. That each strategy is in fact capable of succeeding

3. That the employees can share the goals

4. That an environment of valued contribution exists

Alignment implies a certain order or consistency. Some order is necessary in all organizations. The rudiments of a shared vision do not have to mean a bureaucratic or authoritarian management style. A shared vision can be found even in organizations that bear little semblance to an ordered universe. In our usage, we simply mean a clear, considered, and powerful direction suitable to being shared by (and in fact, being shared by) most if not all employees. It is difficult, if it's even possible, to get alignment around an ill-conceived and poorly articulated strategy. Employees are never stupid and seldom rally around such a defective strategy. To ensure employee support, we need to cast our net wide enough to make sure that we have a direction worthy of getting alignment in the first place. Once we have a good goal or strategy, it has to be sold to everyone involved. If not, the alignment discussion is wasted. Also, we want to outline specific tools that can help create clear strategies, gain alignment, generate enthusiasm, and provide a stream of innovations that are directly applicable to the business management has chosen (because only management can choose it or change it).

THE ISSUE OF IMPLEMENTATION

Implementation deserves a special place in any discussion of innovation if only for the fact that for any innovation to have commercial impact, it must be implemented and not just developed. Most executives feel that implementation is the hard part. Getting a new product, process, or method out the door requires a cluster of skills that are probably quite different from the talents most valued by the creative department. Implementation demands a great deal of discipline: Persistence, tenacity, focus, and sometimes just plain stubbornness are what actually bring the innovation to market. Most companies earn nothing on their innovations until they are brought to fruition—until they are implemented. More good ideas wither on the vine for want of successful implementation than for any other reason. Poorly conceived ideas and ill-defined innovations only make an already difficult innovation task a lot harder, maybe impossible.

Implementation most often fails for common and familiar reasons:

- Implementation concerns were not considered in the design phase—i.e., design decisions have made the innovation more difficult to implement. Ideally, design decisions should make the product or process easier to implement.

- Midcourse design changes have muddled the original vision to such a degree that coherent implementation is no longer possible.

- Management did not span the entire process. Management might have managed the "road gravel" of the process but failed to maintain the vision. In systems thinking parlance, this is the "Drifting Goals" archetype.

In our model, implementation takes on a major role. Commercial success is about getting it done and not just dreaming it up. Innovation is such an interesting and energizing topic that it is easy to omit the all-important elements of disciplined implementation.

CONTINUOUS EVOLUTION

RETURNING TO OUR case of the triceratops that opened this chapter, she had simply run out of choices. After 140 million years of carefree existence, her line was to end. She really had no choice because the opportunity to adapt to her environment was beyond her control. She could do nothing but live out her unfortunate destiny.

But at the dawn of our new millennium, the situation is a lot brighter for us. Adapting to environmental challenges is not beyond our control. No company is compelled to live out the triceratops's unfortunate destiny. Today's enterprise has the power at its fingertips to change and to adapt, and to innovate. We are limited only by our imagination and our creativity. Some competitors make this economic evolution look easy, but most of us discover we have to work at it. Either way, those of us who manage innovation or otherwise contribute to creative adaptation will shape a vibrant and exciting future—or we risk following the triceratops.

SUMMARY

- Innovation is how we keep one step ahead of our environment. Without it, we are always running backward to keep up. Innovation creates competitive advantage.

- There are three big ideas to keep in mind: (1) innovation matters, (2) management matters, and (3) strategy is the key enabler.

- Inappropriate innovation can be distracting. Keep your eye on the ball without losing sight of opportunity.

- Management is a key member of the innovation team. Members of management are innovators too.

- Management sets the tone for innovation, creates a fertile environment, and ensures alignment with company strategy.

- Routine and continuous innovations are easier to achieve, but less dramatic in effect.

- Radical and discontinuous innovations can be vastly more powerful, but are also more risky and more difficult.

- A systems view of innovation includes both the unplanned and the planned elements of the innovation process.

Notes

1. Frank R. Bacon and Thomas W. Butler, *Achieving Planned Innovation* (New York: Free Press, 1998).

2. Jacques Barzun, *From Dawn to Decadence* (New York: HarperCollins, 2000).

3. Alan G. Robinson, *Corporate Creativity* (San Francisco: Barrett-Koehler, 1997).

PART ONE

THE BUSINESS
OF INNOVATION

CHAPTER TWO

THE MIRACLE OF SYSTEMS

SPARSE SNOWFLAKES COASTED ON THE sharp wind of a December 16 evening. The familiar seaport odor hung in the air, commingled with the wood smoke of a thousand fireplaces, night soil, and garbage. The waterfront was a hard place, and it was cold. But the men who crowded Boston's Congress Street were not cold. They were heated, loud, and single-minded. These passionate but responsible men would not be swayed from their purpose. A full-blown protest was under way, and the fire showed no sign of burning out soon.

Taxes were as polarizing a topic in 1773 as they are today—more so, even—but in Colonial America, no avenues remained for peaceful disagreement. The citizens of Boston represented the extremes of colonial politics: loyal supporters of the King, on one hand, and the radicals known as the Sons of Liberty led by Samuel Adams, on the other. And, no mistake, Adams's fingerprints were on the civil disorder this night.

The crowd roared, taunted, and shouted epithets against the King and his minister, Lord North. These men were angry, and some were drunk. The crowd was intent on having its message heard clearly in the Parliament. Quite beyond the madness of the moment, there was a feeling of having been betrayed by their King and his ministers, who seemed to regard them as property of the crown rather than free men in loyal service of their King.

The object of their anger tonight was tea, East India Company tea. Parliament had canceled the hated Townshend Acts, retaining only the duty on tea, to demonstrate its unlimited right to tax the colonies. The Tea Act was supposed to bolster the faltering East India Company by granting, among other things, a monopoly on all tea exported to the colonies. A haughty, uninformed, and unconcerned Parliament was incapable, it seemed, of civil behavior toward England's loyal, if thin-skinned, colonies.

Emerging from the crowd, cheered on by the shouts of angry neighbors, about sixty patriots rushed toward three ships loaded with tea, the *Beaver*, the *Dartmouth*, and the *Eleanor*. In a matter of minutes, these odd-looking men, clad in blankets and feathers, overpowered the sparse ships' watches and cast the much-prized cargo over the side. Soon, 342 boxes of tea were steeping in the cold, filthy saltwater of Boston harbor. There would be no duty paid on this shipment.

Such were the makings of history. Such were the workings of the English colonial system. It was a system of complex relationships and distant reach, a system strained to the limit and on the brink of catastrophic failure. At this moment, the system was providing feedback to its King and his Parliament, but the feedback was being ignored. Well, not ignored, actually. Rather, the mother country's response was reprisal in the form of the Intolerable Acts of 1774. The system was spinning irretrievably toward revolution.

Had the King had the benefit of today's understanding of the behavior of complex systems, he might have redesigned his colonial system to work more smoothly. He might have repaired the damage and put things to right. He might still *have* a colonial system.

SYSTEMS THINKING

BUT THE KING and his ministers had no knowledge of complex systems. Unfortunately for them, the discipline of systems thinking is relatively new. Systems thinking pretty much began in 1948, when Norbert Wiener published a book called *Cybernetics* (MIT Press, 1948). Both the name *cybernetics* and the formation of the discipline itself can be traced to this work. (Actually, our choice of 1948 as the beginning of systems thinking is not entirely accurate. The earliest work in systems has its roots in early 20th-century biology, but Wiener's book is usually thought of as the beginning of systems thinking as we know it.) Some of the most important discoveries in the field of systems thinking can be traced back to only the mid-1980s. Anyone who did graduate work in business in the 1970s probably heard not a single word about the amazing and powerful field of systems thinking.

It's really only been since 1990, when Peter Senge's best-selling *The Fifth Discipline* brought the principles of systems thinking to the business press, that the business community has taken up the topic to any appreciable degree.[1] Prior to this time, most of the work in systems thinking had been applied to areas other than business organizations (mostly scientific and technical). It's hard to overstate the inherent power of the shift or the significance for business organizations. However, despite Senge's best-seller, systems thinking has still not found the common acceptance it deserves.

Our treatment here will be brief and is by no means complete, but we hope it will be enough to encourage you to seek out more detailed material for study. The Bibliography lists some of the more approachable sources for those wishing to continue their study of this powerful tool. For now, let's talk a little about what systems thinking is.

A WORLD OF SYSTEMS

SYSTEMS ARE IMPORTANT because we live in a world of systems. Tiny systems are nested inside small systems that are nested inside larger systems, which are in turn nested inside really large systems, which are in turn nested inside enormous systems. Everything, from subatomic particles to the earth's ecosystem, behaves according to the basic principles of systems. If that's not sufficient reason to be interested, what is?

Our focus here is specifically innovation and how it can be more mindfully managed to contribute to the vitality and dynamic health found in the best business organizations. Healthy and dynamic organizations are creative, continuously reinventing themselves and their products and processes to better serve customers. Innovative behavior is, at its root, creative behavior. At whatever level of magnitude the innovation occurs, the innovator is bringing forth some thing or idea that did not exist before. And creative behavior is integrated behavior, carefully woven into the web of the larger system. Even if innovation took place on a desert island with only one human being present, the innovation would still have been sparked by some interaction with the environment, some need, stimulus, or perceived application. As such, creative behavior is complex behavior.

Business organizations are complex systems. The systems related to the management of innovation are complex systems, and systems thinking is currently our most formidable tool for explaining this kind of behavior. If we pursue this line of thought, we can conclude that innovation is a specialized, particular, and fragile system that requires conscious nurture, careful management, and continuous encouragement if it is to thrive.

THE IMPORTANCE OF INTERRELATEDNESS

SYSTEMS THINKING REQUIRES that we take a different view of the world. Sir Isaac Newton provided us with a vision of the world that consisted of "parts." In Newton's view, we could study and understand any entity by first dissecting the object of analysis into its parts, then subjecting each individual part to rigorous examination. Scientists and philosophers spent the next two hundred years breaking our world up into parts and analyzing each part in an effort to understand how the larger entity "works." We have learned a lot. Unfortunately, though, it became an article of faith that anything and everything could be understood by this mechanical approach of division and analysis. However, not everything can be understood in this way.

Recently, this mechanical approach to understanding our world has been recognized to be incomplete. Our long love affair with the study of "parts" has given way, in some cases at least, to the study of "the whole." From subatomic physics to the study of biology to the study of manufacturing processes, we have come to understand that studying parts is insufficient if we wish to understand even the most common behaviors and things that surround us.

A central feature of a system is its integrity. In a collection of parts, one can simply remove one or two and still have a collection of parts, or a heap. Not so with the system. If you remove one element, the system is irrevocably changed. If you divide a system in two, you do not get two smaller systems. You get one damaged system, and it probably won't function. Likewise, it makes no difference to the heap or pile of parts how they are organized. Organize them any way you want, and you still have a heap or pile of parts. It is distinctly not so with a system. In a system, the organization of the elements is critical to the nature and function of the system. Finally, the behavior of a system depends on *how* the parts are connected, the specific relationship between them. The behavior of the pile depends on the size of the pile for its behavior, if there is any behavior at all. A pile of auto parts will not function as an automobile, but will do little apart from permitting bacteria to migrate from one to another.

In a marvelous and magnificent way, researchers are finding that the interrelatedness of the parts is what actually drives the myriad systems within which we live and work. It seems that everything is connected to something else in an apparently endless web of relationships, and understanding, predicting, and managing such "systems" requires both a different view (that the parts are all connected) and a suitable tool or theory to guide our action. Systems theory is currently the best tool available.

We have a long and glorious business tradition of oversimplifying complex relationships and tinkering with the parts while the whole disintegrates. If we are to manage innovation successfully, we have to incorporate a comprehensive understanding of the interrelatedness of our systems and learn to pass on the quick fix, the apparently obvious common wisdom that often asserts itself in the urgency of the moment. We need to look for the connections, the feedback loops and the relationships in our system—our organization.

FEEDBACK LOOPS: THE KEY TO UNDERSTANDING SYSTEMS

AT ITS SIMPLEST, a system is a collection of related elements that must function in concert to achieve a desired result. This definition can be enhanced by adding that a system also contains one or more feedback loops, which are central to system behavior. Feedback loops permit a system to function in a self-managed, self-sustaining way.

For example, the water-control mechanism in your toilet tank is a simple and highly efficient system. When the tank is flushed, the water goes down and a float descends, turning on the water inlet. As the tank fills, the float rises to its prior height and switches off the inflow of water (feedback). This repeats day after day, year after year, with virtually no attention required. With each flush, we personally experience an effective and well-designed system. In addition, when we push the lever, we even become part of that system.

The human circulatory system also functions according to precisely the same feedback principles. We exert ourselves, and the body calls for more oxygen. The heart speeds up, capillaries expand, and an increased flow of blood delivers the extra oxygen being called for. The respiratory system is similar. When exertion takes place and the body needs more oxygen, the breathing rate accelerates to provide it. When the need declines, the respiration rate slows down again to normal. We are cooled by perspiration in much the same manner. When we overheat, because of exertion or high summer temperature, our body receives the message that we are too hot, and perspiration is then released, cooling us through evaporation.

As yet another example, the sprinkler system in your front yard is similar, differing only in that the feedback device is usually an electric timer. At the determined time, it turns on. Then, when the preset amount of water is delivered (the preset time has expired), it automatically turns off. Some sprinkler systems today also include a sensor to measure rainfall or monitor the moisture in the soil. In both cases, these enhancements are just additional feedback loops in the larger system. Beats standing there watering with a hose.

Just as researchers made great strides in recognizing that the interrelated parts drive systems, they made another key breakthrough with the realization that systems and feedback loops are *circular rather than linear* activities. We have been conditioned for centuries to think in linear patterns, but when our problem is a systems problem, understanding requires us to see things in a circular, balancing, or reinforcing way. For many, this concept is difficult to grasp. However, to truly understand systems, we must overcome our overreliance on cause and effect by first recognizing that things aren't that simple.

Mistakes are virtually guaranteed to occur when we discuss organizational issues and the problems are circular but the logic is linear. Let's look at some related activities frequently encountered when exploring systems. Then we'll return to systems thinking itself.

RELATED DISCIPLINES

SYSTEMS ENGINEERING is a general term referring to the application of engineering skills to the design and creation of a complex system. Any engineer acts as a systems engineer when responsible for the design and implementation of a total system. The major steps in the completion of a major systems engineering project are:

- Arriving at a problem statement

- Identifying objectives

- Generating alternatives

- Analyzing these alternatives

- Selecting one alternative

- Operating the system

Systems engineering principles were developed to create and manage large space and construction projects such as the lunar landing mission. Systems engineering is interesting but is not the focus of our present discussion. In this book we are mainly concerned with social systems—the management of innovation—rather than mechanical systems.

Webster's New Universal Unabridged Dictionary defines a *systems analyst* as someone who conducts the evaluation of an activity to identify its desired objectives and determine procedures for efficiently obtaining them. The systems analyst is commonly encountered in the information technology industry, developing and implementing complex information processing systems. As with systems engineering, systems analysis offers many valuable contributions but is not of primary interest in a discussion of innovation.

Systems thinkers can come from anywhere. The systems thinker has progressed beyond simply seeing events to seeing patterns of interaction, and further to the underlying structures responsible for those patterns. The systems thinker has moved beyond simplistic explanations for complex behavior, but moreover, she has at hand a method for understanding and addressing that behavior. The systems thinker is a valuable asset, and one with many applications.

APPLYING SYSTEMS PRINCIPLES

COMPLEX SYSTEMS, SUCH as a company with thousands of employees, are correspondingly more complicated but actually function according to the same principles as our toilet tank example. For some, this may seem hard to accept. Admittedly, the similarities between AT&T and the toilet tank seem a stretch, but the underlying systems principles are the same—action, feedback, adjustment, action, feedback, adjustment, action, feedback, adjustment, and action again—repeated, over and over again, as often as necessary. Continuously interacting—continuously communicating—continuously adjusting.

The key characteristic of systems thinking and applying it is a fundamental shift in thinking, from a focus on the parts to a focus on the whole. In business school many of us were taught to break problems and opportunities down into pieces on the premise that we "eat an elephant one bite at a time." That sounds good, but it doesn't work in reverse—i.e., we can't take all the bites and reassemble an elephant. What we would get is compost, not a new elephant. And when we cut our elephant in half, we again get compost, not two cute little elephants.

Managers trying to build and grow their organizations have found the same situation. It is more effective to manage the whole. We use the parts, to be sure, but always with both eyes on the whole. Physicist and author Fritjof of Capra says it this way: "Systems thinking is 'contextual,' which is the opposite of analytical thinking. Analysis means taking something apart in order to understand it; systems thinking means putting it into the context of a larger whole."[2]

Systems thinking is an essential tool in the process of understanding organizational behavior. Innovation, and the management of innovation, are clearly organizational behaviors. Analysis of parts is helpful in many problem-solving situations where the parts are the source of the problem and the problem is isolated. But analysis cannot explain how the whole system operates, or how the system should operate, or how the system might be improved.

Figure 2-1 shows a simple system diagram based on Norbert Wiener's example of a steersman to demonstrate the feedback loop. In Wiener's example, the person steering the boat observes his course and notes any deviation from his desired direction. Noting the deviation from course, he countersteers the boat in the opposite direction of the deviation, thus bringing the boat back on course. He again returns to observing the course, and should any deviation remain or a new one occur, the process of countersteering begins again. The boatman thus snakes his way back and forth till he reaches his destination. The process of innovation is often very similar. As we find an answer that moves us forward, we pursue it—we devote resources to it. When an exploration comes to a dead end, we steer back. We add resources to those activities that produce results.

FIGURE 2-1. A SIMPLE SYSTEM DIAGRAM USING WEINER'S EXAMPLE OF A STEERSMAN.

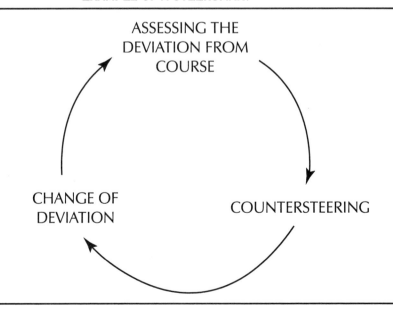

ASSESSING THE
DEVIATION FROM
COURSE

CHANGE OF
DEVIATION

COUNTERSTEERING

Circular system diagrams are useful tools for understanding organizational phenomena. Many of us find visual pictures of such behavior much easier to understand than verbal descriptions.

Let's look at another system diagram in Figure 2-2. Systems researchers have developed a series of "archetypes" to explain commonly encountered situations. Archetypes are generic models that can be applied to a multitude of specific situations. The archetype in Figure 2-2 applies specifically to a perceived deficit of innovation in product development.

In the example, management perceives a problem in the development process for an important new product. Let's say the perceived problem is a lack of ideas about how to solve a difficult technical dilemma. We see two sets of pressures: the first to bring in outside help, and second to develop internal capability. Often, the decision is made to bring in the outside expert—an innovation specialist. The decision

FIGURE 2-2. THE ARCHETYPE OF "SHIFTING THE BURDEN."

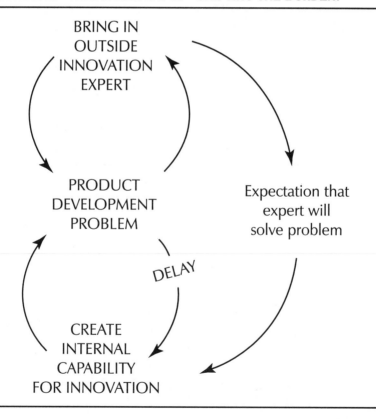

to bring in outside help is justified on the basis of the delay necessary to develop internal capability.

Because we shift the burden to the outside specialist, whether she is successful or not, we have only temporarily addressed the problem. We come right back around to the problem on the next product when a similar situation arises. "Shifting the Burden" is the name of this particular archetype, and it demonstrates that shifting the burden is a temporary solution at best, attractive though it may be at the time. (There are numerous archetypes describing common business problems. We encourage readers to study them and become fluent in their use.)

DEVELOPING A STRUCTURE FOR MANAGING INNOVATION

WE HAVE DEVOTED these early pages to the discipline of systems thinking because we feel it is central to understanding and managing innovative behavior. In Chapter 3, we introduce a model to guide our understanding and structure the discussion throughout the remainder of the book. Simply offering an extended list of "how-to" anecdotes salted with do's and don'ts offers little real help. It is necessary to reach deeper, in this case penetrating the mantle of systems understanding, to find ways to describe and better manage innovative behavior.

SUMMARY

- Systems thinking is a powerful but relatively new and little used tool in the management of business.

- Complex organizations are complex systems that are described accurately by the tools of systems thinking.

- Systems thinking represents a distinct move from analyzing the parts to understanding the whole.

- Feedback loops are the vehicles that permit systems to be self-sustaining and self-managing.

- Innovative organizations are dynamic systems, continually changing. Stable, unchanging systems cannot be innovative. The stable state of equilibrium seeks to preserve stability. It does its best *not* to change, to innovate.

NOTES

1. Peter M. Senge, *The Fifth Discipline* (New York: Currency Doubleday, 1994).
2. Fritj of Capra, *The Web of Life* (New York: Anchor Books, 1997).

CHAPTER THREE

A MODEL FOR MANAGING INNOVATION

THE OLD MAN WAS READING his daily paper. It was the Philadelphia paper, and the news was unremarkable, though indeed, all manner of change was going on. The year was 1784. The old man was Benjamin Franklin.

The remarkable thing about this particular day was not the news in the paper, or even the paper itself, but the ease with which he read it. That morning, he had received a new pair of eyeglasses from his spectacle maker. His old ones had worked pretty well, but at age 77 he was no spring chicken, and the old eyes needed more help.

For some years, Franklin's eyes, never strong, had been causing him trouble when he read a book or letter. He could see at a distance well enough with his old glasses, but they just didn't do the job for reading. He had tried reading glasses but was always changing from one pair to the other, and he was prone to leave the extra pair all over town. He conceived the idea that it would be nice if he didn't have to carry two pairs of glasses, but there seemed no alternative. After all, eyeglasses hadn't changed very much since the Chinese developed magnifying lenses in the 10th century or since Roger Bacon first wrote of spectacles in 1268.

As always, undaunted, Franklin thought, "Why couldn't spectacles have two different lens corrections for each eye?" Why couldn't they be two pair of spectacles in one? It seemed reasonable to this supremely practical statesman. When his ideas on the subject finally solidified, he asked his spectacle maker to try constructing a pair of spectacles with two different lenses for each eye. The skeptical lens grinder patiently and politely listened to the renowned Mr. Franklin, finally agreeing to try constructing the new spectacles along Franklin's design.

This morning he had them in hand, and they worked marvelously. Without giving the achievement second thought, he had invented the first pair of bifocals. It seemed like a logical solution to an obvious problem. Streetlights in the streets, a warm fire from the stove, a lightning rod on the roof providing protection from the storm, a new and independent country—and now a good pair of glasses. Not bad for an old printer.

To see the management of innovation clearly, we also need a little visual help. We need help to structure and organize our challenge in such a way as to handle it effectively. We don't have Ben Franklin to help us clarify the management issues, but we do have a model that suits our needs very well, because we need more than a new pair of spectacles.

SEEING THE CHALLENGE CLEARLY

WHY DO WE need a model to manage innovation? Because the best way to achieve innovation is to understand how it functions, is directed, and is supported. A model helps us understand. It helps us to see the situation more clearly. It's currently popular to exhort managers to promote and encourage creativity, individual performance, and innovation. The search for excellence, the high-performance individual, and the high-energy organization are familiar topics. There is nothing wrong with encouragement—in fact, we totally agree. But few sources approach the question of *managing* the innovative resource.

Behavioral science has contributed immeasurably to our understanding of the factors encouraging and inhibiting organizational innovation. Again, however, the focus is usually not on the *management* of innovation. It is our intention to fill that gap. Thus, the challenge becomes one of structuring a workable approach to the management of innovation. All currently available models either proved inadequate for our purpose or are directed to entirely different behavior. We believe that our model offers much more potential for guiding our explorations into the successful management of innovation in organizations of varying size, complexity, and purpose.

THE INNOVATION MANAGEMENT MODEL

THE INNOVATION MANAGEMENT Model is shown in Figure 3-1. We will discuss each element of the model in detail and see how it is used to manage innovation and improve our performance.

First, some background. Our focus on systems led us to the work of Stafford Beer, who—in the United Kingdom—had begun applying the principles of systems thinking to the management of organizations.[1] Beer pioneered much of the original work in applying systems theory to the structuring of organizations and developed the Viable System Model. The Viable System Model is unique in its insight and power to explain the behavior of organizations of all kinds, but existing literature does not apply Beer's model directly to the management of innovation. With some adaptation, however, we can benefit from the power of this device. Using the basic structure offered by Beer, we approach innovation from the viable system perspective.

First, we need to clarify what we mean by a "viable system." Beer spent many years researching the necessary and sufficient conditions for a complex system (like a business or nonprofit organization) to be *viable*. The "viability" of the system is maintained by managing the various elements of the system together, keeping elements from interfering with each other, and looking to the future with the whole rather than just the parts in mind. A viable system is a solid foundation upon which to build.

Because innovation is vulnerable to so many organizational viruses, only a comprehensive and holistic view can provide the insight necessary to both engender and sustain innovation. The success of the Viable System Model in business, government, nonprofit, and nonor-

FIGURE 3-1. THE INNOVATION MANAGEMENT MODEL.

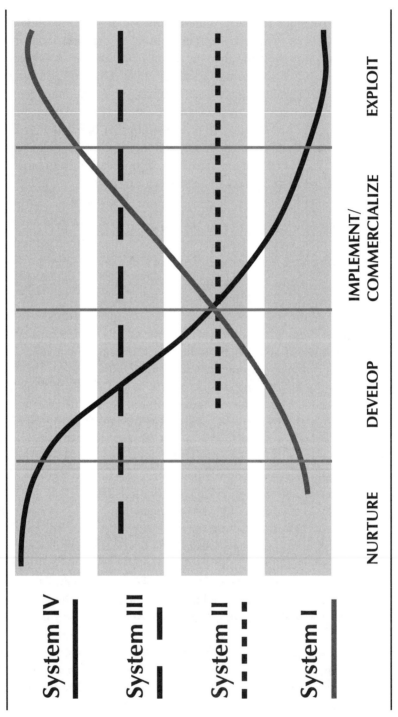

ganizational applications over the past thirty years or so lends credibility to the application of the model to the management of innovation. Only such a panoramic view can offer much help. So let's take a look at our Innovation Management Model and see how it works.

FOUR DIFFERENT SYSTEMS

THE INNOVATION MANAGEMENT Model, shown in Figure 3-1, consists of four levels or subsystems, each of which represents common and necessary elements of the model. The only requirement (and a necessary one) is that System I must produce something of value such that in its own right it could be a viable system. All the other systems (System II, System III, and System IV) exist only to support the teams and groups that make up System I. If System I does not create something of value to its marketplace or society, then there is no purpose for the others—and hence, by definition, no viable system.

Figure 3-2 shows what the four systems levels actually do.

SYSTEM I

System I represents the people who actually get stuff done: the product development teams, process development teams, and manufacturing teams. Some would call it operations, but certainly product development teams or process development teams would fall easily into System I. These are all the nonsupport activities, the line functions.

SYSTEM II

System II supports System I folks with shared resources. A product development team, for instance, is far from self-sufficient. It is an intense user of shared systems and resources—payroll, benefits, information services, PC repair, library resources, copyright services, and legal services, to name only a few. The efficient provision of System II services to System I units is one of the biggest challenges for all organizations. System II is "overhead" and proud of it. System II units make it possible for System I units to actually function in their assigned role. Understanding the relationship of System II to System I is a critical component in the management of innovation. System II is support.

When System II functions find themselves in competition with

FIGURE 3-2. THE FOUR SYSTEMS LEVELS IN THE INNOVATION MANAGEMENT MODEL.

System IV	**Creating the Environment for Innovation**
	• Values • Long-term Goals • Policies • Long-term Strategies • Organizational Character

System III	**The Strategic and Managerial**
	• Command Decisions • Operational Goals • Resource Allocation Decisions • Operational Strategies • Negotiation and Compliance Functions

System II	**Provision of Shared Resources**
	• Legal • Library • Market Research Possibly: • Human Resources • Accounting • Communications • Sales • Information Services • Order Processing • Advertising—Promotion • Technical Research

System I	**Operational Team Level**
	• Product Development Teams • Process Development Teams • Manufacturing Teams

System I elements, something is obviously wrong. Yet, it is not inconceivable to envision a research department in conflict with a product development unit. Similarly, one may see the advertising and promotion department in competition with the sales department, rather than in direct support of its efforts. It is not unusual for support functions, in their efforts to standardize services and thus cut costs, to find themselves in conflict with their direct customers, the System I units. The Viable System Model clearly illustrates the folly of this type of conflict. It is analogous to a salesman picking a competitive argument with the customer. Certainly he cannot win without also losing. But in many organizations, this is precisely what one sees between System II units and System I clients. Such turf wars can be calamitous.

SYSTEM III

It is noteworthy that System III is the first place where we find management. To the extent that the system requires a command function, it resides here. System III provides operational direction, resolves conflicts, and allocates resources in cases where System II needs help or clarification. Functional and operational relationships in the system frequently require negotiation of issues like resource availability, priorities, and the like. Negotiation of issues is a function of System III. Compliance with prior agreements (goals, quotas, completion times, roles, profitability, etc.) is also a System III function. Management is, after all, accountable for performance of the various elements within its jurisdiction.

Similar to the compliance function, but not quite the same, is an audit function. It is up to System III to ensure that safety standards, quality control, security, copyrights, and the general state of the infrastructure are all maintained. (In Beer's original iteration of the model, System IIIa is used to point out this adjunct function.)

SYSTEM IV

System IV may at first seem a little confusing. Isn't creating the organizational environment for innovation—setting the values, policies, and long-term goals, for example—a management function also? Certainly it is. But it's a broader, more encompassing challenge than those addressed in System III, which is distinctly operational. In very large organizations like General Electric, it is easier to see the differentiation. Jack Welch may spend most of his time on System IV issues, and it's easier to rationalize because he has a small army of executives below him in that huge organization. In a smaller organization, we often find the two functions being performed by precisely the same executive team. In these cases, where management must clearly wear two hats, it's even more important to differentiate between the different roles and responsibilities of System III work and System IV work. It is important, in our judgment, that System IV remain separate and be addressed separately. It is important enough to successful innovation that it clearly deserves its own category.

CLUSTERS OF INNOVATION ACTIVITY

SO THERE WE have the Innovation Management Model, but we haven't yet said much about how it influences the actual management of innovation. We will, but first—because innovation occurs to our great advantage across the complete range of organizational activity—we need to divide these activities into several categories or clusters so we can discuss each. In Figure 3-3 we divide our activities into four activity clusters, each requiring management and each essential to the comprehensive understanding of innovation. The combination of the viable system with the activity clusters gives us a useful way to dissect and examine the management of innovation.

NURTURE AND BUILD

The first and most overreaching cluster shown in Figure 3-3 is that of providing a nurturing and hospitable environment for innovation. Roses won't grow on concrete or in tap water. Innovation is at least as demanding and a lot more complex than growing roses. (Dedicated rose gardeners may disagree.) The organizational environment is a function of the policies and values held and reinforced by management itself. It might also be noted that these are the values and policies reinforced consistently by the actions of all, but particularly management. It is not limited to the values and policies printed somewhere in planning documents and policy manuals. Employees watch their leaders like eagles, observing their most minute actions and statements. It's not what's in the policy book that counts: It's what the executives say and do that determines the behavior of others.

FIGURE 3-3. TYPICAL ACTIVITY CLUSTERS.

Nurture/ Build	Create/ Develop	Implement/ Commercialize	Exploit/ Manage
Creating the environment for innovation, i.e., trust, openness, security, honesty, community, etc.	Creating the capacity of the organization to meet its goals.	Putting the innovation into place within the context of the organization.	Carrying through with exploitation of the opportunity to mine the profits from it.
Environmental Values Policy Organization Compensation Communication	Customer segmentation Process development Technology development Research Recruiting skilled people Employee education Corporate knowledge base	Operations Pilot runs Process application Technology application Distribution	Sales growth Marketing/promotion Cost reduction Product line extensions Distribution expansion

CREATE AND DEVELOP

The second cluster is the creation of the *capacity* for innovation—the capacity for the organization to meet its goals. We list several types of capacity by way of example, but there are certainly others critical to unique organizations. At the top of the list for every organization must be accurate and useful information about the client or customer. All organizations exist to serve someone, and that someone is always the client. The capacity to serve the client (and hence fulfill the purpose of the organization) is based immovably upon that understanding. It cannot be repeated too often for any of us.

Organizations known for innovative or creative performance invariably have created the capacity for recurrent innovation to happen. It's an ongoing and ever-present necessity if consistent and useful innovation is to occur. Innovation is not a resource that can be turned on like a faucet when you need water. The water comes out only because someone is supporting the water delivery system at all times—someone is maintaining the pipes.

IMPLEMENT AND COMMERCIALIZE

The implementation cluster is one we're all familiar with whatever our profession. It is the essence of what the organization does, the everyday blocking and tackling. The drive to reduce costs and increase productivity has done more to emphasize the gains to be made from operational innovation than probably any other single factor in the past fifty years. The results have been phenomenal and provide a critical driver for an economic boom period that was foreseen by almost no one. Managing innovation (or an innovation) all the way through the process can yield gains that can exceed all expectations.

EXPLOIT AND MANAGE

Exploitation of the innovation is probably a new category for some, but it's not at all unusual for organizations to get so wound up in the first three exciting and urgent activity clusters that they forget to fully exploit what they've created! It would seem obvious that carefully reaping what you've sown would be only common sense, but many fail to enjoy all the benefits from their effort. Management gurus have popularized the fast-moving demands of today's business environment and lavished praise on companies that replace a quarter of their products every couple of years or continually derive a large portion of their revenue from new products. Such examples do serve the useful purpose of punctuating the importance of continual progress, but can (presumably unintentionally) distract management from milking the cash cow that's in the barn today. There's room for innovation in the exploitation phase too.

COMBINING THE
MODEL WITH THE CLUSTERS

WE CAN NOW combine our adaptation of the Viable System Model with our activity clusters and see how it helps us manage innovation. If we bring the two together, we can make some useful observations. First, we can see that the involvement of the various participants in the system varies by system, time horizon, and activity. Figure 3-4 shows the involvement of each system.

As Figure 3-4 indicates, System IV is almost entirely focused on the future as it is the key purveyor of the organizational culture and work environment. System IV, in conjunction with System III, provides the critical elements of the capacity for innovation. Certainly the other systems interact with capacity development insofar as they improve their own education and the like, but the greatest part must come directly from Systems III and IV. Effective capacity for innovation is seldom if ever present in any organization where management is not consciously working to provide it.

As Figure 3-4 shows, System III, interestingly, maintains a constant role across the entire spectrum of activities. After all, that is the nature of operational management. System II, on the other hand, has little or nothing to do with creating the culture and environment for work. System II is certainly part of it and may support and contribute to it, but in no way can the support elements of an organization *determine* a culture that is contrary to that held by management. This is easiest to see in small businesses where it is obvious that the character of the owner is present in all aspects of the business. It is precisely the same in the large organization—it just may be a little harder to discern. System II may indeed have some impact on developing capacity for innovation, and the support role must continue throughout implementation and exploitation.

The activities of System I are biased toward the present. Some

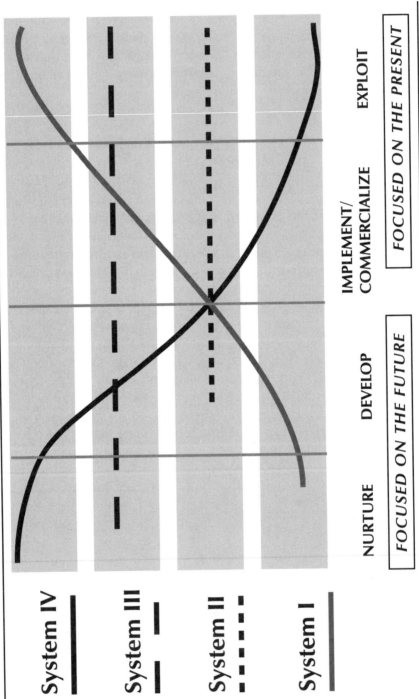

FIGURE 3-4. THE INNOVATION MANAGEMENT MODEL COMBINED WITH THE ACTIVITY CLUSTERS.

System IV

System III

System II

System I

NURTURE   DEVELOP   IMPLEMENT/   EXPLOIT
                          COMMERCIALIZE

FOCUSED ON THE FUTURE   FOCUSED ON THE PRESENT

work teams are involved in future activities, at least in the sense of new products, services, or processes, but many more are working on the present, as Figure 3-4 shows.

USES OF THE MODEL

THE INNOVATION MANAGEMENT Model provides a useful view of the challenge of managing innovation. It provides us with a means of seeing and understanding what needs to be done and provides insight into how to go about it. The backyard gardener wishing to grow apples, for instance, can do so in a number of ways. The easiest way is to visit a garden center and purchase some apple trees, bring them home and plant them, sit back, and wait for the apples to appear. For some, this approach works. If they're lucky and happen to have the right combination of soil, light, nutrients, etc. and aren't plagued with disease or insects, the ripe, juicy apples appear in about four years.

For most, however, the exercise is more frustrating. One or more of the following situations generally occur:

- The tree dies unexplainably.

- The tree grows slowly and weakly.

- The tree produces no fruit.

- The tree produces fruit, but poor and small fruit.

- The tree grows better than planned and becomes too big for the allotted space.

- The tree produces fruit, but not the kind you expected.

The wise gardener who takes the time to understand a bit about apples will likely find the experience much more rewarding. It takes little time to learn enough to:

- Choose the best variety of apple and the right size root stock for the location.

- Understand the preferences of apple trees for light, moisture, and nutrients.

- Learn which two or three local pests that attack apples and how to control them.

- Be observant of the one or two diseases that may bother the tree in your area.

The process is not difficult, nor is it particularly time-consuming. Apples are pretty easy to grow in much of the United States and Canada, but the lack of a little knowledge can make it seem impossible. So it is also with innovation. Just about everybody knows it when they see it, but it can be infuriatingly elusive—all for the lack of a little knowledge. Using a model like the one proposed here can help enormously.

The model will be applied to numerous central aspects of managing innovation as we proceed, including:

- Creating the ideal environment for innovation

- Linking innovation to market opportunities

- Organizing for innovation

- Implementing innovations

- Exploiting innovations

- Supporting the innovative enterprise

With these observations and multiple dimensions, it's now possible to view management of innovation as both reasonable and possible. But we still lack a focus, a context, and a purpose to direct the actions of our model.

THE CONTEXT FOR INNOVATION

ALL SYSTEMS NEED a purpose, clearly understood and widely accepted—otherwise, they disappear. In the case of innovation (both commercial and nonprofit), the purpose is to serve a client or customer—to directly or indirectly serve people. Innovation must support implementation of corporate strategies. As stated in Chapter 1, strategy matters, innovation matters, and management matters. All are ultimately focused on the customer. Whether we're talking about a business, a government agency, or a nonprofit organization like the Salvation Army, there is an ultimate customer who is being served. For an organization to survive, much less prosper, there can be no other focus but the ultimate customer. Even governments are overthrown when they fail to serve their constituents.

SUMMARY

- The Innovation Management Model describes organizational functions in terms of *how* each is best performed.

- Senior management is primarily responsible for the future. Everyone else is primarily working in the present—on today's work. The model thus implies *who* does what work.

- The other key element in the model is identification of four key activity clusters. Activity clusters describe *what* has to be done.

- The interaction of the what and the who/how provides us with an effective model for examining and managing innovation.

- The model operates effectively when applied with strong market focus.

NOTE

1. Stafford Beer, *Diagnosing the System for Organizations* (New York: John Wiley & Sons, 1995).

CHAPTER FOUR

NURTURING INNOVATION

AS ECONOMIC HISTORIAN AT THE prestigious Shanghai Jiao Tong University, Jiang Tzu Peng often pondered the remarkable past of the Heavenly Kingdom. His life's work had been devoted to understanding the economic accomplishments and disappointments of his native China. China produced so many inventions, but the most populous nation on earth had relatively little to show for them. It was left to other nations, usually European nations, to exploit China's many discoveries commercially.

History documents a remarkable series of Chinese inventions. Printing, first used in China, became an accomplishment that altered the creation of knowledge beyond anything the world had known. Yet, it was the 15th-century printing press of the German Johann Gutenberg that is credited with the spread of the printed word. Similarly, it was the Ts'ai Lun who invented paper, the material that made possible the inexpensive dissemination of printed materials to the population at large. But the mass production of paper was developed by the English, not the Chinese. And was it not the Chinese who invented the process to make silk, and thus influenced centuries of trade throughout the Far East?

The story doesn't end there. Jiang noted that the first rigid horse collar, which permitted more efficient use of draft animals (without choking), also originated in China. So did gunpowder and porcelain. The Chinese were the first to use coal and coke in blast furnaces, Jiang noted, for the smelting of iron, and did so hundreds of years before Europeans. But there was no doubt it was the Europeans who built an industry on the knowledge. A water-driven machine for the spinning of hemp was used in China long before any similar device was discovered or employed in Europe. But the English produced a textile empire from the knowledge. And the list goes on.

The relevant question for Jiang was: If China discovered all these inventions, why was she apparently unable to exploit any of them? The answer was straightforward: *No one was trying* to capitalize on the innovations. Precisely the reverse was valued. Stability was cherished; change was to be avoided whenever possible. Thus, the environment evolved into one that was distinctly hostile to new ideas and innovations of every kind. No one understood better than Jiang that China is changing. While he wished often that his country could move faster, he was somewhat mollified by the fact that similar hostility to innovation still exists in many companies across Europe, North America, and the rest of the world, even today.

So, Jiang mused, perhaps China was not so poorly positioned after all. Perhaps the future would be brighter.

DEVELOPING AND NURTURING AN ENVIRONMENT OF INNOVATION

SO, WHAT HAPPENED to the Chinese? There is little mystery in our example. There are several specific reasons for the Chinese failure to commercialize, which are outlined by David Landes.[1] In Landes's view, the Chinese were unable to exploit these monumental inventions because of:

- The absence of free markets

- The absence of institutionalized property rights

- Societal values

- The larger pattern of totalitarian control

Landes's observations of the Chinese experience reveal situations that are not so different really from our business environment today. Certainly, circumstances differ in the matter of degree. But on balance, there are useful parallels. In the first factor noted above, the absence of free markets, innovation is always stunted by the incentive of "stability," and those who benefit from the existing situation object vigorously to relinquishing their advantage. Regarding the second factor, the absence of institutionalized property rights, certainly the West pretty much has institutionalized property rights in the national sense, but on the individual level, the employee may have no stake at all in the profits of the enterprise. The recent movement to broad-based stock ownership, both in compensation and in retirement plans, is a step in the right direction.

The third factor involves societal values. Most of the world today values economic achievement, but there are certainly countries where this is not true, even in this new millennium. Iran, Afghanistan, and many other countries view change and innovation much differently from the West. Their lack of economic vitality reflects the fallacy of trying to preserve the past at the expense of the future. Totalitarian control, the fourth factor, influenced the lack of innovation in China, and can be seen at work today in Iran and Afghanistan.

Reality is much different from long-ago China for those of us in the developed world. Every company innovates. Every person innovates. Innovation is as necessary to the normal operation of enterprise as it is to a major new product breakthrough. Even the meanest organization possesses some level of innovative activity. However, many organizations lack a sufficiency of innovative achievement to ensure their success. As with the historical Chinese, many businesses are simply not trying, presumably trusting that innovations can be pulled out of some mythical hat when they are most needed.

Every normal person innovates every day, though maybe in insignificant and unobservable ways. We are all capable of innovation, and when this propensity is encouraged, it often flowers with remarkable power and energy. However, when stunted or abused, either intentionally or unintentionally, the results can be equally powerful—but in a counterproductive way. Organizations usually get the innovation they nurture; they get the innovation they plan for. They get the innovation they deserve.

Three key elements can have a powerful effect on the environment for innovation. These are:

1. Management development

2. Strategy development

3. Employee development

We will look at each of these three elements in the pages that follow.

You can easily look at the nurturing activity cluster of the Innovation Management Model (see Figures 3-1 and Figure 3-4), as the pie chart shown in Figure 4-1. Nurturing activities are best envisioned as a managerial responsibility. The nurturing activities primarily take place in System IV—charged with creating the environment for innovation.

MANAGEMENT DEVELOPMENT

ONE SELDOM HEARS much about management development in discussions of innovation. Evidently, the presumption is that management is just fine, or possibly that managers are either incapable of or somehow exempt from innovation. While attending to all the day-to-day needs of the organization, too few executives tend to the care and feeding of their own skills. If innovation is as important to success as we believe it is, should we not direct at least some effort to developing the management skills necessary to stimulate and nurture innovation throughout the organization? There should be a concerted effort to develop management awareness and knowledge of at least the basic requirements for nurturing and sustaining an innovative organization.

MANAGEMENT FACTORS INVOLVED IN NURTURING INNOVATION

Numerous volumes have addressed the role of the executive in business today, so there is little point in reiterating common themes.

FIGURE 4-1. THE "NURTURING PIE."

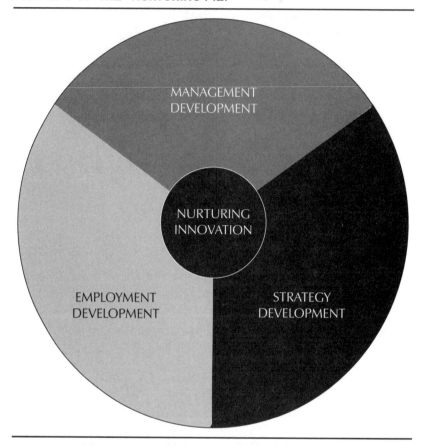

There are, though, several points specifically related to nurturing and fostering innovation that are worthy of more attention. In no implied order of importance, they are:

- Personal understanding of the process of innovation

- Continuous learning and study

- Curiosity

- Openness

- Leadership

- Focus on strategic issues rather than operational tasks

Let's look at each of these.

Personal Understanding of the Process of Innovation

First is the executive's personal understanding of the process and activity of innovation itself. If you have little interest in or regard for the process of innovation, then it is unreasonable to presume you can lead and manage innovation to superior results. How does innovation come about? Can it be structured—pursued methodically? How can you manage something you don't understand? The manager's learning process is enhanced considerably when innovators help managers learn more about what innovators do, how they do it, and how it contributes to company success.

Continuous Learning and Study

Continuous learning is the hallmark of every great executive. Maybe there was a time when the senior management could coast along on skills and knowledge acquired long ago, but if that was ever true it certainly is not now. Managers who sharpen their skills continuously can be confident they will remain valuable contributors.

Curiosity

Innovation is better managed by those with diverse interests and a curious nature. It's not possible to fake interest in innovative ideas and projects when the manager's heart just isn't in it. The manager must be genuinely interested in possibilities to value innovation. The manager who is always interested in new things and new ways will invariably find it easier to develop and maintain a closer relationship with innovators in their organization. Innovators can tell who's really interested.

Openness

Similarly, the manager must be receptive. The innovative organization thrives on openness—openness to the new and novel, openness to criticism and suggestion, and openness to learning from everyone and anyone. A manager who is open to new possibilities and to hearing from others is much more able to foster such an attitude in those working under her.

Leadership

Leadership implies an interest or even a passion for progress and for useful ideas. Continual improvement of organizational capabilities and competitive prowess is achieved through leadership. Leading an innovative organization certainly calls for even more of these qualities.

Focus on Strategic Issues Rather than Operational Tasks

A focus on the important and strategic rather than the operational is the mark of an effective executive. By *important,* we don't imply that nonexecutive tasks are not important, but rather that the executive must, to do the job well, focus on those responsibilities that *only* the executive can accomplish. Every moment the executive spends doing nonexecutive work is wasted. Generally, if someone else can do the work, the executive should not be doing it. When the uniquely executive work is not getting done, the organization is the worse for it.

Can an organization be highly innovative within an environment hostile to creativity and innovation? We do not believe so, at least not beyond random acts of innovation that might peek through in spite of the environment. Can anyone but executive management create the environment for innovation? No. Subordinates may try, but significant innovation cannot be sustained without a companywide appreciation of the benefits, the reason, the purpose. That sense of perspective cannot be established entirely by lower-level managers, no matter how dedicated, if they do not receive commensurate support from the top.

A TAPESTRY OF CONTRADICTIONS

Management is nothing if not the art of manipulating contradictions into a coherent and efficient system to provide something someone wants. Figure 4-2 shows a sampling of the contradictions confronting managers every day. How the contradictions are resolved, as conscientious and responsible managers move the slider bar to the right or left, also determines the climate for innovation within the organization.

The contradictions shown in Figure 4-2 are familiar to all managers. Every manager is forced to try to find a balance among opposites. She tries to move the slide bar a bit farther in one direction, only to have to move it back again as situations change. She is constantly being pulled between competing opposites. Experienced managers also know that Solomon-like decisions are never really an either-or proposition. Instead, sound decisions are nearly always a balancing act that places the slider somewhere between the polar extremes.

FIGURE 4-2. A FEW OF THE CONTRADICTIONS MANAGERS FACE IN MANAGING INNOVATION.

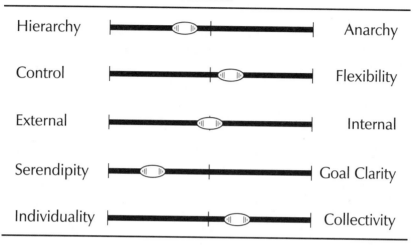

THE DETERMINING DIMENSIONS

Four key dimensions determine the real environment for innovation. These are:

1. The generally perceived level of control

2. The operational structure of the organization

3. Access to and quality of corporate strategy

4. The overall level of organizational focus

Let's look at the four dimensions.

The Generally Perceived Level of Control

Control issues are typically anathema to "creative types" if only because control is the antithesis of flexibility. Flexibility offers the means and the time to nurture innovation. Conversely, inflexible organizations are emblematic of bureaucracy, and bureaucracy *is* hostile to creativity and innovation. The bureaucratic behemoths are the poster companies for stagnation. Inflexibility in thinking, inflexibility in action, and inflexibility in seeing are all disabling afflictions. Finding an efficient and supportive balance between control and flexibility is one aspect of good management.

Certainly, strategy and strategic vision provide clarity and purpose (which we strongly advocate), but taken to extreme, clarity can engender blindness to new or serendipitous events and developments that provide grist for the innovation mill. With strategic focus, more is usually better than less, but on a scale of one to ten, few managers would seek a perfect score. The efficiently innovative organization is focused, not fixated like a doe caught in the headlights. The purpose of strategy is not to preclude innovation but to encourage it within bounds determined by organizational goals.

The Operational Structure of the Organization

The organizational dimension (discussed at length in Chapter 7) affects the environment for innovation. Organizational structure is seldom neutral. Structure can either encourage or discourage innovation. Systems theory places considerable emphasis on the idea that structure produces behavior.

In the case of systems theory, *structure* refers to the structure of the system, which is more encompassing than just the organization chart. It also includes the operating policies (see Chapter 8). In this respect, system structure is considered to be generative—i.e., it has the power to redefine and redesign itself through the decisions of managers. The structural level is thought to be the most powerful level of explanation in the systems vernacular.[2]

Structures encouraging unhealthy competitive attitudes are less supportive of cooperation and innovation. Strict functional structures often create barriers that, while supportive of the function, may unintentionally discourage new ideas and experimentation. Financial controls and procedures allocating resources are particularly susceptible to the creation of mischief.

Access to and Quality of Corporate Strategy

Knowledge of the purpose of one's work is essential to simulating useful innovation. Sound corporate strategies, communications to employees in clear and relevant language provides the foundation for individual contributions to those strategies. People need to know where the organization is trying to go and how it is trying to get there before they can steer their innovation efforts in that direction. We all have probably encountered organizations where most of the employees knew nothing of the goals and strategies (presuming there were some), but were criticized for being slow to innovate.

The Overall Level of Organizational Focus

Focus sets the stage for either an internal or external orientation (shown in Figure 4-2 as external versus internal). A market focus is arguably the greatest stimulus to innovation because it orients attention to serving new customer needs and/or solving new customer problems, thus creating value. Just as necessity is the mother of invention, there is no substitute for understanding your customers as a springboard to good and marketable innovation.

THE COST OF COORDINATION

There is also a cost of coordination. By this, we mean the need for moderation in all things. As in the age-old "golden mean," the moral is clear: Find the right balance. This is a challenge, and it's one thing to say it but another to really believe it. Figures 4-3, 4-4, and 4-5 make the reason clear.

The primary performance drivers for any organization are quality, cost, and time. These are measures we can all see, quantify, and apply. We will use these three measures to examine our premise that there is a cost to excessive coordination—in short, a cost of excessive management.

On all three measures—quality, cost, and time—there is indeed a golden mean. Figure 4-3 shows how each driver can be represented as

FIGURE 4-3. THE COST CURVES OF THE PRIMARY PERFORMANCE DRIVERS.

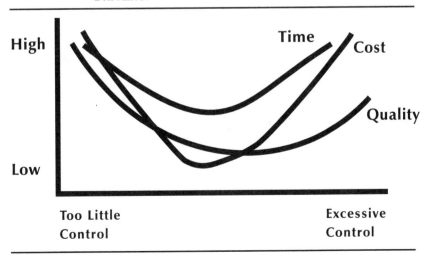

a U-shaped curve. The U-shape curve reflects the nature of cost behavior. The cost curves in the figure could reflect any category of decision. For example, let's say we are concerned about the cost of direct labor hours. If we reduce direct labor hours, we see costs decline. But if we drive costs down so far that there's no one to handle unexpected problems, or the scarcity of labor reduces flexibility to serve customer requests, real costs will again increase. The optimal situation is somewhere between the extremes of scarcity and excess.

The curves shown in Figure 4-3 make the moderation point more clearly. The curves are representative, as each organization differs, but it becomes immediately apparent that too much or too little control can have stultifying and unintended results.

Thus, you can see that moderation is a successful strategy. But as Figure 4-4 shows, there is another more subtle point to be made. As with any normal U-shaped curve, one finds a relatively wide range around the lowest (most favorable) point, where there is little evident change. In other words, it is not necessary to strive obsessively for the optimal point. Anywhere within the "success range" is nearly as good as any other. It is not necessary to micromanage the various dimensions. This is good news, since even getting close is hard enough. It is good (or at least comforting) that in many cases, close is also good enough.

FIGURE 4-4. THE RELATIVELY WIDE RANGE OF EFFECTIVENESS.

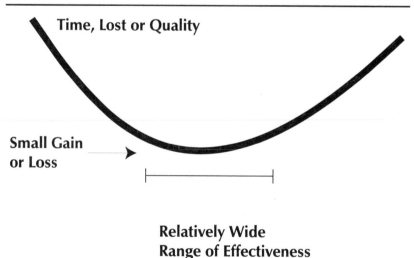

Time, Lost or Quality

Small Gain
or Loss

Relatively Wide
Range of Effectiveness

If you'd like to plot an overall view of your organization, you can take each of the dimensions shown in Figure 4-2 (hierarchy versus anarchy, control versus flexibility, external versus internal, etc.) and overlay one on the other to make up a single chart, as shown in Figure 4-5. Plotting your organization on each of the scales provides a visual map of the organization and may provide insight into desirable changes to make it more hospitable to innovation.

The diagram is just an example, but portrays an organization that one would expect to encourage innovation as the balance favor (the right side of the diagram). One could probably think of additional variables to add in appraising a particular organization. Such tools are admittedly imprecise, but are useful in helping us form a mental picture of the challenge at hand.

Managers are thus helped in three essential ways. First, those who set policy need to understand the implications of the decisions they make. Second, the expectations for innovation need to be viewed in terms of objective information regarding the state of the organiza-

FIGURE 4-5. PLOTTING AN OVERALL VIEW OF THE ORGANIZATION.

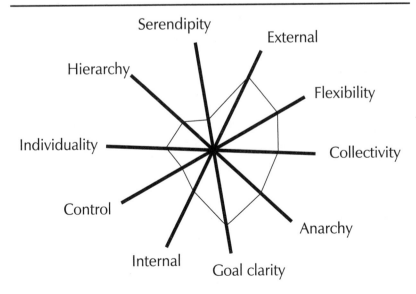

Serendipity

External

Hierarchy

Flexibility

Individuality

Collectivity

Control

Anarchy

Internal   Goal clarity

Less Conducive
to Innovation

More Conducive
to Innovation

tion at the moment. And third, consistency is necessary to prevent setbacks to innovation.

STRATEGY DEVELOPMENT

HOW MANY OF your company's strategies depend substantially on the creativity or innovation of your employees? Some? Most? Even all? Well, then, is there a provision in your plan for specifically developing and exploiting your innovative ability? No? Why not?

If you answered no, your organization certainly is not alone. Few companies acknowledge the significance of innovation efforts to the extent of putting a strategy in writing. But innovation should at least be worthy of a meaningful discussion at your next planning retreat. Does each member of the planning team understand and appreciate the significance of innovation to your company? Do they really believe it's that important? In our experience conducting many strategic planning sessions with executive teams, there is a very real tendency to fixate on operational issues and urgent issues, whether or not those issues are of strategic stature.

We're not talking here about the obligatory "our employees are our most important asset" kind of statements that are dutifully included in nearly all strategic plans and value statements. We are speaking here of a comprehensive commitment to supporting and developing people as a matter of organizational values and management policy.

British Field Marshal B. L. Montgomery believed that the worst thing a leader could do was to divide his resources up into "penny packets" that could be defeated separately by an adversary weaker in overall strength, but superior to the divided unit it confronted. This is not a unique point of view: It is a bedrock of military strategy. Many businesses apparently are unaware of the strength of Montgomery's wisdom and seek to serve all manner of customers. By trying to serve everyone who comes along, they are generally unable to serve any single segment better than their competitors. They lack a focused strategy.

From an innovation perspective, the lack of a clear strategy, understood by employees, reduces innovation to guesses as to what someone hopes might be useful. Why make people guess? So your competitors won't know what you're up to? Well, if your employees don't know what you're up to, your competitors' knowing becomes irrelevant. You won't be competitive enough for them to care. It's much better to amass the resources of your organization behind a clear and effective strategy. Competitors usually will be unable to do much to combat an effective, well-conceived strategy anyway. But if your people do not understand what the strategies are, then it won't matter. Many employee innovations go wasted, the casualties of poor communication of strategic direction.

Employee Development

EVERY ORGANIZATION IS aware of the need for employee development. Many have distinct functions devoted to employee development, some on the scale of small universities. Few, however, are as sincere in this regard as the U.S. armed services. In the U.S. military, education is encouraged at every level. No one is deprived of the opportunity for additional schooling because "there is no one to handle your job while you attend class" or "we don't have enough budget for it this year" or "you're responsible for your own education." There may be nowhere on earth where education is more available than the U.S. armed forces.

But commercial organizations have at least as great a challenge. When we hear a manager say that he just can't get his people to innovate or do what he thinks they should be doing, it's a signal that something is wrong. Occasionally, one hears of a manager who thinks employees are stubborn, stupid, or otherwise just unwilling to "get with the program." Such attitudes (mental models) may be difficult to change but fortunately seem less common these days. In any event, it is necessary to change the attitude or suffer the consequences of sullen contempt from the employees. The best managers know such consequences are unnecessary, unproductive, and undesirable.

When it seems that employees are simply not doing the "right thing," it's time to pause and think carefully about why it's happening. Ferdinand Fournies provides an illuminating view of why many employees don't do what they're supposed to.[3] Fournies offers sixteen reasonable explanations:

1. They don't know why they should do it.

2. They don't know how to do it.

3. They don't know what they are supposed to do.

4. They think your way will not work.

5. They think their way is better.

6. They think something else is more important.

7. There is no positive consequence to them for doing it.

8. They think they are doing it.

9. They are rewarded for not doing it.

10. They are punished for doing what they are supposed to do.

11. They anticipate a negative consequence for doing it.

12. There is no negative consequence to them for poor performance.

13. There are obstacles beyond their control.

14. Their personal limits prevent them from performing.

15. There are personal problems.

16. No one could do it.

Without elaborating on each reason, it is pretty obvious that Fournies's reasons are all good ones with which many readers can doubtlessly identify.

Many companies today have exemplary employee development programs, and each company receives benefits that far exceed the cost. There are many dimensions to a complete employee development program. The best programs result from sincere belief on the part of management that employees perform much better when they receive a little help. These organizations tend to freely offer employees the benefit of the doubt in their personal development and resulting benefits to the organization.

The following are some suggestions for ways to foster employee development. You should consider providing your employees with:

- Professional journals

- Books

- College courses

- Management seminars

- Professional seminars

- Study time allowance

- Internal training courses

- Internet education materials

- Cross-training in multiple jobs

Employee development is every manager's job—maybe the most important job. Are managers in your organization evaluated on the achievements of their employees, on the professional growth of employees in their charge? Are they seen as husbanding a valuable resource? Are your managers allowed an adequate education budget to use as they think best? Or have cost-reduction programs forced employee development programs into suspended animation?

NECESSITY VERSUS OPPORTUNITY

EVERY DAY THERE are those who innovate in small ways to accomplish small but useful tasks. These small achievements are generally overlooked in the literature of innovation, possibly because they're not very exciting. Of these unsung achievers, none has a richer history of such innovative accomplishment than does the small farmer, who often worked on the frontier of civilization, far from the resources of skilled tradespeople who could provide services for them. These independent souls were compelled to provide for themselves.

Often, survival was at stake, and the difference between feeding a family and going hungry was creativity—in addition to a lot of hard work, of course. Those capable of innovating and adapting were the ones who succeeded rather than simply survived. Most farm machinery was designed and even built by farmers, not by a large industrial corporation as we would expect today.

For example, the "jet boat" propulsion system was actually designed by a farmer, C. W. F. Hamilton of Tekapo, New Zealand. In New Zealand, there are many bodies of water too shallow for conventional outboard motors to operate without the propeller striking bottom. Hamilton needed a way to get feed to his sheep on the far side of just such a shallow body of water, and it was time-consuming and annoying to go all the way around each time. His solution was a device to pump the water out the back of the boat to propel the boat forward with no propeller at all. From these humble beginnings we have the sophisticated jet boats we see on recreational lakes around the world today, because Bombardier of Canada took the concept and translated the jet pump into the personal water craft. Bombardier, which faced seasonal scheduling problems because of its reliance on snowmobile production, innovated by making use of Hamilton's invention, arriving at the SeaDoo personal watercraft, which provided a summer product that balanced the company's production surge in winter products.

All manner of farm equipment—specialized to perform specific chores such as spraying, weeding, harvesting, pruning, or fertilizing—have been the innovations of small farmers. One reason is the multitude of skills necessary to be a successful small farmer. The small farmer generally maintains his own equipment as it may be a long, slow trip to a dealer service center. It's also cheaper, always a concern on the farm. The array of equipment found in the average small farm maintenance shed is impressive but not at all unusual: maintenance tools, hand tools, welders, and maybe basic machine tools. This experience of using such equipment provides skills of such breadth and diversity as to be quite unusual today. Many innovators in far-flung fields owe their skills to having grown up on the farm.

The sad part of this story is that the small farmer may be slowly passing from the scene in the progress of economic development and the corporate agricultural industry (at least in North America). It will be a genuine loss, along with that of the "shade tree" mechanic, the watchmaker, the small town barbershop, and doctor who makes house calls. The moral of this story is that as we become more specialized and focused in our specialized professions, it becomes even more desirable to provide cross-disciplinary experience. We need all the skills available in order to successfully innovate. At the very least, multiple skills are infinitely preferable. We may no longer be generalists out of necessity, but we can achieve a broader range of experience to fertilize our imaginations, and we can do so intentionally.

CREATING THE FAVORABLE ENVIRONMENT FOR INNOVATION

ENVIRONMENTS CAN EITHER favor innovation or be hostile toward it.

THE FAVORABLE ENVIRONMENT

Trust lies at the heart of any healthy organization, and certainly at the center of innovative organizations. Openness provides the opportunity for the innovator to freely discuss and propose ideas that in the early stages may be easily criticized and vulnerable to the sarcasm of the closed-minded. Adaptability provides the organizational resources necessary to accommodate or even welcome change—the kind that comes from innovation. Flexibility provides adaptability on a day-to-day basis. Rigid, rule-obsessed organizations always have trouble innovating. A clear sense of purpose guides innovation activities in directions that more closely fit the organization. The better the fit, the less adaptation is required, and the greater the likelihood of the innovation being accepted and implemented.

Valuing creativity goes a long way to encouraging innovative behavior, and demonstrating to employees that innovation is important and valuable requires some form of recognition. Valuing innovation goes far deeper than occasional words of praise or pay raises. Those who do the good work know when they've done something important and valuable. To them, patronizing words are worse than nothing. But genuine praise and appreciation can move mountains. There is little that motivates any of us more than genuine appreciation of our good work. Person-to-person appreciation goes a long way toward communicating this appreciation.

In short, recognition needs to be overt and demonstrated to be effective. Recognition need not take the form of an extravagant gift, a large raise, or even public acknowledgment, although all have their place. But care must be taken with tangible rewards, particularly if there are already perceived to be inequities among "contributors." Fairness and appropriateness are good bottom-line measures. When a manager gets a $20,000 raise for cutting costs by $100,000, one should not expect a designer to be delighted with a write-up in the house organ for having created the most successful product of the decade. You must take into account the perception of relative fairness. When people are treated and rewarded fairly for their day-to-day contributions and their exceptional contributions, innovation is supported.

THE HOSTILE ENVIRONMENT

We also need to look at innovation from the opposite direction. To achieve innovation, it's helpful to understand what prevents innovation. And what prevents innovation is found more often in the background than in the foreground.

Environments unfavorable to innovation represent more than simply the absence of the desirable qualities recorded above, though they certainly are that. The hostile environment is seldom malicious. Generally, hostile environments are only the result of the misinformed good intentions of one or more managers.

Some managers are perfectionists, for example. They seek to produce only exemplary work, but by trying so hard to avoid mistakes, they create an environment of extreme risk avoidance. Employees are extolled to do the best work—the highest-caliber work—but what they hear is "take no risks" or "make no mistakes."

A manager may have been instrumental in developing a particular process, system, or product. She may feel justifiably proud of that achievement. It may have been the reason she was promoted to management. Her sincere belief in the existing approach as the best way may blind her to new and innovative ideas by subordinates. None of us like to see our brainchild replaced by someone else's.

Simple enlightenment may be sufficient to produce a corrective effect. Few managers want to be associated with the hostile environment or be saddled with the reputation of cretin or ogre.

Oddly, such environments are seldom obvious to those responsible for them. In ancient China, those in power sought stability, and by so doing, they reduced innovation completely so as to preserve the status quo—a status quo that was distinctly favorable to those in power. They saw no need to encourage innovation. Today, there are fewer intentional obstructions to innovation and a greater understanding of the necessity to change and improve. The challenge in the coming millennium is to remove the *unintentional* obstructions to innovation and vitality.

SUMMARY

- It is a conscious act to create an environment conducive to innovation. It does not happen or survive without management support.

- Nurturing innovation involves three distinct activities: (1) management development, (2) strategy development, and (3) employee development.

- Managing the tapestry of contradictions is the key challenge and determines whether the environment is supportive or hostile to innovation.

- Overmanaging can be counterproductive.

- Employee development efforts and exposure to diverse experiences give a huge boost to innovation.

- The innovative environment is usually one that:
    Is trusting.
    Is open to new ideas and alternative approaches to solving problems and exploiting opportunities.
    Operates in an environment of adaptability.
    Operates in an environment of flexibility.
    Is goal-directed with a sense of purpose.
    Demonstrates that innovation is valued.
    Recognizes innovative achievements.

NOTES

1. The scholar Jiang Tzu Peng is fictitious. The Chinese inventions are real.

2. David S. Landes, *The Wealth and Poverty of Nations* (New York: W. W. Norton, 1999).

3. Ferdinand P. Fournies, *Why Employees Don't Do What They're Supposed To* (New York: McGraw-Hill, 1988).

CHAPTER FIVE

INNOVATION WITH A PURPOSE

THE OPEN EXHAUST OF THE twin-cylinder engine was roaring wildly, 24 horsepower braying in his face. The hot and acrid exhaust offended his nostrils and numbed his ears. The exhilaration was almost palpable. Years of dreaming and months of assembly finally over, the frail collection of bamboo, fabric, and agricultural spare parts called out to him. Sweat beaded on his forehead despite the modest temperature. The time was now. His pulse quickened, he eased in the throttle, the noise increased, and the machine began to move. Faster, faster it accelerated. The wind was pummeling his bare face with fierce intensity. Never had he experienced anything like the mingled sensation of fear and elation he was feeling now.

He was moving at an incredible pace—faster than the fastest horse, as fast as railroad trains he'd heard about. He sensed the dried earth passing behind him. On and on he went, seemingly forever, but actually only for seconds. The moment had come.

The machine grew lighter on the wind and was caught up suddenly, as if by a supreme act of willpower, and he was airborne. The machine eased into the spring air, its vibrating structure pulsating in the airflow. His elation was palpable. But what? He had no control. He couldn't steer! But faster and higher his machine took him, until a few moments later: Whomp! He was unceremoniously deposited full speed into a gorse hedge 12 feet from the ground. He was fortunately unhurt, but chastened by the experience. He climbed down from the hedge and onto the ground. As his pulse slowed, he realized: He had flown! He had really flown! Not a bad performance, actually.

Aloft for forty-one seconds, covering a distance of 350 feet, this manned flight should have set off bells of triumph throughout the world. It did nothing of the kind. The world would wait seven years before news of this event would even be published.

The pilot-builder was not named Wright. The year was not 1903, and the place was not Kitty Hawk, North Carolina. The year was 1902, and the young pilot's name was Richard Pearse.[1] The place was Waitohi, New Zealand, and it was a full year before the famous flight over the dunes at Kitty Hawk, North Carolina. (We should note that whether or not Pearse was the first to fly is a matter of controversy to this day.)

Impossible? The Wright Brothers were not the first? No, not impossible. In fact, many inventions suffer a similar fate. The failure to successfully promote and implement the invention relegates it to anonymity until someone successfully relates it to a commercial use—a market need.

This seminal cornerstone of aviation history was obscured by a number of contributing factors. Richard Pearse was not seeking commercial gain. He was doing his flying experiments for his own satisfaction. As with many inventors, he was obsessed with flying, not with business. Knowledge of his feats also suffered from Pearse's self-imposed seclusion: The religious neighboring farmers thought his flying obsession to be the "work of the devil," not to mention frightening their farm animals. Nor did it help his place in history to be located on the outer fringe of the other side of the world. Word of Pearse's accomplishment was not even published until 1909.

The Wright Brothers suffered no such disadvantage. Orville and

Wilbur Wright were intent on commercial success from the outset. Their success, not to mention fame, was commensurate. They clearly had market applications in mind when pursuing manned flight.

The moral of the story is that *invention in the absence of market need or market fit is seldom successful*—at least, it is seldom successful for the inventor. When invention finds itself in search of a market, the search is commonly long and fruitless. As managers in a modern competitive business environment, we must do better, and we can do better.

DEVELOPING THE CAPACITY
NEEDED FOR INNOVATION

DEVELOPING DETAILED AND accurate knowledge of target customers is fundamental to usable innovation. In this chapter, we are specifically concerned with the means and process of identifying and securing the market information necessary to focus our innovation efforts.

Figure 5-1 is the Innovation Management Model with a particular area highlighted. The shaded area shows that all four systems are involved in activities that either generate or utilize customer information and knowledge. System IV—creating the environment for innovation—is clearly involved in this effort, since any company plans for the future certainly require some model or assumption about whom the company will be serving, and this is clearly a System IV activity. System III—the strategic and managerial—is also involved here because the operational management of the organization makes use of customer information all the time.

System II—provision of shared resources—is also an important participant, since customer models and knowledge certainly are shared resources and information. And members of System I—the operational team level—participate both as users of the information and as the source for much of the data required to construct the model itself.[2]

A clear and concise strategic market segmentation model is a key resource for any organization. Even governments, for example, create and use such knowledge. In the case of a representative democracy, each politician gets elected by knowing the wants and expectations of

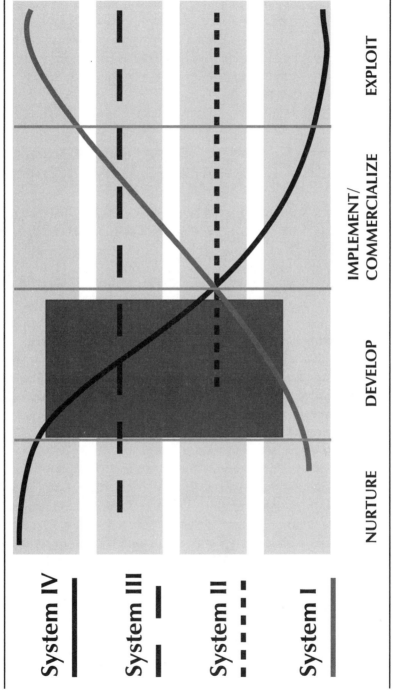

FIGURE 5-1. THE INNOVATION MANAGEMENT MODEL HIGHLIGHTING THE DEVELOPMENT OF MARKET INFORMATION.

System IV

System III

System II

System I

NURTURE   DEVELOP   IMPLEMENT/   EXPLOIT
                      COMMERCIALIZE

76 THE BUSINESS OF INNOVATION

his constituents. The politician who can best serve the needs of the constituents—who can provide what the market wants—is the one who gets elected. Each politician represents a "segment" of the population, and information on that population is necessary to the system for it to remain viable. Let's examine the customer knowledge requirements in more detail.

STRATEGIC FOCUS IS
ALWAYS MARKET FOCUS

AS NOTED IN Chapter 1, strategic imperatives determine the goals and strategies of the organization. And the key strategic decision—for all organizations—is the choice of which customers to serve, which is variously referred to as customer focus, market focus, or close to the customer. Without a clear understanding of whom the enterprise is trying to serve, a great deal of time is devoted to casting about for agreement on product issues, service issues, cost issues, or promotional issues, when each area should clearly be aimed at target customers.

Goal setting and strategy development virtually cry out for clearly defined and carefully chosen customer targets. In the absence of clear targets, assumptions are substituted so development can proceed. The more assumptions are required, the more trial and error must replace skill. Invariably, then, conflict, confusion, and frustration occur.

Many executives are said to spend far too much time on daily operations issues. In fairness to them, strategic decision tools can be hard to come by, and workable tools to identify customers and segment markets are often nonexistent. It is difficult to be strategic when customer information is scarce or inaccurate. Likewise, it's no easier to be innovative when strategies are enshrouded in a fog of generalization and ambiguity. Operations decisions are likewise difficult. Innovation becomes ill-defined and without direction. Innovate what?

Three key elements can focus innovation activities:

1. Clear strategic understanding of target customers

2. Concise, well-founded strategies to reach and serve those target customers

3. Communication of corporate goals, strategies, and customer knowledge to employees

It may seem obvious that every company would want clear targets as to the customers it wishes to serve. After all, some customers are always more profitable to serve than others, and some are easier to serve (i.e., are a better fit for your organization) than other customers. It is remarkable that few companies actually do have a clearly defined vision of their target market. Yes, there may be anecdotal information about customers, sometimes quite accurate. Too many companies, though, have "evolved" into the customer base they currently enjoy, rather than consciously deciding on the basis of evidence what they should be doing and whom they should be serving. This slow and steady evolution often deprives businesses of the most fundamental choice available to them: whom they *choose* to do business with. Such lack of clarity usually takes the form of assumptions about customers, compounded with anecdotal experiences, modified by expensive marketing mistakes, and leavened with a large dose of opinionated wisdom.

THE DANGERS OF INACCURATE INFORMATION

Not long ago one of the authors, invited to discuss market segmentation, met with the executive management team of a sizable manufacturing company. The company had grown steadily to a point where it was now an NYSE-traded corporation approaching $2 billion in sales. Not long into the meeting, it became apparent that some in the group felt there was no need to waste time or money segmenting markets. This attitude had thus far prevailed—despite several failed efforts to expand into other parts of their present industry. The minority, who had invited us to the meeting, felt the reason for the failures was the very real fact that they knew virtually nothing about the actual users of their current products. More important, they knew little or nothing of those adjacent sectors into which they had hoped (and tried) to expand. They had been making assumptions, of course, but the assumptions had been inaccurate.

One might ask how any company can grow to that size with so little information about its users and the market for such products as a whole. It's not so hard to understand when you find out that the company makes rather generic, low-tech products. It becomes easier still when you learn that it markets almost exclusively through distributors, wholesalers, and retailers who actually handle the selling activity. This manufacturer had little or no personal contact with customers (ultimate customers—the users of the products). Growth had been greatly assisted by the company's successful efforts to become a low-cost producer. Key members of the executive group had determined (with some degree of validity) that generic, high-value products, in limited variety and undistinguished design, would find their own market. By definition, this was true for the customers who had been drawn to their existing products.

History had treated this generic but blindfolded approach all too kindly, helped considerably by the fact that larger competitors were content to serve different segments, virtually ignoring our audience's core customer base. But now, times were changing and the company wanted to grow into new segments, but was enjoying very little success. This was obviously a "production-driven" organization, which may have read the "market-driven" books—but the key executives didn't really believe them.

As it turned out, the majority opinion won, and to our knowledge the company has continued to follow its old strategy, blissfully unaware of the diverse segments in its own marketplace. Actually, their challenge was not all that difficult to solve, but their mental models—their preconceived notions about doing business—wouldn't let them pursue a more enlightened and hence more successful strategy. They simply didn't understand the new and more demanding customers they wished to add to their portfolio. How could one expect the necessary innovation to occur inside this company in the absence of clear targets, and the absence of the knowledge of the needs and wants of each group? It couldn't.

Unfortunately, anecdotal customer information usually contaminates really useful information. Executives meeting to discuss strategic matters easily fall into the habit of: "I think we should do so-and-so because last week I was talking with John Thackory of ABC Rivets, and he wants a lower-cost product solution, and that sounds like a good idea." Someone else then recites another experience: "That may be, but yesterday I talked with Betty Wiener at Brookings Bolts, and she wants more features—and she's willing to pay more to get them!" Then another will bring up his latest example: "Ned Sackville over at Fabulous Fasteners says what we really need to provide is faster delivery and JIT inventory services. Ned's been in this business a long time and knows what he's talking about." On and on the conversation goes until everyone finally wears out the subject, and the team finally ends up taking a guess—or deciding to decide later. Frequently, the most powerful member's anecdote carries the day. Another profound strategic decision made, documented, and launched.

Anecdotal customer information is dangerous precisely *because* it *is* true—well, partially true, at least. It is true about somebody, some company, somewhere. But this is a fragile reed upon which to build a high-stakes business strategy. For example, what can you say about the geology of the earth based on examination of a single stone? Everyone can find examples to make a case, but if each is describing a different stone, the description of the earth will be sorely inaccurate and impossibly confusing.

THE SOLUTION TO THE PROBLEM

In the case of markets, the best solution yet discovered is to examine the market as a whole, then divide the total market into bite-size pieces containing customers with very similar needs, buying behavior, and decision methods. This is the purpose of a market segmentation model. It's now possible to see how many types there are and precisely describe those in each category. From such a model several key decisions can be made with confidence. You can:

- Choose that segment (or segments) that best suits your goals and resources.

- Develop strategies to win the targeted customers.

- Determine what is necessary to successfully implement those strategies with targeted clients.

It isn't possible to know too much about your target customers, but to be useful, customer information needs to be structured in such a way to be accessible to those parts of the organization that can exploit it. The ability of your employees to innovate in product development, in process development, in distribution, or in promotion all depends on their understanding of the intended customer.

In our earlier book *Powerful Products: Strategic Management of Successful New Product Development,* we devote an entire chapter to segmenting markets effectively and provide detailed how-to information. This discussion would be particularly useful to readers involved in business-to-business or industrial products, for whom traditional survey methods of developing segments leave much to be desired in both cost and precision.

COMMUNICATING THE STRATEGY TO EMPLOYEES

IN CHAPTER 4, we discussed the development of corporate strategy to foster innovation. But once that strategy is developed, it also needs to be communicated to everyone in the company. Otherwise, innovations are unlikely to see full fruition.

Each organization has unique requirements, but when in doubt it's better to overcommunicate than the reverse. Invariably, it seems harder for the small organization to communicate effectively than for the larger organization. One would think it would be easier, but the small company may lack a communications or promotion department with writers, copy editors, a printing department, in-house photographers, and production managers to run the program. Managers in smaller companies may be physically closer to their employees, but they are often the least likely to share the most useful information.

Here are some communications guidelines:

- Structure the information so it is useful to diverse functions.

- Make sure all employees have access to:
    Goals
    Strategies
    Customer information
    Why they should help

- Use every vehicle available to communicate clearly and often, including newsletters, e-mail, meetings, direct mail, and special brochures.

- Recognize that repetition is both necessary and desirable.

In the frenetic pace of day-to-day business demands, such employee communication requirements may go unattended. It somehow seems easier to handle the urgent issues (even if these are not the most important) than tend to things that are more important but clearly less urgent. Don't make the mistake of not communicating with your people—all of them.

GETTING AND ORGANIZING INFORMATION

IT'S NOT ONLY important to get the necessary customer information. It's also important to organize it.

MINING INSIDE SOURCES OF CUSTOMER INFORMATION

Many organizations overlook a treasure trove of information right under their noses. In a sort of reverse "not-created-here" syndrome, many companies discredit internal sources of market information on the premise that such information could not possibly be as accurate or valuable as that which might be purchased from a high-priced research firm. Makes sense, right? Wrong, at least sometimes. Many research organizations use inferior sources but have impressive methods of categorizing and processing what they do gather. The result can look persuasive yet provide little real, useful understanding of customer segments.

Ironically, the best information can often be found in the heads of your own sales force, wholesalers, distributors, specifiers, and retailers. The problem is not that these people don't have (know) what you seek. More likely, there is no efficient or effective method to secure and categorize the knowledge they have.

Your sales force should be your primary source of information. These are the folks in daily contact with real live paying customers, and they are the first to hear the customers' successes, failures, problems, complaints, suggestions, and praise. It is the salesperson who has to negotiate the contract. It is the salesperson who has to overcome objections and justify the value of your product or service. Experienced salespeople come to know instinctively whom they can sell, whom they cannot, and why.

In addition to sales, there may be others who can supply vital market information. Customer service representatives are also in personal contact with customers. Depending on their role in the organization, they can be important sources of suggestions for improvement and often have a keen understanding of the customers they serve.

Marketing folks spend their careers trying to better understand customers and use that understanding to the benefit of the company. In a sense it's their primary job to understand the customers and the markets the company does or might serve. They are usually the primary coordinators of market information. But even they might benefit from closer proximity to the strategies and company needs at the corporate level.

Last, don't overlook the credit and collection people either. They may be in direct contact with your clients and may get input that others are not in a position to receive. They certainly learn about problems that cause customers to withhold payment of invoices.

Organizing Information

Having the source of information does not mean the information is actually available. Usually, it is not available to those who need it most.

Here are some principles for organizing market information for innovation:

- Select a structure that you can build on—i.e., a structure that is expandable and grows with you.

- Use your market segmentation model as a framework.

- Don't bother collecting information you don't need.

- Don't collect information that you don't plan to maintain.

- Make someone responsible for the gathering and maintenance of customer information. (If everyone is responsible, then no one is responsible.)

- Conversely, do not try to create a massive bureaucracy. Manage only what needs to be managed.

- Recognize that information technology is a wonderful and useful tool, but it should not drive your information requirements. Collect what's necessary and useful, not what's convenient for the IT department.

- Beware of "secret" information. If it's secret, who is going to benefit from it?

- Know that if you make the system too hard, no one will want to have anything to do with it.

IN SEARCH OF COMPETITIVE ADVANTAGE

THE ULTIMATE OBJECTIVE of commercial innovation is to create or extend competitive advantage. Sure, there are innovations you willingly undertake that may not provide competitive advantage, but these are usually those most valued by owners and managers rather than customers.

Competitive advantage generally accrues from some way to better serve a customer—better than your competitors serve the same customer. The best innovations are those that can be protected, as with patents or copyrights. These are sustainable for the period granted and/or renewed. But these are not the only sources of advantage, of course, or even of a *sustainable* competitive advantage.

Some other sources of competitive advantage that may be sustainable are:

- Proprietary processes

- Proprietary technology

- Unique customer knowledge (such as your segmentation model)

- Cost leadership

- Corporate and employee attitude

- Shared values when these values and the exercise thereof constitute a competitive advantage

There are many other sources of sustainable advantage, many of which are industry-specific. Our point is that the underlying creation of these and many more sources does, in itself, constitute an act of corporate innovation. For example, the collapse of a market leader, leaving the successor in an advantageous position, is not an innovation. It's good fortune. A shift in market taste or fashion may favor a given company for an extended period without any particular innovation being responsible.

WHEN THE TARGET KEEPS MOVING: THE INTERNATIONAL SPACE STATION PROJECT

THE ROOTS OF the International Space Station Project (ISSP) lie in the early 1980s, when NASA began amassing the efforts of academics, government officials, and industry in support of an orbiting space station in which astronauts would live and from which they would conduct experiments. From these beginnings has come what is now a $47 billion undertaking—and the largest space project in history, involving the cooperation of the most advanced nations on earth. But despite its name, the space station then was definitely not "international." Instead, it began as a proprietary national effort to keep U.S. science out in front of the Soviet Union.

The ISSP involves the participation of 16 nations (the United States, Russia, Belgium, Brazil, Canada, Denmark, France, Germany, Italy, Japan, the Netherlands, Norway, Spain, Sweden, Switzerland, and the United Kingdom). The objective is to place a space station the size of a football stadium in space. Technologically challenging in the extreme, ambitious on a massive scale, it is complex, expensive, and difficult. Simply put, it is a behemoth. It was undertaken—in the official vision—to be a triumph of international cooperation at the frontier of human technology.

But that's not all it is. It is also incomplete, over budget, and late, very late. The ISSP is also a good example of the difficulty of innovating and implementing an ambitious project in an environment of conflict and self-interest.

On its way to a democratic government and a market economy, Russia fell into a depth of economic bedlam seldom seen in modern history. The once formidable and still proud Russian space community cannot pay its bills or meet its obligations. Nor does the Russian space agency today command the respect many Russians feel it deserves. Yet much to the chagrin of its other ISSP partners, in early 2000, Russia announced that it had found additional outside funding for *Mir*, its proprietary but aged space station, and would consequently not allow

Mir to end operation in 2000 as originally planned. When Russia had decided to participate in the ISSP, it had agreed to abandon *Mir*. The United States was consequently concerned about the Russian decision, since there was considerable doubt that Russia could support both projects, leaving its commitments to the ISSP in question. In late 2000, though, Russia announced that *Mir* would end operations and be intentionally crashed into the ocean in the spring of 2001. Conflicts of interest within a development effort can be so debilitating as to destroy projects that lack the deep pockets of the ISSP.

This is just one example of how the ISSP is a classic case of conflicting cultures and interests. It is a governmental showcase of how not to complete a commercial project. That said, the ISSP may well be worth all that it costs and wastes if it promotes international cooperation to any appreciable degree. But it would not be a model for corporations to emulate.

The project is instructive because it provides a clear example of difficulties caused by lack of alignment. Instead of clear alignment of goals, we find:

- An organization (NASA) looking for a project to justify its existence
- National pride, on the part of everyone involved
- Differences in national resource availability
- Old animosities haunting current relationships
- Political demagoguery
- An attractive target for "potshots" from all quarters
- Mission creep
- Goal conflict among the partners

Thus, the project is behind schedule, over budget, and the victim of drifting performance criteria. Only governments could afford, condone, and ultimately claim victory for such an accomplishment.

Could such a result occur on a smaller scale in the corporate environment? It happens all the time. But because such stories are seldom newsworthy, no one hears about them. In fact, the typical corporation goes to considerable length to bury such failures.

What lessons can we learn from the International Space Station Project?

- Clear goals focus action.

- Common, shared purpose mobilizes people to efficient action.

- Intangible, interpersonal elements like pride, heritage, nationalism, and the like are extremely powerful motivators.

As we strive to make our organizations more creative, innovative, and productive, we managers have an obligation to provide the nurturing environment wherein innovation can flourish. It is certainly possible for individuals to innovate in difficult conditions. But it is also much more difficult (and expensive) for an organization to successfully bring great ideas to fruition and market success in an environment of conflict, confusion, jealousy, bureaucracy, and rigidity.

SUMMARY

- Strategic focus *is* market focus.

- There are three elements of focusing innovation: (1) clean, strategic understanding of target customers; (2) concise, well-crafted strategies; and (3) clear communication of goals, strategies, and customer information to employees.

- Inside sources of customer knowledge are often the most powerful, if there is a method for procuring and organizing such information.

- Getting the right target from the outset is the most effective way to avoid shifting goals and moving targets.

- Sustainable competitive advantage comes only from innovation.

- Frequent changes of corporate direction result in confusion, and confusion is an enemy of successful innovation.

NOTES

1. C. Geoffrey Rodliffe, *Wings Over Waitohi* (Wellington, New Zealand: Avon Books, 1993).

2. For a complete description of the procedure for developing an effective market segmentation model, see Chapter 4 of Roger Bean and Russell Radford, *Powerful Products: Strategic Management of Successful New Product Development* (New York: AMACOM, 2000).

CHAPTER SIX

DEVELOPING THE CAPACITY TO INNOVATE

I N JONATHAN SWIFT'S SATIRE *Gulliver's Travels,* Gulliver visits the land of Laputa, where he tours the Grand Academy and is privileged to examine the department of "speculative learning."

I had hitherto only seen only one side of the academy, the other being appropriated to the advancers of speculative learning, of whom I shall say something.

The first professor I saw was in a very large room, with forty pupils about him. After salutation, observing me to look earnestly upon a frame which took up the greatest part of both the length and breadth of the room, he said, perhaps I might wonder to see him employed in a project for improving speculative knowledge by practical and mechanical operations. But the world would soon be sensible of its usefulness; and he flattered himself that a more noble exalted thought never sprang in any other man's head. Every one knew how laborious the usual method is of attaining to arts and sciences; whereas, by his contrivance, the most ignorant person, at a reasonable charge, and with a little bodily labour may write books in philosophy, poetry, politics, law, mathematics, and theology, without the least assistance from genius or study. He then led me to the frame, about the sides whereof all his pupils stood in ranks. It was twenty feet square, placed in the middle of the room. The superficies was composed of several bits of wood, about the bigness of a die, some a bit larger than others. They were all linked together by slender wires. These bits of wood were covered on every square with paper pasted on them; and on these papers were written all the words of their language in their several moods, tenses, and declensions; but without any order. The professor then desired me to observe, for he was going to set his engine at work. The pupils, at his command, took each of them hold of an iron handle, whereof there were forty fixed round the edges of the frame. And, giving them a sudden turn, the whole disposition of the words was entirely changed. He then commanded six and thirty of the lads to read the several lines softly, as they appeared upon the frame; and, where they found three or four words together that might make part of a sentence, they dictated to the four remaining bobs who were scribes. This work was repeated three or four times, and at every turn, the engine was so contrived, that the words shifted into new places, as the square bits of wood moved upside down.

Six hours a day the young students were employed in this labour, and the professor shewed me several volumes in a large folio already collected, of broken sentences, which he intended to piece together, and, out of those rich materials, to give the world a complete body of all arts and sciences; which, however, might be still improved, and much expedited, if the public would raise a fund for making and employing five hundred such frames in Lagado, and oblige the managers to contribute in common their several collections.

He assured me that this invention had employed all his thoughts from his youth; that he had emptied the whole vocabulary into his frame, and made the strictest computation of the general proportion there is in books between the numbers of particles, nouns, and verbs, and other parts of speech.

I made my humblest acknowledgement to this illustrious person for his great communicativeness; and promised, if ever I had the good fortune to return to my native country, that I would do him justice, as the sole inventor of this wonderful machine; the form and contrivance of which I desired leave to delineate upon paper. I told him, although it were the custom of our learned in Europe to steal inventions from each other, who had thereby, at least, this advantage, that it became a controversy which was the right owner, yet I would take such caution, that he should have the honour entire, without a rival.[1]

In Gulliver's visit to the Grand Academy of Laputa, Swift shows us an imaginary place where the ridiculous is the norm. He also writes of a researcher who spent eight years extracting sunbeams from cucumbers and placing them in a hermetically sealed vial, to be let out to warm the air in inclement summers. He introduces us to another person who developed an automated system of plowing fields. This fellow's innovation began by first carefully burying prodigious quantities of acorns, nuts, dates, and other vegetables in the field to be plowed. Hogs would then be turned loose in the field to root up the ground in preparation for sowing a crop. (We have come up with more efficient farming techniques since then.) Swift also shared an endeavor to make clothes by trigonometry. We're lucky Lands' End hasn't heard about the trigonometry method.

Swift's goal with his tale was to satirize the excesses of his time, in this instance the use of scientific tools and methods for inappropriate purposes. We smile at his wit nearly 300 years later, but even today we're not immune from using improper tools and inappropriate skills. In this chapter, we explore the development of capabilities for innovation—useful innovation—which will be immeasurably more powerful than those pursued by the Laputans.

STRATEGIC VS. TACTICAL INNOVATIONS

INNOVATIONS CAN BE either strategic or tactical—big-picture, or narrow-focus. The big-picture strategic innovations tend to be those that are measured by their impact in the marketplace. Strategic innovations demand intimate involvement by senior management because only senior management has the power to enact strategic decisions. In addition, such innovations may originate at the highest levels.

On the other hand, tactical innovations are the fiber of continuous improvement initiatives. They are usually smaller in scale than strategic innovations and may be either internally or externally measured. Such innovations can be significant and may produce discoveries that find their way all the way to the boardroom. No organization lives by strategic innovation alone, and we are lucky to have either type of innovation.

In either case, we're doubly lucky. We don't require "speculative knowledge" (a wonderful example of an oxymoron).

GETTING THE INNOVATIONS WE NEED

THERE ARE KEY areas of business operations (opportunities) where innovation can have a major impact on a company's future. If we identify these key areas, we can proceed to developing the capability to innovate in each one.

THE IMPORTANCE OF INNOVATING IN MORE THAN ONE AREA

This brings us to a key point: Of ten diverse trajectories along which major innovations may occur (listed below), the effective organization will sustain innovative success only when it can innovate in more than one area. True, innovations in a single area can produce big gains, but the gains will not be sustainable.

In other words, we need innovation in multiple areas if it's to produce a sustainable competitive advantage. These might be any combination of strategic and tactical innovations. The assertion that multiple innovations are necessary ups the ante considerably. If we're to have any hope of producing continuous innovation, the management of that resource must be more holistic, more inclusive. To achieve innovation in a single area is difficult. Achieving innovation in multiple areas is much more so, particularly to get the innovations when you need them. Why are multiple innovations required? There is a straightforward reason: One innovation usually demands another to become fully operational.

Here's an example. In 1959, Kelly Johnson and his design group at the famous Lockheed "Skunk Works" brought forth the still awesome SR-71 reconnaissance aircraft, the Blackbird. A technological marvel, the Blackbird—even when retired in the late 1990s—remains the most exotic high-performance aircraft (space travel excepted) ever created. It was an aircraft like none ever created before, the first to use the then–state-of-the-art carbon fiber material in copious amounts throughout the airframe.

Using a new material like carbon fiber for making a state-of-the-art aircraft is certainly innovative—so innovative, in fact, that there was no carbon fiber industry in existence to supply the required raw material or finished components. So the innovative design for the airplane could not be brought to fruition until a complete new industry was created to produce the raw material for the new design! It was an ambitious undertaking by any standard.

THE ORGANIZATION AS MORE THAN THE SUM OF ITS PARTS

According to the systems view of the organization, any complex organization is more than just the sum of its parts. Every complex system is defined not by the parts, but by the diverse and prolific interrelationships among all the elements in that system. Because the elements—the parts—do not function independently, it's necessary to manage them together, as an integrated whole. We may not be able to create an entire industry to support our innovations, but we can identify the important capabilities wherein innovation could produce immense benefit.

TEN KEY AREAS OF INNOVATION OPPORTUNITY

THERE ARE TEN specific areas where innovation can produce huge results. Each is but one of the interrelated elements in our system. Certainly, we can innovate in any one area, but when we do, our innovation will invariably impact other areas as well. When we anticipate these interrelated needs, we can prepare more effectively. The ten areas, shown in Figure 6-1, are:

1. Management development
2. Strategy development
3. Employee development
4. Product and service development
5. Process development
6. Tool and technology development
7. Supplier development
8. Market development

FIGURE 6-1. TEN AREAS OF INNOVATION OPPORTUNITY.

9. Distribution development

10. Brand development

These are primary areas of opportunity for the successful and vibrant organization. For an organization aspiring to innovation, each represents key capabilities wherein unusual skills may produce profitable innovations. These are also areas in which innovation can make a substantial difference in overall success.

CORE AND DISTINCTIVE COMPETENCIES

Every organization should be at least competent in all areas of their business, but core competencies—those fundamental skills that the organization does particularly well—are usually found in only two or three areas at most. Distinctive competencies—those competencies that the organization does uniquely well, and that competitors do not do well— are usually found only in a single area. Distinctive competencies are much less common and can create sustainable competitive advantage.

Core and distinctive competencies are not necessarily innovations per se. Competencies are the skills, systems, and values that sustain the success of your organization, though one would expect the rate of innovation to be highest in areas of particular competency. But innovation is not, and should not, be limited to areas of particular competency in a healthy and vibrant organization.

FOUNDATION ELEMENTS

If any of the ten areas listed above can provide a forum for major innovations, what do we mean when we say that every organization should develop the "capacity for innovation" in these areas? To be capable of innovating, several foundation elements must be present. At a minimum, these include:

- Understanding
- Experience
- Diversity
- Information and data
- Skills

To consistently innovate in a particular area—for example, market development—the person (or team) innovating requires some degree of each foundation element listed above. The person needs to understand the various elements of the market being targeted, and she must draw on experiences she's had in this or analogous segments to form relevant conclusions. This allows her to formulate an idea for tapping the market opportunity and generating a concept. Information (including experience) about the markets in consideration is drawn upon to refine ideas and approaches. The more diverse and rich this information base is, the better the result. Specific skills are of course necessary to bring the innovation to fruition and hone concepts of pragmatic solutions to real-world problems. These skills might include marketing planning, statistical analysis, selling skills, customer research, sales organization, promotion programs, and financial analysis.

EXAMINING THE KEY AREAS OF INNOVATION OPPORTUNITY

HOW ABOUT YOUR company? Have you developed the capacity to innovate in each of these areas? Are you *capable* of innovating in the ten areas of opportunity? Let's examine each of the ten areas of innovation opportunity.

MANAGEMENT DEVELOPMENT

Managers often consider the development of their employees—or the lack thereof. They're less likely to examine their own developmental needs and proactively take the steps to stay at the forefront of their profession. Yet what could be more important? As has been previously stated, no group of people has a greater impact on an organization's success than management, particularly senior management.

As senior managers, do we understand the issues that underlie the process of innovation? Do we feel comfortable that we can create the environment and policies to encourage the innovative forces of the organization to their highest levels? If not, it's time to crack the books and do our own research. We may need to study to find out. The Bibliography at the end of this book is a good place to start.

STRATEGY DEVELOPMENT

Successful strategies are arguably the central indicator of superior management. Strategy provides the fundamental basis for the innovations that make the company a superior competitor.

Everyone learns in grade school that Thomas Edison invented the light bulb. Fewer people know that Edison also started the electric power industry. Before a majority of homes could be connected by wire to a reliable source of power, innovation after innovation would be necessary. Edison needed a strategy to bring his business vision to reality.

He chose a strategy based on the technology of direct current (DC) power. His logic was that DC power was safer than alternating current (AC), operating at lower voltages, and besides, he had based all his experiments on DC. But DC ultimately did not prevail as the dominant technology.

Meanwhile, George Westinghouse had other ideas. In Europe, several successful AC systems had been developed. Westinghouse bought the patents of Nikola Tesla and hired him to make improvements to work better with Westinghouse's AC power transformer. Despite attacks from the DC advocates, Westinghouse Electric and Manufacturing Company was retained in 1893 to light the World's Columbian Exposition in Chicago. In addition, the Niagara Falls were developed with Westinghouse's AC generators. DC supporters were less successful in finding customers for their system.

Ultimately, it was alternating current that won in the marketplace. AC proved much more transportable, simpler, and more convenient. In actuality, it was also safer since it did not rely on batteries, which were a nuisance and could produce explosive hydrogen gas if the bank of batteries was not carefully tended. So in the end, the strategy based on DC power was a failure. No amount of innovation could overcome the inherent limitations of an inferior strategy. The same is true today.

EMPLOYEE DEVELOPMENT

Developing employees' skills, knowledge, and experience is a central theme in the topics to follow. Employees are by far the most crucial element in our "system." The interrelationships that form the network of the organization are primarily employee relationships. In addition, the experiences are employee experiences, the intellects are employee intellects, and the skills are employee skills. When the employees can't do the task, it doesn't get done. When we fail to invest in the people, ultimately we fail.

As with management development, employee development provides the richness of education, experience, understanding, and skills that permit day-to-day operations to proceed with superior efficiency and produce the commercially relevant innovations necessary for future success. A learning organization is capable of continually recreating itself as conditions dictate. The ability to recreate itself (what some have called reinvent itself) is the ultimate organizational creative act.

Without an active employee development program, the company is forced to try to recruit, hire, and retain the skills it needs. If the organization is small or growing rapidly, this approach can work pretty well for a while—maybe quite a while. Eventually, though, it catches up with those who try to cut corners this way. At some point, employees who lack the needed skills must be discharged and replaced with fresh employees with the new skills. The long-term impact on morale and loyalty isn't hard to imagine when an organization is seen as one that voraciously ingests people and then just sends them packing like so much excess baggage.

PRODUCT AND SERVICE DEVELOPMENT

Products and services are the lifeblood of every organization. Few businesspeople would argue that score. One would presume, then, that all well-managed organizations place great store by the capability to produce an uninterrupted stream of new and profitable products and services that meet understood needs of a well-defined customer universe. Many organizations, indeed, try to act in precisely such a manner. Others, though, find successful products to be elusive. Frequently, a big product success presages several mediocre performers—and maybe some outright failures. This is tolerable, maybe, if the successes are big enough, but it is erratic at best. Any organization, with a little work and discipline, can do better.

Certainly, developing products and services (or at least acquiring them) should be a core competency of every organization. There are three key elements that make up this competency:

1. Strategic market understanding

2. Strategic product direction (superior strategies)

3. A repeatable development process

We can examine each element in the context of the Innovation Management Model (first introduced in Chapter 3). Such analysis shows that both understanding the market and having a repeatable development process are System II functions—that is, those that involve shared resources. These are shared systems owned by the organization as a whole and used by multiple System I (operational) teams. The strategic product direction is a System IV function (concentrating on future direction), and clearly within the System IV responsibility of senior management.

This means that market knowledge (or creation of a strategic market segmentation model, if it takes that form) is the property of the entire organization. Often, market knowledge is seen as the property of the marketing department, and hence neither trusted nor supported by other functions, often including management. On the contrary, it can only perform to potential if it is clearly and unquestionably *shared corporate property,* just like the company values or the headquarters office building. The market segmentation model is a valuable corporate asset.

Thus, according to the Innovation Management Model, the corporate strategic market segmentation model (the official view of the market) is managed as a System II (shared) resource. The strategic market segmentation model should be managed as a multidisciplinary asset, and hence by a multidisciplinary team or function. It may be necessary to develop this multidisciplinary resource, gradually weaning the model away from the marketing department to become the joint owned asset it should be. If you currently have no market segmentation model, creating one can be a powerful growth experience for key people resources in the organization.

Here are some guidelines for developing products and services:

- If you do not have a clear, workable market segmentation model, create one.

- Recognize that when top management is engaged in the product/service development project, it will be an important element of the strategic plan.

- Understand what support the product development teams need from the System II functions, and see that it is provided efficiently.

- Audit these needs occasionally to be sure System II functions are still performing.

- Formalize the development process to the extent that it is repeatable, or better yet, until the *results* are repeatable. Then stop formalizing it. When it becomes a bureaucracy, it is no longer working.

More frequently, we are seeing retailers—catalog, online, and brick-and-mortar—increasing their involvement in the product development process. They may not actually make the product, but they apply their customer knowledge and promotional expertise to specify products to be built to suit a specific target market. What else is product development? Sears had long been deeply involved in the product development business, but not in the manufacturing business. Lands' End is another example. Many of today's computer companies do more "developing" than they do manufacturing.

Process Development

Process development is similar to product development in many respects, but it is different insofar that it tends to be more internally and more functionally focused. Process is the sovereign realm of the operational manager. It is less about *what* and more about *how* than product development.

How we see the processes involved has a great deal to do with how they can be optimized. For example, when we only envision key processes according to traditional definitions and labels, we will, not surprisingly, arrive at the same justification for the process that created it in the first place. Not much room for innovation in that approach. It's much more productive to experiment with different ways to "see" the processes by which the organization fulfills its purpose. An example is provided in Chapter 7 that demonstrates how a bricks-and-mortar manufacturer might reorganize by process rather than function. The key element in creating a structure such as this is the ability to envision the processes that will govern the structure and *see them* in the most useful way.

On a more specific and tactical level, process projects may be most effective when they are closely linked to product projects, because generally both can find significant improvements in the work of the other. There are often synergies, and huge benefits may be enjoyed when the communication and relationship between the process projects and product projects is close, cordial, and flexible. For example, a new product project to create a high-quality, low-cost lawn and garden tractor would certainly benefit greatly from a parallel project to streamline and consolidate procurement processes. Product and process are interdependent.

Here are some guidelines on process development:

- Develop interdisciplinary skills and relationships by rotating assignments.

- Avoid presuming that your existing, formal communications vehicles will be sufficient to clearly communicate between product and process projects.

- Process teams require shared resources as well as product teams. Make sure that they have them.

Process development is where systems thinking really shines. Process is about the interrelationships that make up the net of interactivity that constitutes the organization—the system.

TOOL AND TECHNOLOGY DEVELOPMENT

We encounter tools and technologies at various points in the development of most products. Often, success or failure of a project depends ultimately on the availability of tooling and technology. Profitability may be possible only under an assumption that proper tooling can be developed. In the example of the SR-71 aircraft given earlier in this chapter, an entire manufacturing industry (a micro-industry, at least) had to be created to build a few airplanes. Most products are much less demanding, but the tools and technologies are no less important.

There are key junctures where tool and technology development is critical. Several are listed below:

- TO CONCEIVE THE PRODUCT. In the 1980s, CAD (computer-aided design) equipment emerged to design products using a graphic computer program. It wasn't too long before someone developed the first CAM (computer-aided manufacturing) software to automatically write the necessary machining software for CNC (computer numeric control) lathes, milling machines, routers, and the like.

- **TO PRODUCE THE PRODUCT.** Steelcase, Inc., designed the largest selling office chair in history with its Sensor chair line. The chair was patented, of course, but the real profitability and competitive protection came from the expensive and proprietary tooling used to smoothly fit and glue the fabric to a molded foam substructure. Without the special tooling innovations, created in-house, cheap copies of the Sensor chair would have been on the market within a few months.

- **TO DEVELOP THE PRODUCT.** After the close of World War II, there was a great demand for office furniture to supply workplaces for all those returning from the war. During the 1950s and through the 1960s, several manufacturers developed procedures for testing the durability of key components of desks and chairs. Today, it's taken for granted that wear-related components are tested for reliability prior to introduction (at least the quality ones are). There are now industrywide standards that have evolved from these early innovative testing procedures and equipment.

- **TO DELIVER THE PRODUCT.** Arriba and Commerce One are among the most powerful entrants in the fast-moving (and hazardous) world of business-to-business Internet technology. Suppliers and customers are being linked together electronically to conduct much of the business formerly done less efficiently by manual means. How this will ultimately be achieved, and who the prime mover will be, is yet to be seen. But change is certainly afoot.

- **TO SERVICE THE PRODUCT.** It's difficult today to deal with a bank without being confronted with its automated phone service system. Such systems now deliver information on your balance, transactions, and general service through the push-button phone. When taken too far or less than brilliantly conceived, such systems can also be extremely frustrating.

- **TO RECYCLE THE PRODUCT.** A considerable little industry that remanufactures and upgrades used computers has sprung up to extend the life of rapidly outdated personal computers. As the rate of improvement in new equipment continues to increase, we may expect to see more of this activity. In another case, the office furniture market some years ago was flooded with used parts and pieces of the then–relatively new "systems furniture" (mostly panel systems). Methods, tools, and complete companies sprang up in the early 1980s to take these relatively useless and banged-up parts and pieces, refurbish them, and remarket them again as complete office solutions.

• **TO RESELL THE PRODUCT.** Since books have existed, there has probably always been a used book industry, but with the advent of the Internet, companies like Alibris.com, Bibliofind.com, and Amazon.com have placed the ultimate used book inventory at the fingertips of every potential buyer.

SUPPLIER DEVELOPMENT

The Toyota production system is the quintessential model of supplier development. In its march to become more efficient, the company chose to focus efforts on smoothing work flow. Toyota found that waste created uncertainty, and uncertainty—that enough good parts would be forthcoming, for example—caused function after function to create buffers, surplus inventory, etc., to bolster confidence they would not run out. Smoothing work flow called for eliminating these buffers and the uncertainty that caused them. Toyota was drawn to the idea now known as JIT (just-in-time), which caused a fundamental revolution in the relationship between the manufacturer and the supplier. To eliminate inventory buffers, it was necessary for the supplier to provide parts as needed with a great degree of certainty.

This caused manufacturers to concentrate purchases in the hands of a limited number of carefully selected, high-quality suppliers in which confidence could be vested. Reduction in the number of suppliers was followed by much closer engineering and development relationships with these suppliers. A cooperative, closely interrelated relationship with the supplier was in the interest of the manufacturer. The role shifted from one that was adversarial to one that was cooperative and system-enhancing, wherein both parties were seen as part of the same system. The system is now common throughout the developed world.

Initially, U.S. manufacturers tried to achieve efficiencies and lower prices simply by making strong demands on their suppliers. They later learned from Toyota that it was also necessary to help suppliers to become innovators on behalf of the manufacturer.

MARKET DEVELOPMENT

Market development should take place throughout the company, not just in the marketing department and sales department. Market development takes place in three distinct arenas:

1. Developing existing domestic markets

2. Expanding into new domestic markets

3. Developing or expanding foreign markets

In our view, the key to market development begins with a strategic market segmentation model. Once available, the detailed segmentation information is used first to examine domestic markets and analyze the product/service fit to currently served segments. Second, the segmentation information provides insight into the requirements of new domestic markets that are not currently being served by your company. For new markets, an opportunity analysis ensues from potential opportunities in new domestic target markets. In either case, innovation springs best, and with a greater sense of purpose, from accurate information about the various segments available to choose from.

Foreign markets almost always require a new segmentation model for each country being considered, but the principles of how to approach the opportunity are essentially the same as for domestic markets. The strategies may be quite different.

Access to markets (customers) is the principal governor of the engine of innovation. The most innovative organizations, particularly in the area of new products, are generally most hampered by an inability to reach the proper markets for their new products. If they cannot expand into new market sectors, then they are constrained to those they serve now, and by definition any new product or service outside that market is useless and a waste of resources. Thus, the organizations need to be able to stretch into new market opportunities. The key questions are to what degree they should enter such new markets, and how often.

If the organization is planning significant growth, the source of that growth becomes central. What will be required to provide access to the customers needed to meet the plan? Do you have the capacity for developing new markets?

DISTRIBUTION DEVELOPMENT

For some service organizations like hospitals, the product (health care) and the distribution of service are provided by the same organization at the same location. There is no distributor per se. The same may be true for other professions like law and public accounting. But for manufacturers of tangible products, all manner of distribution choices come into play. Where distributors and retailers are necessary to reach and serve customers, distribution choices are critical to success.

Distributors and producers usually interface on multiple levels. For instance, a manufacturer of office supplies may interface with its various distributors:

- At the sale level

- At the service level

- In customer service

- At the design-engineering level on build-to-order items

- At the relationship level (e.g., personal friendships and contacts)

- At the technology level (shared systems)

- At a coordinated product development level

In any event, the challenge of developing, expanding, and managing distributors quickly becomes a sizable chore in all but the smallest companies. Henry Ford is most often touted for his innovation of the assembly line and his unprecedented daily wage of $5. He is less often acknowledged for creating a distribution system capable of matching his fast-moving assembly lines. Without an innovative approach to selling his cars and getting them to their new owners, his other innovations would have been much less significant. Again, multiple innovations in several simultaneous categories are the norm rather than the exception.

BRAND DEVELOPMENT

When we drive down the street and see the "Golden Arches," we immediately think of hamburgers, fries, and a shake. McDonald's took an existing idea (fast food) and through its brand identification created the expectation of consistency. It was, as much as anything, this reliable expectation that the food in every McDonald's would be equally good, and essentially the same, that made McDonald's the best-known name in fast food the world over. (It's become such a powerful brand, in fact, that it frequently becomes a surrogate for protests against so-called "American imperialism" in numerous foreign countries.)

Innovations in branding are so common that we usually overlook the potential for innovation available through brand creation and management. Andersen Consulting has now become Accenture, a deliberately nonoffensive word in any language. Without doubt, Andersen spent a great deal of time and money delivering just the right name—one that meant nothing, but implied a positive image.

DEVELOPING CAPABILITY WITHIN THE INNOVATION MANAGEMENT MODEL

INNOVATIONS IN ANY of the ten areas of opportunity may be either strategic or tactical, but more likely there will be a pattern something like that shown in Figure 6-2. The roles and responsibilities of System I, II, III, and IV in developing the capacity for innovation are apparent from the figure. Please keep in mind that only the ten innovation development areas are shown on the diagram. Figure 6-2 is not a complete job description for each system level.

For example, System I (the operational team level) is primarily involved with employee development (their own), product and service development, and distribution development. System II (shared resources) is involved with management development, supplier development, tool and technology development, process development, and brand development. System III (the strategic and managerial level) is involved with management development and market development, while System IV (the future) concentrates on management development.

All ten of the areas in which we see opportunity for increasing the capacity to innovate fit easily on the Innovation Management Model. One observation may come to mind, though: Out of all ten opportunity areas, only two are placed under the activity cluster of "develop capacity." This is not the paradox it first appears. It is because management and employee development tend also to encompass the others in the sense that the real capabilities of an organization are always in the

	NURTURE	DEVELOP	IMPLEMENT/ COMMERCIALIZE	EXPLOIT
System IV	MANAGEMENT DEVELOPMENT	MANAGEMENT DEVELOPMENT	N/A	N/A
System III	MANAGEMENT DEVELOPMENT	MANAGEMENT DEVELOPMENT	MARKET DEVELOPMENT	MARKET DEVELOPMENT
System II	MANAGEMENT DEVELOPMENT	MANAGEMENT DEVELOPMENT	SUPPLIER DEVELOPMENT TOOL TECHNICAL DEVELOPMENT PROCESS DEVELOPMENT	BRAND DEVELOPMENT
System I	N/A	EMPLOYEE DEVELOPMENT	PRODUCT/SERVICE DEVELOPMENT DISTRIBUTION DEVELOPMENT	N/A

heads of its people. To acknowledge this reality and also make the figure more meaningful, we allowed the other eight areas to migrate to those systems where they are more commonly found in practice. While the lines between cells on the figure are hardly rigid, we assign market development, for example, as a System III–level responsibility in the activity clusters of "implement/commercialize" and "exploit." Our reasoning is that the decision responsibility for developing new markets is invariably higher than System I or System II. In other words, the capacity to innovate in the area of market development requires increasing the skills and knowledge of some pretty senior managers.

Using the model helps us know what to manage, who needs to manage it, and something about what needs to be done to increase the capacity to innovate. We will expand on these ideas more as we move to Chapter 7.

SUMMARY

- Creating the capability for innovation is a management responsibility.

- Frequently, innovation must be achieved in multiple areas simultaneously to achieve sustained competitive advantage. Innovation in a single area is not sustainable.

- There are ten key areas of opportunity for strategic and tactical innovation: (1) management development, (2) strategy development, (3) employee development, (4) product and service development, (5) process development, (6) tool and technology development, (7) supplier development, (8) market development, (9) distribution development, and (10) brand development.

- Creating capability for innovation requires developing: (1) understanding, (2) experience, (3) diversity, (4) information and data, and (5) skills.

- The Innovation Management Model helps organize and assign responsibility for increasing our capacity to innovate.

NOTE

1. Jonathan Swift, *Gulliver's Travels* (New York: Oxford University Press, 1998). First published as *Travels into Several Remote Nations of the World, by Lemuel Gulliver*, in 1726.

CHAPTER SEVEN

CRAFTING THE INNOVATING ORGANIZATION

"**W**HERE SHOULD I PUT *THIS*? How am I to make sense of all these things? There's no rhyme or reason to all these listings!" As a naturalist, he had been collecting information on flora and fauna for many years. His existing method of categorizing and retaining his specimens and other materials were less than efficient. He frequently was misplacing important items, causing considerable frustration. He needed a better method.

Aristotle had worked out a classification methodology 2,000 years ago, but that system was pretty rudimentary. Too many items lacked a logical "place." Carl von Linné wanted a better, more encompassing approach to classifying organisms. He was convinced he could do better; and maybe others would use his system if he could come up with one. He began to consider the project and the many challenges involved.

Ideally, it would be a structure that could encompass all plants and animals. He would create his system to begin with the most general and proceed to the most specific. He settled on beginning with kingdom, then class, then order, then genus, and finally species. Plants and animals would surely be separate kingdoms. But what criteria should he use for the subordinate categories? If he chose poorly, his system would bog down as he burdened it with more and more items. Perhaps he could use these defining characteristics of each type as key discriminators. But which characteristics?

For example, all those animals having mammary glands might, in this scheme, become "mammalia." A nested system of categories could produce a species name that would be truly unique for each and every different plant or animal. He felt a sudden rush of satisfaction. This could actually work! He would assign each organism a two-part Latin name; this would begin with the genus, and then the specific name. Humans would receive a name as well: He would call them Homo sapiens. In this way, his binomial species name could replace the much more cumbersome previous method of offering a long descriptive narrative.

He settled on his classification scheme to expedite both the identification of and reference to unique organisms. The system he created was clear and indeed effective. It achieved the goals established for it, and it continues to do so. Oh yes, before he was knighted in 1761 by the Swedish government for his work, Carl was known as Carolus Linnaeus. We know him as the creator of the biological classification system used throughout natural science to this day. Carolus Linnaeus had indeed created a good system.

WHAT STRUCTURE IS BEST?

CRAFTING THE INNOVATIVE enterprise addresses the issue of which structure can best encourage and nurture an innovative environment without incurring the anarchy that invariably results from an absence of organization. The problem is not so dissimilar from Linnaeus's challenge. How to organize the human resources around business activities to achieve a desired result is daunting. If the organization is too tight and controlled and too hierarchical, innovation is stymied. Too little, and pandemonium results.

As one approaches the question of organization, two distinct and important factors emerge early on. First are the issues that are directly related to enhancing innovation. The second is how to do business in a changing world. Today's business environment is changing rapidly, and we must determine how to accommodate and exploit opportunities of the flowering world of Internet-enabled e-business and e-commerce. The way we do business is changing, and our organizations must change to make best use of the opportunity.

We could spend pages here discussing structures for yesterday's economy, but it would add little real value. *Today's* organization, after all, is essentially about *yesterday's* economy. The fundamental structure of many organizations does not differ appreciably from what one might have found in a manufacturing company of the early 20th century. We thus prefer to address the potential inherent in tomorrow's organization. However, we don't know precisely what tomorrow's economy will be like. We believe, though, that it will be quite different from yesterday's and also feel that an electronically enabled organization offers opportunities both new and powerful—opportunities that can have a great impact on encouraging and supporting innovation. The focus of this chapter is hence tomorrow's challenge to our collective organizing skills. We will offer what we consider to be a logical alternative to today's function-based structure.

ORGANIZING FOR AN INNOVATIVE FUTURE

EMINENT HISTORIAN JACQUES Barzun persuasively contends that we are on the threshold of a new era.[1] The "modern" era, which he defines as beginning in the year 1500, is in the process of being replaced by a new and different era even as this is being written. It will take a while to reach full flower, but a new era is unfolding all the same. At the forefront, particularly for our purposes here, is the revolutionary impact of information technology, specifically the Internet. Crafting the innovative organization is one thing. Add to that a major sea change with respect to the foundations of work and commerce, and we have a new challenge entirely—a challenge with which we are unfamiliar.

We offer several observations:

- Fundamental structural changes are occurring in the way business is conducted. These will spark major changes in organizational structure.

- We are early in a sea change in business process.

- The pace of change in organization structure will accelerate.

- Organizing around process is likely to be most successful for most organizations.

- Many traditional job functions are vanishing, obsolete in an e-business environment. Entirely new functions are appearing in their place.

Obviously, the dot-coms are experimenting with new organization structures to accommodate their unique challenges and opportunities. But other, more traditional, organizations will be affected to a great degree as well. Innovation in the form of new and effective organization structures will be an evolving accomplishment of the coming decades. We will figure out how to do our work better, and it certainly will not be done the same way we do it now.

As of early 2001, we have been witnessing the first shakeout of the fledgling dot-coms. Those that were not viable, carried along only on the euphoria of IPOs and bubble-inflated stock prices, have crashed to earth. Certainly more will do the same. But make no mistake, those that *are* viable will continue to shape the future of many industries.

What is truly different and powerful in all this change is the way it will affect the normal business, the low-tech business. Makers of screen doors will learn to accommodate the new potentialities just as will the chip manufacturers. Every organization will find it has to change in very real and tangible ways, or it will perish. This profound insight may come too late for some companies.

RECENT DEVELOPMENTS IN ORGANIZATIONAL THINKING

WITHOUT QUESTION, THE most vibrant and dynamic concepts of organization have emerged from recent work in the natural sciences. These new developments, which have come about well within the lifetimes of most readers, stem from discoveries in the organization of living systems and have produced new understanding in just how living systems are organized and function. Three key areas make up the bulk of this new knowledge:

1. Discoveries in pattern and organization

2. Discoveries in structure

3. Discoveries in process and cognition

Since commercial organizations and social organizations are living systems, we can learn from this research and apply the concepts to forming and operating more effective and efficient organizations.

While there are many fascinating aspects of organizational dynamics, we will focus on one dimension: structuring organizations around process. Let's look first at another recent development exerting a very real influence on organizations of all kinds.

DIFFERENT TYPES OF ORGANIZATION STRUCTURE

MANAGING INNOVATION REQUIRES organization, but what is the appropriate organization structure? An effective structure must be able to satisfy the requirements of an innovative organization, while simultaneously functioning in a new environment driven by emerging technologies. We have arrived at an approach we feel satisfies both critical demands. In its briefest form, the approach:

- Organizes around the activity clusters that constitute process fulfillment.

- Forms a modest hierarchy consistent with the accountability horizon (time focus) of the decision maker.

We will discuss each in detail, but for the moment, note that there are several common ways of organizing—such as by function, by market segment, or by geography—but organizing around process is emerging as particularly amenable to teamwork and e-business. We'll see how and why.

In the 1990s, hierarchies got a bad name. Pyramidal organizations are bad, bad, bad; flat organizations are good, good, good. But all organizations have hierarchies. It is not the existence of hierarchy per se that causes most of the problems, but how the hierarchy is structured. Establishing the hierarchical structure according to the accountability horizon, or time focus, of the decision maker has proven to be particularly effective. Most organizations have too many levels, too closely spaced, and based on pay grades rather than accountability. When pay grades are separated from hierarchical structure, an effective and efficient hierarchy can be implemented that performs well in either a process-focused organization or a traditional one. If you're a professional scientist, researcher, engineer, designer, or the like, it should not be necessary to go "higher up" the management hierarchy to make more money. Many talented professionals are lost to their profession (e.g., engineering) to become managers, wherein they spend virtually no time "engineering."

ORGANIZING AROUND PROCESS FULFILLMENT

There are several familiar structural choices for organizing a company, the most common being a structure by department or function—the marketing department, the accounting department, the engineering department, etc. Where this method was de rigueur only recently, about 1990, it has been substantially diluted by recent emphasis on team structures and matrix approaches.

Also familiar are organization charts based on product line. In this approach, one finds the motorcycle division, the lawn mower division, the lift truck division, and all similar departments and business units. When structuring by product line, one essentially presumes that all other methods are subordinate to product line in importance, or that other considerations pretty much automatically fall into proper alignment with the product line. In other words, if we manage the product line properly, our other objectives will also be served. Sometimes this may be true, as with Philips NV, and has found organizing of product line to be effective on a global basis. At Philips NV, the HQ for a particular product division need not even be in the Netherlands, as with the monitor division, headquartered in Taiwan.

Organizing by market or market segment gets occasional attention, but many companies find it too cumbersome to implement. Organizations serving many segments or different businesses may find it far too complex and generally unworkable, though there is much to be said for any approach focusing on the customer. Frequently, for example, companies doing considerable business with government manage this part of their business as an independent entity, or at least partially so.

Geographic structures may make sense for some organizations, though this method seems less common than the others. One could challenge the need for geographic organization in today's environment. Information technology has gone a long way toward mitigating the need to be located in close proximity to others working on the same problem or toward the same goal. It is not unusual today to find projects being pursued simultaneously by coworkers located all over the world, and for some applications, information technology is sufficient to overcome the liability of distance. In some cases, it's probably even faster.

One drawback with all these approaches—department/function, product line, market, or geographic—is that they are essentially "linear" in conception. Each presumes that activities and challenges occur in a straight-line sequential manner. But this flies in the face of what we have learned about complex systems, specifically living systems. Living systems are not linear. They are circular in nature, best represented by a vast network of interconnected elements representing innumerable possibilities. In such cases, linear solutions are an extreme oversimplification. A systems view is superior to a linear view of a living organization every time.

Our favored approach, structuring an organization around process fulfillment, incorporates current thinking drawn from systems theory (see Chapter 2). Organizing around process fulfillment also incorporates some of the most recent thinking in the areas of biological and ecological models of organizational behavior. This approach would seem uniquely suited to current needs of information- and Net-based businesses. It's particularly true when the process by which the organization fulfills its customers' needs is changing in fundamental ways, as it appears to be doing at the moment in nearly every business. To this another element must be added: making sure the hierarchy is based on the time horizon for which each manager is accountable.

A LOW-TECH EXAMPLE OF
A HIGH-TECH CHALLENGE

PERHAPS A BRIEF example will bring the issue into closer focus. Let's examine the case of Public Furniture Company (an alias, though the company is real). The company is a leader in a rather specialized field, makes relatively low-tech products for public institutions and commercial businesses, and enjoys reasonably good relationships with its customers, employees, suppliers, distributors, and the community in which it is located. Though it has less than a billion dollars in sales, its growth has been strong, its profits are good, and it has been expanding into international markets for some time. The company's present organization is typical of a moderate-size manufacturer, structured around key functional departments similar to the diagram shown in Figure 7-1.

Several current situations present Public Furniture Company with both opportunities and challenges:

- Current product lines are designed and produced in traditional ways.

- The Internet has had relatively little impact on its industry, with the exception of e-mail.

- The company is primarily a manufacturer, occupying only a limited position in the value chain for its products.

- While the company has been expanding internationally, it is now more vulnerable to international competitors, particularly from Mexico.

- It has relatively little real competition at the present time. There is no sense of perceived urgency.

How will the future economy, this e-economy, affect a relatively straightforward and traditional organization like this one? The impact will be considerable, and it won't be long in coming. This new technology permits customers (and competitors) to do business in fundamentally new ways. Activities that used to be done by people will be done faster, cheaper, and in some cases better by electronic means. These are of course all information-related activities—but the most frustrating, delay-prone, error-inducing, and problem-solving activities *are* in-

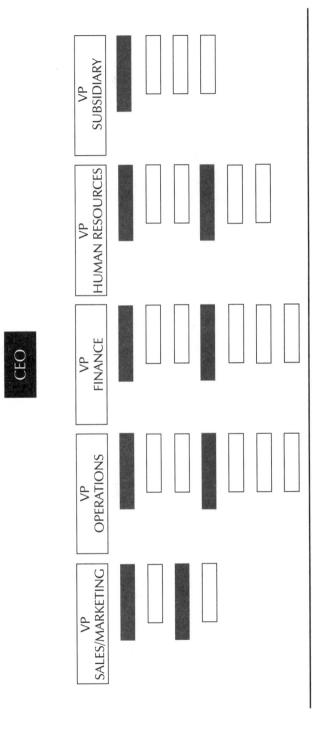

FIGURE 7-1. THE CURRENT ORGANIZATION OF PUBLIC FURNITURE COMPANY.

formation-related activities. The manufacturer still makes the product, but the information-rich environment in which the physical activity happens is changing at a very rapid rate. This is a result of how the technology is being applied to wide-ranging and common business activities.

The primary reason these effects haven't already confronted Public Furniture Company is the absence of really strong or sizable competitors (though this could change). A Public Furniture executive once observed, "We're the best in a lousy industry." In either event, the company has not been seriously threatened to date, though there is incessant price pressure from its unsophisticated domestic and international competitors.

Hence, Public Furniture Company's traditional organization chart will likely be challenged in the future, for the following reasons:

- Achieving results will become more and more process-driven.

- Customer focus will intensify. New and powerful means of identifying and segmenting customers will become common.

- It will no longer be possible to control events by withholding information when everyone is connected with e-business technology.

- Business relationships will undergo enhancements made possible by the new technology, becoming both closer and more committed.

- The comfortable world of middlemen is changing. Hence, middlemen (and everyone else) will have to justify their value or perish.

Any one of these developments would present a significant challenge. Two such trials could be enough to upset a relatively weak competitor. Take them all together, and this packet of problems offers a major obstacle to even the strongest competitor. For those who are unaware or ill-informed, the future could be more than painful. It could be fatal.

UPSETTING TRADITIONAL BUSINESS

HOW ARE THESE developments upsetting traditional business? Recently, one of the authors went to his favorite men's department in an upscale department store, in search of a new pair of dress slacks. A simple purchase, to be sure, but the experience was illuminating. Locating a suitable pair of trousers in the proper size was no problem. Once the choice was made, all that remained was to have the pants cuffed. The salesman marked the trousers for cuff length, and when the author returned from the changing room, the salesman proudly told him that the pants would be ready for pickup in three weeks! How's that for real service?

This situation isn't uncommon. At least, it would not have been uncommon ten years ago. You just waited or pleaded for special handling and a better date on some premise of great and urgent need (as the author did in this case). It happens all the time.

But consider the difference when you call or place an order online with a company like Lands' End, located hundreds of miles away in Wisconsin. One of us placed an order with Lands' End for a pair of trousers that had to be cuffed at a slightly nonstandard size. Two days after the order was placed, the trousers arrived, via UPS, properly cuffed.

Now, we ask you, which of these vendors of trousers is likely to have a big surprise one of these days? Why drive nine miles to a store, find a parking space, go through the search for the proper pants, have them measured, then wait three weeks, return to pick up the trousers, and return home, when a simple phone call or a few keystrokes can accomplish the same result? Lands' End has learned how to serve demanding customers reliably, even flawlessly, with quality products and services in a very short period of time by selecting products, services, and technology that combine seamlessly to result in satisfied customers. The people at Lands' End have innovated. Their process takes maximum advantage of the new technology to differentiate the company in terms of value added to their chosen customers. For many, the company has completely replaced the friendly, so-called personal service of the traditional local clothing store. Just a few years ago, who would ever have thought it?

The moral of the story thus far is this: If a well-run but conventional department store can be threatened in fundamental and powerful ways by a competitor operating in new and dynamic ways, offering genuine value through unconventional vehicles (catalog and Internet), then the company in our example—Public Furniture—can also find itself either threatened or energized by a similar application of creative thinking and organization.

Note that Public Furniture Company has a similar opportunity, even though it produces and sells no retail consumer products at all. Its world is also changing, though in less obvious ways. Public Furniture needs innovation every bit as much as Lands' End. Organizations thinking they have little to fear from the Lands' Ends of the world are missing the point entirely. They will be challenged at some point just as the department store is. They need to find a way to provide the highest value, best service combination for their customers just as Lands' End does. In fact, their opportunities are greater, because the range of processes they perform is much wider than that of a catalog/ Internet clothing retailer.

A HIERARCHY BASED ON ACCOUNTABILITY HORIZONS

ONE MORE ELEMENT needs to be added: accountability. When we mention hierarchy, we normally think of those organizations in the 1950s and 1960s that included layer after layer of middle managers, each dispensing information and exercising control. The problem with these hierarchical structures was simple: Many of the layers were contributing little or no value. They were often as not obstructing communication and information flow rather than expediting efficiency. But technology provided little in the way of a viable substitute fifty years ago. The requirements then were not all that much different from what they were in the 19th century. Hence, the structure was similar. But since about 1985 or so, any attraction to tall organizational pyramids has vaporized. Tall pyramids have become a liability and are vanishing faster than the 10¢ cup of coffee—and for good reasons.

One reason is that technology has certainly provided us with new tools. But even after reducing middle management levels, many organizations still find it difficult to settle on the right number of layers of the right kind and responsibility. That's because they're going about it in an inappropriate manner. Elliott Jaques contends that we still have too many layers, and he feels that those we have are inefficiently structured. His proposal is to determine the proper structure (i.e., with the most effective number and type of layers) by examining the accountability horizons for each level of decision making.[2] The accountability horizon of management is that period of time within which the manager's decisions (those he is authorized to make) produce results. It is the time frame within which the manager should be focusing his efforts.

In any discussion of management layers, the concern turns to compensation. In the scheme favored by both Jaques and the authors, pay grades do not necessarily follow hierarchical level. Or, maybe it would be more accurate to say they should not follow *only* managerial level. When a professional, for example, must move into management to advance her salary, the organization loses twice. First, it loses the professional's skills if she leaves the company, and second, it may not get a great manager if she moves into a managerial slot. The employee loses too, when she feels she needs to change her career to management just to advance.

When manager levels and professional skills are muddled together, complex and redundant levels are an inevitable result. It has been our experience that Jaques's observations are sound. Most organizations have too many of the wrong kind of levels, heavily influenced by pay grade and sometimes populated with people who would rather be doing something else. The challenges of the new e-economy virtually demand that we do better. It is more important than ever to get the organization levels right.

One approach is to separate the managerial component and the professional component of positions. If the job is exclusively managerial, then Jaques's levels of accountability would apply. If the job is exclusively professional, then a professional scale could be applied. Should a job include both, then there might be a component for the managerial part and another for the professional part. But the integrity of the managerial hierarchy determined by accountability horizon should remain intact. Don't call professionals managers just to increase their pay, and don't call them managers just to avoid paying them overtime. A case for proper hierarchy is outlined in Figure 7-2. It shows, for example, that while those on the shop or office floor have accountability horizons measured in days or weeks, the accountability horizons of general managers are measured in about three years and the CEO/COO considerably longer.

Jaques is making a case for a flat organization—but not just any flat organization. He is advocating an "enlightened hierarchy." His or-

FIGURE 7-2. THE CASE FOR PROPER HIERARCHY BASED ON ACCOUNTABILITY HORIZONS.

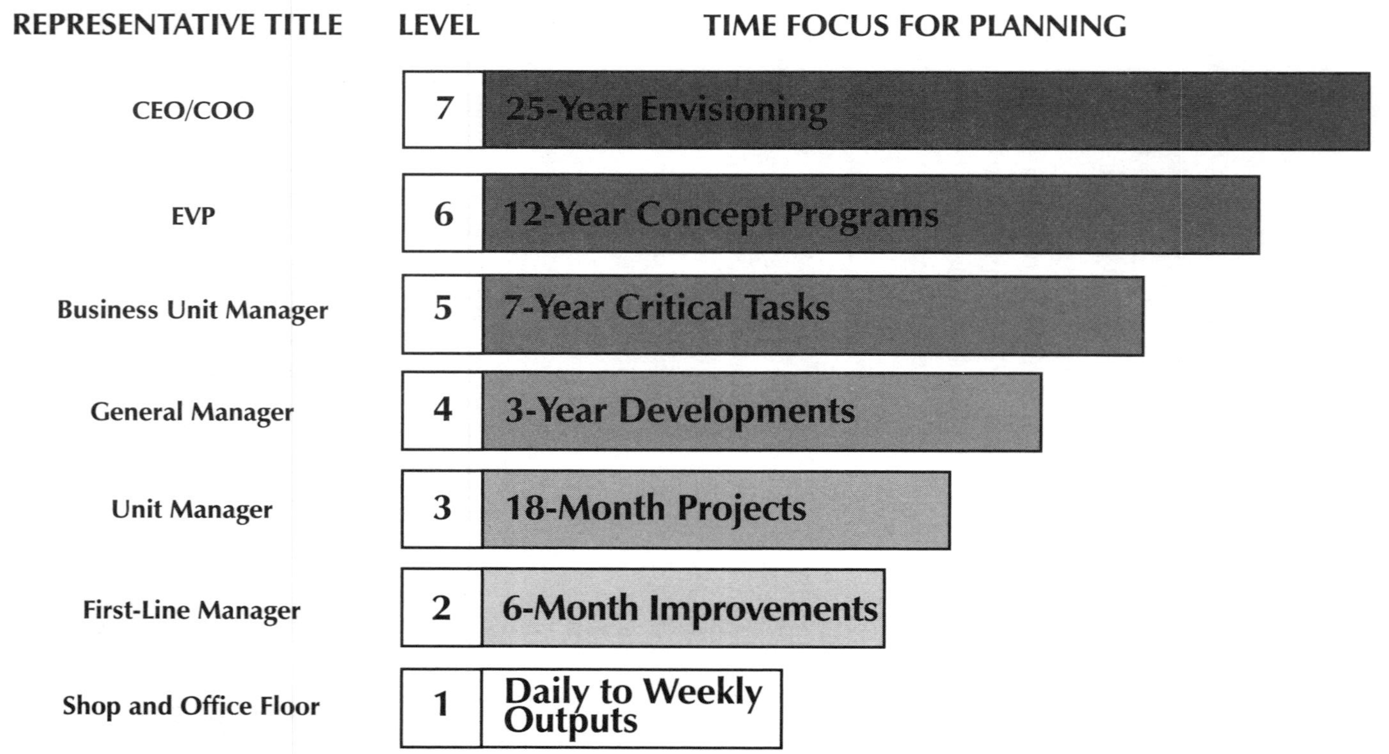

REPRESENTATIVE TITLE	LEVEL	TIME FOCUS FOR PLANNING
CEO/COO	7	25-Year Envisioning
EVP	6	12-Year Concept Programs
Business Unit Manager	5	7-Year Critical Tasks
General Manager	4	3-Year Developments
Unit Manager	3	18-Month Projects
First-Line Manager	2	6-Month Improvements
Shop and Office Floor	1	Daily to Weekly Outputs

ganization is not only flatter: It is governed by a clear principle, that of a specific time horizon for each level of management.

RESPONSIBILITY BASED ON PROCESS ACTIVITY CLUSTERS

WE NOW HAVE a guiding principle of organization—the accountability horizon. But what specifically is on this new "horizon"? We said earlier that we favored structuring around process because a process focus offers new opportunities to align resources in new ways. In Figure 7-1, five strategic activity clusters are shown, defined in a traditional functional way. Each cluster (a function, in this example) consists of a multitude of subprocesses, but for purposes of demonstration, the more aggregate clusters are sufficient to make our point.

Public Furniture Company looks just like most manufacturing companies in the world today, organized into such a traditional structure. How do we determine the most desirable future structure, given that e-business and process fulfillment are major concerns? There are a couple of distinct steps required to get from a traditional functional structure to organizing by process fulfillment.

In the case of Public Furniture Company, we begin by identifying the various elements in the customer's value chain. Each element or process represents a part of the total cost paid by the customer with respect to the product. Think of the total customer purchase as totaling one dollar. How many cents go for each value-added component making up the dollar? On our way to organizing by process, we first need to know what the major elements are in the larger scheme of providing the customer with products and services directly and indirectly involved in satisfying his overall need. From analysis of this high-level snapshot, Public Furniture can identify opportunities open to it in the whole value chain and determine whether there is advantage in seeking such a greater (or lesser) role.

Note that in this example, the value chain includes life cycle cost elements not normally included in common definitions of product. Analysis of these extended product/service definitions is a key to finding new opportunities. Try to ensure that your model takes this analysis and includes all aspects of the sale and use that are valued by the customer (i.e., what the customer would be willing to pay for). Figure 7-3

FIGURE 7-3. THE VALUE CHAIN.

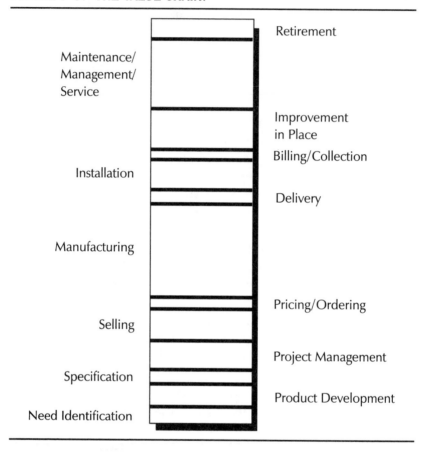

provides an example of what we mean by all aspects of sale and use—in other words, the value chain. Such things are often the real opportunities for growth.

Having identified the relevant processes contributing value to the customer's purchase and use of the product, we can determine how Public Furniture Company currently adds value in each process. We also see where Public Furniture participates in various links of the value chain. We can also identify those areas where Public Furniture does not participate, leaving these areas to be provided by others.

We see from the shaded areas in Figure 7-4 that Public Furniture participates in only a limited number of the value-creating processes related to its customer's total experience of the product—specifically,

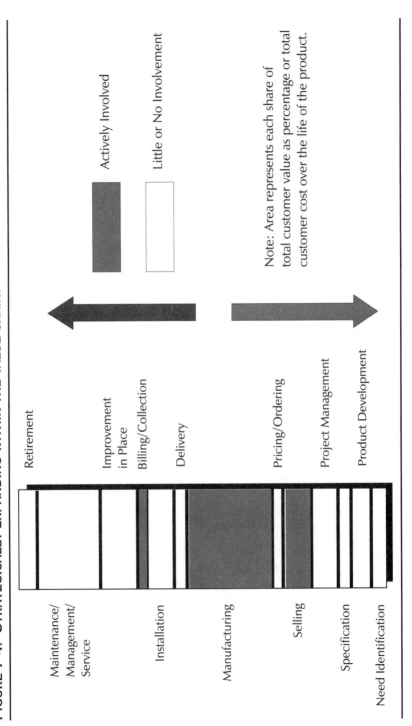

FIGURE 7-4. STRATEGICALLY EXPANDING WITHIN THE VALUE CHAIN.

manufacturing, selling, and billing/collection. Past choices to focus on these value-adding elements were, of course, based on a traditional economy. If this were the only consideration, the decision to choose these elements would not be a bad one. But today it could be a mistake to stop there.

When the present organizational decisions were made, Public Furniture encountered only traditional domestic competitors, and weak ones at that. The company's small size made it practical to follow a "stick to your knitting" approach. There was no point in accepting additional risks and responsibilities, mostly because there was no real payoff in doing so. So why do it now? What's in it for Public Furniture today?

Let's look at those portions of the value chain Public Furniture now participates in with its products and services. What we see in Figure 7-4 is a relatively limited involvement (the shaded areas) in the overall value creation chain for the company's own products. Granted, it dominates some of the largest processes, but in the overall picture, it participates directly in only a fraction of the potential logically available to it through its current customer base. The question is whether it makes sense for the company to expand into those new areas. Should Public Furniture undertake greater responsibility in its value chain and accordingly add these new revenue sources to its income statement?

Another key issue allied to the decision to expand involvement is the overall delivered quality of the customer experience. Expansion may be even more desirable when the potential for synergy exists, or when the expansion may reduce problems either from a communications or performance perspective. Can expansion to new areas improve quality and increase profitability? Can expansion reduce uncertainty costs by giving this manufacturer a more direct role with the client? Can Public Furniture perform some of these additional functions more efficiently and reliably than the present purveyors? These would be legitimate and powerful reasons for looking to expand within the value chain. Is this true for Public Furniture? To find out, it's necessary to go a bit further.

SEEING THE PROCESSES DIFFERENTLY

CONTINUING WITH OUR example, we analyze the current and potential areas of opportunity for Public Furniture. What emerges from the analysis is illuminating. Figure 7-5 shows the new possible process groupings. Compare these with the present structure shown in Figure 7-1. It is a big departure for Public Furniture.

The new process fulfillment categories are very different. The present functional organization has four vice presidents plus a VP of Subsidiaries. The new structure would still have four vice presidents (presuming each of the new categories warrants a continuation of the VP-level position, which is probably the case). What is truly striking is the increase in customer focus offered by the process fulfillment structure. Each new vice president would be able to control an entire process comprised of various subfunctions. This is very streamlined, with the vice president in control of the elements necessary for success of the process. It would appear to be a vast improvement over the current system. It's also a structure that would support more appropriate electronic relationships with customers than is possible with the present function-driven structure.

FIGURE 7-5. NEW POSSIBLE PROCESS GROUPINGS FOR PUBLIC FURNITURE COMPANY.

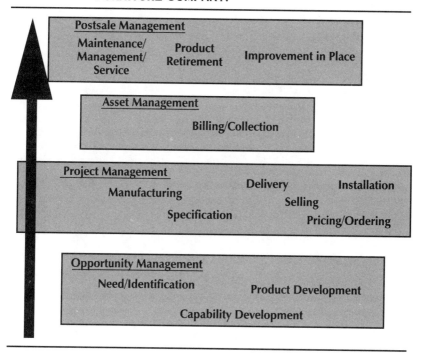

THE E-FRIENDLY
ORGANIZATION STRUCTURE

THERE SEEMS TO be a payoff right now for Public Furniture, and the company has grown to a size where it can both accommodate and finance a more strategically advantageous strategy—that enabled by e-technology. New e-business B2B (business-to-business) opportunities are unfolding with the new technology, and this is changing the landscape for Public Furniture. The company can try to pass on the new developments in the hope that its customers will not demand these new services. Or, it has the opportunity to restructure its traditional operations around new opportunities to far exceed the value-added performance of its domestic and international competitors.

Organizing around processes rather than functions would be a big change for Public Furniture. To move to a process-based organization, totally new systems will be needed, and time will be required to complete the transition, but the benefits could be huge, since a process fulfillment structure can identify completely new opportunities to increase customer value, reduce costs, increase profits, and improve the loyalty of customers through new ways of managing relationships with customers and suppliers. The new organization for Public Furniture would conceptually look something like that in Figure 7-6.

The figure shows four major process activity clusters—opportunity management, project management, asset management, and postsale management—connected by networks that also include foreign subsidiaries and joint ventures. External relationships include customer segments, wherein the customer consults an electronic catalog and communicates with Public Furniture electronically for most routine transactions. Personal sales time is reduced dramatically, not just to reduce costs but because the electronic communication with the customer is both faster and more convenient for many transactions and routine service matters. Coordination of the company's worldwide activities is also enhanced. Supplier transactions and service communications are improved and speeded up in the same manner as the transactions with customers. The new diagram looks like a network rather than an organization chart.

Structuring around process fulfillment, when thoughtfully and carefully implemented, permits new and novel ways of solving prob-

FIGURE 7-6. PUBLIC FURNITURE COMPANY AS AN "E-ENABLED" ORGANIZATION.

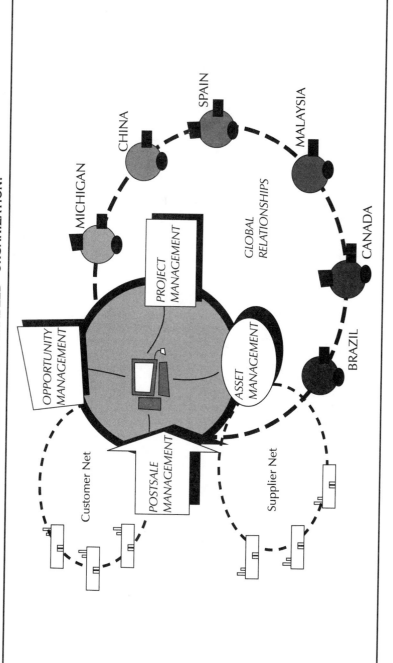

lems and exploiting opportunities. To function smoothly, however, such a structure may require changes in product lines, product catalogs, and service policies to expedite and enhance the new possibilities. Managed holistically, the process-based organization can reach new levels of customer satisfaction while increasing internal efficiency. It does so by using the technology to best advantage by structuring products, services, processes, etc., to work synergistically with the technology. The system (the new organization) is designed as a whole, not a collection of parts.

STEPS IN NEW ORGANIZATION DESIGN

CREATING A NEW and more appropriate structure suited to the new demands of the e-economy can be approached in several discrete steps. These are:

1. Determine the current value chain for the business.

2. Identify those parts of the value chain in which your organization now participates.

3. Reengineer the value chain to capitalize on foreseeable technologies.

4. Identify the main process clusters to be provided by this value chain.

5. Determine if the new clusters represent a new way of viewing the opportunity presented. If not, rethink the value chain.

6. Structure the new organization according to the future process.

Many issues invariably arise in the course of these six steps. For one, there should be considerable discussion surrounding the creation and reengineering of the value chain. At this juncture, you are doing nothing less than reengineering your basic business design. That's certainly not trivial.

Rethinking the process clusters to become the basis for the revised structure also presents both opportunities and challenges. It's necessary to consider a wide range of possibilities, and the best conception is probably not the one that is closest to the current system. It's important to see the business in many different ways—to mentally model new possibilities. If not, then most of the potential for excellence and innovation may be lost to yesterday's mental models.

The actual implementation of such a dramatic change demands careful planning and extensive communication with everyone involved—customers, suppliers, employees, joint-venture partners, and anyone else touched by the changes. To do less is to invite failure. Laying the groundwork for such a transition may take months or even years, so having a pretty clear vision of the desired result helps a great deal. To begin such a journey with only a fuzzy vision virtually guarantees that problems will appear like raindrops in a monsoon.

REVISITING THE
INNOVATION MANAGEMENT MODEL

LET US MAKE a final connection between the system levels in our Innovation Management Model and Elliott Jaques's principles of management accountability/time horizon. As we would expect, and as Figure 7-7 shows, System IV demands a longer time horizon than System I.

In addition to drawing the parallel between the business systems of the Innovation Management Model and the time horizons of management levels, a clear message comes through in Figure 7-7. First, System I managers (short-term accountability) should never be given System IV responsibility. It is true that increasing participation levels across management levels is one positive development of the past couple of decades, but participation should not be confused with accountability. Long-term future-oriented responsibilities call for skills and experience levels not common to junior managers. Conversely, System IV managers (given time horizons of five to twenty-five years) should never waste their time on System I (or any other short-term) problems.

It's only a short step further to superimpose a time horizon curve on our Innovation Management Model matrix to visually reinforce the point that nurturing and capability-creating activities are centered in System IV and System III activities, where the time horizon of managing these systems is five years or more. (See Figure 7-8.) Implementing

FIGURE 7-7. COMBINING THE SYSTEM LEVELS WITH THE ACCOUNTABILITY/TIME HORIZONS.

SYSTEM LEVEL	TIME HORIZON
System IV..........................5–25 years	
System III...........................3–5 years	
System II............................1–3 years	
System I.....................less than 1 year	

activities have a much briefer management accountability horizon, typically one to three years, and are generally System I activities. Likewise, exploitation of innovations tends to be a System I activity, with a management accountability horizon of one year or less.

System II activities, by their nature, transcend any specific project team or specific System I activity. As mentioned earlier, System II activities are primarily found in the capability-creating activity cluster with a management horizon of one to three years.

FIGURE 7-8. THE TIME HORIZON CURVE.

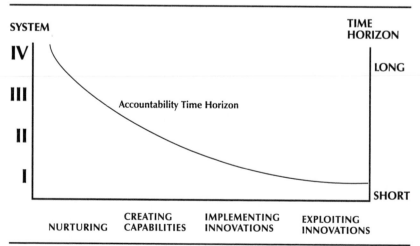

Figure 7-9 shows how the various system levels relate to the various process activity clusters proposed for Public Furniture. We see how the process-organized company would be managed by four levels (or systems), each with clearly identified accountability horizons. Again, the process clusters focus attention on complete processes, which are more customer-oriented than traditional structures.

THE POTENTIAL FOR COST SAVINGS

SIGNIFICANT ECONOMIES MAY be possible when the possibilities of the Internet-enabled organization and a process fulfillment structure are combined. At the same time, it would be a mistake to pursue such a grand challenge just to reduce costs. It makes more sense to exploit the opportunities to enhance and improve customer value as the primary motivation. In this way, cost reductions will be an added benefit that does not become a distraction to the supplier-customer relationship.

Having made the point, however, there are a number of possibilities for cost reductions to be found in our Public Furniture Company example. The new approach addresses two distinct categories of costs. First, in our e-enabled organization, it should be reasonable to reduce transaction costs by doing more and more electronically with less personal intervention. Second, uncertainty costs should be reduced. The latter are costs generated by a perceived need to "add a little something extra" to orders, replacements, delivery times, and shipping times to protect either the supplier or the customer from a general lack of confidence in the present system. The waste generated by continual padding of transactions can be very large and the costs felt in insidious and mysterious ways.

Figure 7-10 provides a list of potential cost savings resulting from our process fulfillment–structured e-enabled organization.

CONCLUSION: RETHINKING THE FUNDAMENTAL STRUCTURE OF THE COMPANY

THE ATTRACTION OF structuring around process fulfillment lies in the allocation of complete processes to a single accountable manager

Accountability Horizon

	Corporate Strategy	Strategic Business Unit Strategy	Opportunity Management	Project Management	Asset Management	Postsale Management
10 Years or More	IV					
5 Years		IV				
3 Years		III	III	III	III	III
1 Years		II	II	II	II	II
Less Than 3 Months			I	I	I	I

Process Activity Cluster

FIGURE 7-10. COST REDUCTIONS RESULTING FROM THE PROCESS
FULFILLMENT–STRUCTURED E-ENABLED
ORGANIZATION.

System I Processes	Transaction Costs	Uncertainty Costs	Quality Improvement
Design/Engineering		X	X
Supplier Relationships	X	X	X
Inventory Control	X	X	X
Scheduling/Control		X	X
Material Requirements Planning	X		X
Shipping	X	X	X
Robotics—CAM	X		X
Process Development	X	X	X
Replacement Parts	X		X

rather than enduring the coordination problems inherent in functionally based structures. Public Furniture Company provides a good example of how process organization might work in a traditional manufacturing company.

To enjoy the greatest benefit from new electronic business-to-business and business-to-customer opportunities, organizations need to rethink the fundamental structure of the company. Process fulfillment would seem at this early juncture to be a leading candidate to satisfy the new and demanding requirements of the e-economy. Perhaps other, superior systems will emerge, but at the moment there are few alternatives other than simply grafting the e-business or e-commerce additions onto an already burdened structure.

We prefer a total rethinking of the opportunity and the alternatives. Complex systems like those discussed here are highly interdependent. Interdependency calls for a holistic, systems approach to product development, service offering, and customer fit. As with any complex system, small changes in seemingly trivial variables can produce major reactions in either positive or negative directions. It is inherent in the nature of how feedback loops work in complex systems. Success calls for a fundamental rethinking of how we manage and organize.

SUMMARY

- Successful management of innovation requires organization.

- We are experiencing a sea change in business processes that affect organization structure. These are often driven by new technologies, currently the Internet.

- Function-based organization structures are familiar, simple, and still the most common, but they may hamper full utilization of new possibilities offered by e-technologies.

- In the future, structuring the organization around key process fulfillment may offer the most efficient support of organization and customer goals.

- The accountability horizon (the time horizon of management) should drive the number of management levels.

- The value chain for the business is the starting point for determining activity clusters around which the new structure may be crafted.

- The reengineered business design will probably call for structural changes in products, services, and processes to smoothly interface with new technologies and optimize new opportunities. Products, processes, services, and structure should be designed to work smoothly together and be mutually supportive.

NOTES

1. Jacques Barzun, *From Dawn to Decadence* (New York: HarperCollins, 2000).

2. Elliott Jaques, *Requisite Organization* (Arlington, Va.: Cason-Hall, 1989).

PART TWO

SUPPORTING

INNOVATION

CHAPTER EIGHT

INNOVATION AND ORGANIZATIONAL POLICY

JEAN-JACQUES-RÉGIS DE COMBACÉRÈS sat quietly in his study in his childhood home of Montpellier, France. He was an old man, but an old man with a remarkable history of achievement. His life had by no means been devoid of either reward or challenge. Certainly, there had been grand highs and depressing lows, but on balance, life had been good. Now, his time was short.

Most of his life he had spent as a jurist. Since his modest but privileged beginnings as a lawyer in a legal family, his star had risen (and occasionally fallen) precipitously. At age 39, he was elected to the Convention and voted at the trial of Louis XVI. He was a member of the Council of Five Hundred. In 1799 he was appointed Minister of Justice. He was archchancellor of the empire in 1804 and made Duke of Parma in 1808. The culmination of his public career came with his exile from France at the Second Restoration.

It was now 1818, and at the age of 65, he had returned to France from exile in Belgium. In the autumn of his years, he could look back on a life of public service and influence at the highest levels of government. Thinking back on his roots as a jurist, his greatest satisfaction came from his contribution to the creation and implementation of what came to be known as the Napoleonic Code, first introduced into areas under French control in 1804 and later to territories conquered by Napoleon.

The Napoleonic Code was generally recognized later to be the first successful modern attempt to produce a uniform national code of law that was expressed in clear terminology and arranged in logical order. Little could Combacérès have known that in the 21st century, his code would still be used in Belgium, Luxembourg, and Monaco and had been introduced in the new world in Haiti, the Dominican Republic, Bolivia, Chile, Ecuador, Colombia, Uruguay, and Argentina.

Further north, Louisiana relies to this day on a civil code with roots in Napoleon's Code. The same is true of the Canadian province of Quebec. Few people can claim a longer or more significant contribution to society than Jean-Jacques-Régis de Combacérès through his contribution to the Code of Napoleon.

THE POWER OF ORGANIZATIONAL POLICY

THOUGH THE POLICIES created by corporations and other nongovernmental organizations can't approach the scope and magnitude of the Napoleonic Code, organizational policy still presides with great effect over the frequency and success of innovation. Policy is seldom mentioned concurrently with issues of innovation, but they are closely related. We don't know precisely which policies encourage and generate innovation. If that were possible, a simple list would solve the problem. Instead, we have identified some of the kinds of policies that *hinder and constrain* an innovative environment and have a negative impact on innovation. We have many examples.

Corporate policies, particularly those directed at the treatment and reward of employees, are generally well intended and created to address some specific situation or problem. Policies—rules—are often treated as if cast in stone, and as if once committed to paper no judgment is either required or even permitted. It is precisely this attitude that makes policies an appropriate topic for discussion in the context of innovation. Ill-conceived policies can cripple innovation, often in ways that would be a total surprise to those who enacted them. The way around this minefield is to appreciate the complex nature of our business and social organizations and, once again, to take a systems view.

Management and policy share much the same literature. They go together. In fact, when most people think of management, they are actually envisioning the policies and practices instituted and supported by the people who direct the organization's activities. Policies are created to support recurring activities that, in turn, support achievement of organization goals. Unfortunately, innovation is seldom one of the clearly stated goals. The dilemma is compounded by the inherent fragility of the innovation process. Innovation seems to be more sensitive than most activities to the unexpected and undesirable impact of ill-conceived policies. The unusually fragile nature of innovation (and innovators) provides good reason to explore the role and impact of policy decisions on innovation.

WHAT IS POLICY?

WHAT DO WE mean by policy, and what kind of policies are we talking about? According to *Webster's New Collegiate Dictionary*, a policy is "a definite course or method of action selected from among alternatives in light of given conditions to guide and determine present and future decisions." That's a pretty good definition for our purposes. It is our view that policy should be enlisted to do a number of things, among them to help managers support achieving corporate objectives. Policies should also act to focus the organization on what is thought to be important, hopefully better serving customers. Conserving customers—that is, retaining and acquiring customers—must be at the very foundation of policy foundation. Finally, policies should support the development and retention of desired capabilities. Because it's easy to see how well-intentioned lower-level managers can lose sight of the big picture, conscious attention to policy proliferation and misapplication should be on the minds of senior management.

Readers will be familiar with the often-published fact that 3M permits all of its research employees free use of 15 percent of their time to work on projects of their choice. Someone at a very high level decided to institutionalize that value, that policy, throughout the entire 3M development organization. That is policy—a clear statement of the 3M commitment to innovation.

A less positive example is demonstrated by the incident some years ago of an R&D director at a midwestern manufacturing company. He was an amiable gentleman of the traditional school who asked a young researcher who was reading a book in his workstation what he was doing. The researcher replied that he was reading a great new book that contained new information related to his project. The director seemed not to hear his answer and then proceeded to inform the researcher that "reading books is something you do on your own time. You're supposed to be *working* while you're here." Apparently, reading (learning) was outside the realm of research in the director's mind. It requires little imagination to guess the effect of the director's comments. The staff member was dumbstruck. Looking busy—like you're doing "real work"—was apparently more important than learning something new. The researcher began to reevaluate his fit in such a department and decided to transfer to another opportunity within the company. The director was eventually replaced under the auspices of reorganization, probably none the wiser.

Policies certainly matter. Sometimes the simplest oversight in some apparently obscure regulation turns out to be far more destructive to the vitality of the system than anyone anticipated. In the case of the young worker cited above, the organization was at the least deprived of a promising researcher. Imagine the total number of such instances that occur daily in the average large organization. The overall negative impact is certainly much greater than we ever know about.

In an environment of open communication, these problems usually surface quickly and can be promptly corrected. However, when communication is guarded, when trust is absent, it may take a very long time for management to learn that a problem even exists. The damage, once done, can contaminate the environment long after the issue has passed.

SOURCES OF POLICIES

WHERE DO THESE policies come from? Surely they come from all quarters of the organization, but some of the most common sources of policies having an impact on innovation originate with:

- Executive management

- The human resources department

- Accounting and finance

- Department heads

The kinds of policies exerting the most influence on innovation are generally those that:

- Determine project direction and objectives (strategic).

- Affect rewards and compensation (managerial).

- Prescribe specific work practices (managerial).

- Either encourage or preclude personal control of work (managerial).

Let's refer these policies back to the Innovation Management Model (Figure 8-1). We see that direction and strategy fall within the province of Systems III and IV. The remainder fall mostly within Systems II and III. At System III and IV, the focus of management is typically well targeted on the desired result. When clear focus is combined with experienced managers, major failures are less likely. When less experienced employees are drafting tactical policies and procedures, they may fail to anticipate the consequences of some well-intended paragraph. Expense reporting is sometimes a case in point. Those charged with monitoring compliance with policies on what is a legitimate expense and what is not can cause considerable mischief when too enthusiastically enforcing what they see as the "law of the land." Mindless enforcement of rules, devoid of judgment and human understanding, is seldom desirable or defensible.

Flexibility in implementation is the obvious answer. What is much less obvious is just how to exercise that flexibility. Some would rightfully ask: What is the purpose of policies if every manager can exercise his individual judgment? Others would counter: Are we supposed to be automatons? What are we paid for as managers if not for good judgment? In an organization that exercises great trust in its managers, we are likely to find an environment much closer to the second case. Where trust is less abundant, the situation is probably closer to

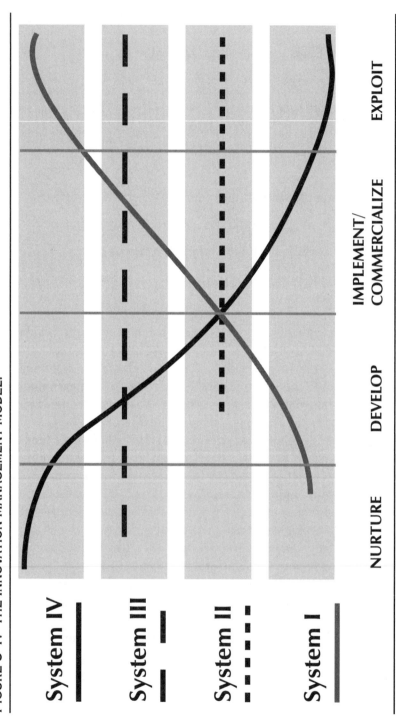

FIGURE 8-1. THE INNOVATION MANAGEMENT MODEL.

System IV

System III

System II

System I

NURTURE DEVELOP IMPLEMENT/ COMMERCIALIZE EXPLOIT

the first case, with greater reliance on rigid rules. Ultimately, the answer probably lies in the shared corporate values. And shared values are hard to acquire and difficult to change.

A STRIKING EXAMPLE OF FAILED POLICY

Another example of failed policy is seen in the case of a company that had just completed an exciting new office building. Some of the country's most knowledgeable consultants were employed to recommend new and effective ways the building could support better communication and, hence, innovation. One of the many recommendations was to include small "coffee centers" throughout the building, within easy walking distance of all employees. These would not be the traditional cold, linoleum-clad "break rooms" one so often sees. No, these were elegant, with comfortable lounge seating, surrounded by marker boards and offering really good, fresh-brewed coffee (or tea). The idea was to actually encourage workers to hang out and talk to each other! Pretty revolutionary at the time. And, to make this even more attractive, the coffee was free. (Coffee had always been available, but down in the cafeteria at the normal price.) As it turned out, the idea was a little too revolutionary, at least at the time (1989–1990).

Needless to say, these attractive coffee centers had the desired effect. People collected there, talking and drawing ideas and concepts. Pretty good, eh? Well, almost. As it happened, someone in another building complained about people in the new building getting free coffee. This led the vice president in charge of (among other things) food services to decide to solve the problem by requiring the folks at the new building to pay for the coffee just like everyone else. Why should they be treated specially and get something for nothing? The memo went out, and tin boxes began to show up at all the coffee centers so people could make honor-system payments for their coffee. It should have been a hint to management when copies of the memo, carefully annotated by some recipient, began to appear pinned up at the coffee centers throughout the new building. Such guerrilla tactics were not common at this unusually contented company.

The result was predictable. Most people, having been told they would have free coffee, liked the situation that way, and most weren't overly fond of this vice president anyway, so they continued to enjoy free coffee, pretty much ignoring the tin boxes. (Most would throw in the occasional quarter.) At this point, the company could have accepted a workable compromise: to tell people they had to pay for the coffee, yet leave the coffee still essentially free since no one was watching them pay. The coffee centers then flourished and abounded with active discussion—their intended purpose.

But a workable compromise wasn't good enough for the stiff-necked vice president. He now became intent on making sure these thieving scoundrels paid for their coffee. Prescience, it seems, was in short supply. Memos about cheating on the coffee were drafted and sent to all building occupants. These memos, of course, exacerbated an already annoying situation and, in true Dilbertesque fashion, the vice president became the brunt of numerous and frequent jokes. After a month or so of continued noncompliance, the VP—not to be outmaneuvered—ordered all the new and expensive fresh-brew coffee equipment torn out and replaced with tens of thousands of dollars worth of coin-operated coffee machines that dispensed a foul sludge reminiscent of used motor oil in a leaky cup. The inevitable memos announcing the new machines included an extensive discussion on how the coffee from the machines had been tested by impartial testing sources and found to be superior in quality and taste. You can guess how the employees felt about those memos.

Within a week or so, the coffee centers were empty of people, conversations, sketches, and ideas. Heavy-handedness had won the battle—and lost the war. The VP had showed those scoundrels, all right. A carefully conceived and sizable investment to support innovation and communication had been shut down virtually overnight. A small policy issue had, in effect, negated a large and forward-thinking investment in the coffee centers as communication enhancers.

THREE LEVELS OF POLICY

LET'S EXAMINE THE policy issue a step at a time. We have identified three levels of policy, those directed at:

1. Managing specific innovations

2. Managing programs of innovation

3. Managing portfolios of completed innovations

Each level will be studied in depth.

MANAGING SPECIFIC INNOVATIONS

At the individual project level, the relationship between policy and performance is both direct and ever present. The story above about the book-reading researcher is such an example. Policies focused on the goal, rather than on the process, will be the best received and are likely to yield the most successful results.

For System III-level managers, managing projects in broad sweeps rather than ensuring compliance with tollgate after tollgate permits greater latitude to fit analysis and verification to the need rather than requiring rote compliance with procedures, even when the procedure may be a waste of time. Proceed with the end firmly in mind. Permit System I teams to select the most useful and appropriate methods and tools. This does not imply a slapdash approach to project management. It does advocate flexibility and knowledgeable exceptions.

Tollgate processes (formally scheduled management presentations whereby the project requires approval—passing through the "tollgate"—in order to proceed), which tend to become progressively more detailed and demanding, are usually little more than an acknowledgment that management doesn't believe the team members are either aware of the goals for the project or able to manage their own approach to achieving them. The process often comes to be seen as a substitute for responsible team members. If the intention is to *regulate* rather than guide team members, the results are likely to be unsatisfactory. Overburdened tollgate processes weigh on the innovative process like a big rider on a small donkey. The rider is uncomfortable, the donkey is in agony, and you arrive at your destination late—if at all.

MANAGING PROGRAMS OF INNOVATION

We'll differentiate between individual *innovation projects* and *programs of innovation* because the responsibility inevitably lies at different levels. Most organizations have teams or groups working on some project or problem, but not all have an organized and planned program of innovation.

If we raise the bar for innovation to include activities extending beyond the individual project, we've moved to a new level of concern and oversight. To stimulate and support innovation on a broad scale, there needs to be higher-level consideration of needs, and this implies a higher strata of organization. Innovation projects are typically within the province of System I teams, operating under the authority of System III managers. On the other hand, programs of innovation are much more likely to be the responsibility of the System III managers, operating within the context conceived by System IV.

Managing Portfolios of Completed Innovations

One might view this role as a kind of "product management for innovations." Many of the same tools and practices apply. Portfolios of innovations are those collective accomplishments that have been completed. The investment has been made, and the portfolio includes both those projects that have been implemented and also those innovations that, for whatever reason, have not. Both implemented and unimplemented innovations have value, and the policies may already be in place to manage these assets. (For example, innovations not appropriate to one organization can often be sold to another.) Implemented innovations, however, are not "over" just because they've been implemented. It may be possible to extend the reach and application of the idea into other related or unrelated areas of the organization. Innovations are valuable and should not be cast off into the corporate ozone.

Some organizations are appointing "knowledge managers" charged to look after organizational knowledge in the recognition that knowledge, of which innovations are part, is indeed valuable—that it's an important corporate asset and worthy of being carefully handled. While the jury is still out on the overall success of the new knowledge managers, the focus would seem to be in the right direction. More commonly, however, little is done to husband this essential innovation resource.

Other organizations institute a policy of strict secrecy surrounding their development efforts. There are certainly cases when such secrecy is justified, but not always. Openness can yield big benefits. A case in point is the Wood Division of Steelcase, Inc., in Grand Rapids, Michigan. Steelcase brings many customers to its home offices to visit plants, meet executives, and see existing and new products. And Tim Stern, the director of design for the wood furniture division, actively seeks opportunities to show new and partially completed concepts to visiting customers.

Because the offices of Tim's design group are near the airport, it is a popular stop for visiting corporate customers on their way home. Tim's department—called the "treehouse" because it is located on an overhanging mezzanine—is constantly abuzz with collaboration and littered with new product mock-ups and concept drawings. Visitors are welcome to question the designers and view the mock-ups. Tim reports that from this he and his designers get a direct pipeline to new and existing corporate customers. This fast and continuous feedback has produced innumerable modifications and improvements in the products and reduced cycle time over previous methods.

In addition, the exposure to customers has provided support for some concepts that might not have seen the light of day without the positive customer reactions. The customers, on the other hand, love the visit and the chance to see ideas before they become public, and they like to provide their suggestions and input. Hearing firsthand what real customers like and dislike doubtless enhances the product designs. Tim's designers really like the direct input rather than having to develop products in a vacuum. The benefit is enormous. Everybody wins.

SUPPORTING THE INNOVATIVE ENVIRONMENT WITH POLICIES

IF THIS IS all true, then we should be able to look at policy formation with an intent to actively *supporting* the innovative process and environment. We feel this is precisely the way policy should be evaluated. Supporting people is, after all, what policies are for. Using policies to "control" employees hints at an organization in conflict with itself, and that's hardly in the scope of an innovative organization.

Several specific areas are candidates for this supportive role. Every manager should take a look at her own policies in terms of the following areas of impact. Do your policies support your people? Here is our shortlist of candidates for evaluation:

- Values form the base, and policies derive from the values. What are the values inherent in your policies? Trust, openness, judgment, flexibility, and sincerity are all positive values that support positive policies.

- Education is supported and valued.

- Reward systems do not pit one employee against another, but rather encourage cooperation and collaboration.

- HR policies cover a wide range and may overlap some of the other categories named here. HR people are generally sensitive to the needs we are advocating and are likely to be even more so if they know there is a concern for supporting innovation.

- Work rules and policies should support cooperation and innovation.

- Cooperation inside and competition outside without needs be a golden rule. Policies that encourage competition inside the organization are seldom supportive of innovation. Competition should be reserved for the marketplace, not coworkers.

PLANNING INNOVATION

IS IT POSSIBLE to *plan* innovation? Sure. Frank Bacon and Tom Butler wrote a book with precisely that title—*Achieving Planned Innovation* (Free Press, 1998)—and it's a book worth reading. Is it possible to plan to have a creative thought? Maybe, but it's not likely to work all the time. Anyway, this is not the kind of planned innovation we're talking about.

We are specifically advocating the need to plan ahead to achieve those innovations that offer the greatest and most productive impact on the welfare of the organization. After all, strategy *is* policy, at least insofar as it sets a direction people follow. We're not suggesting simple blue-sky dreaming, but rather a pragmatic evaluation of the innovations or areas of exploration and development that offer a reasonable likelihood of producing the desired results. Not only is such a proposition reasonable, but it is downright prudent. One would think that every organization would develop a clear picture of its future innovation investment, but it's not usually the case.

SELECTING INNOVATIONS TO PURSUE

ORGANIZATIONS FORTUNATE ENOUGH to have a surplus of innovation are simultaneously presented with a dilemma: How to choose those to be pursued and funded? Selection is certainly guided by economics (the funding of innovations is discussed below), but the key to consistent and effective selection of innovations is a *decision screen*.[1] A decision screen is a brief document containing the criteria for the selection of new products, acquisitions, or innovations to pursue. To arrive at the decision screen, the responsible management group gathers to carefully and thoughtfully determine the criteria once, to be used over and over again. The group uses a rigorous approach to setting the criteria for success, thus ensuring that the selection criteria are both appropriate and efficient. Needless to say, the decision screen must be consistent with the innovation strategy.

Spending a day or two of management time to get this right once will save countless hours hashing the same discussion over and over as recurring decisions come round. Take the time to get it right, so it's not necessary to revisit the screen criteria each time a selection decision is required. Publish the screen with the criteria for success for all who should know. In this way, many ideas will be prescreened before reaching the management group. Finally, use the screen consistently. Otherwise, the effort will be wasted because everyone will know it's not the real decision criteria.

FUNDING INNOVATION

UNFUNDED INNOVATION IS not innovation. It's just a regrettable waste of time. Only when innovations are implemented—i.e., funded—do they produce benefit. Implementation invariably costs something, sometimes a great deal. The idea may come free, but getting innovations up and working is never free. But that should not be an obstacle so long as innovation is treated like the necessary investment that it is.

The criteria for funding innovations should, of course, be included in the decision screen, but what evaluation method is appropriate? Is it the same as investing in a new punch press? Maybe, maybe not.

Whether or not to fund innovations that return investment in any one planning period (annual operating plan) should be a simple decision at the lowest level possible. While it is desirable to keep track of your innovations (see Chapter 11 on measuring innovation) to know how well you're doing, it's a mistake to unnecessarily inhibit the process. The best way to slow it down is to keep bumping approval authority to higher and higher levels.

Innovations showing longer paybacks pose a different kind of problem. Setting too restrictive criteria may obviate innovations that could yield tremendous benefits, but may require more investment over a longer period. These are the decisions executives are paid to make. These are the decisions—the opportunities—that affect corporate strategy. Setting the bar too high just serves to institutionalize the presence of exceptions. But setting reasonable criteria for funding innovation permits more innovative activity while letting the system manage more of it.

Of course, the decision to fund an innovation ought to be based on more than just hard numbers. Considerations should include both the tangible benefits analysis (the hard numbers) and those less tangible factors that may, in fact, be more important than the traditional financial analysis alone might imply. For example, quality certainly offers financial benefits, benefits in operations, and lower repair/replacement costs. Quality may also offer benefits in perceived value to the customer that, in turn, may reduce selling costs. Quality may improve the product's "appropriateness for use." The better mousetrap should be reflected in sales, but what if the better mousetrap is part of a mouse-catching system, and the whole system benefits? Valuing this benefit is more difficult, but it might be even more important.

Thus, our innovation might incur benefit from several sources. Each would ideally be included in the decision to fund the innovation. Each should be included in the decision screen. In general terms, these include:

- Direct financial return (as measured by ROI, ROA, EVA, and cash flow)

- Quality impact (operations savings, replacement savings, and perceived value)

- Market impact (sales, position, and share)

- Synergy with other products, processes, or customers

The issue of synergy can present something of a two-edged sword. While it is important, because it is difficult to verify in advance, synergy can become the favorite justification of the true believer who, convinced that he has just discovered sliced bread, uses this intangible justification to seek approval of an otherwise unsuitable project. To its credit, the synergy justification requires a broader, more encompassing vision of the innovation, the ability "to see what isn't there"—yet. It involves being able to see potential—to be able to see a tangible product as part of a bigger process. It is the best means of visualizing the leverage present in an innovation. Used wisely and prudently, it's a valuable skill.

SOURCES OF FUNDING:

In some cases a new innovation requires more resources than the organization can muster internally. Then the organization must consider different sources of funding, each with its advantages and limitations. The primary sources of funding are:

- Bank financing

- Bond issues

- Venture capitalists

- Stock issues

- Joint ventures

- Strategic alliances

CONCLUSION: SETTING THE POLICIES THAT SUPPORT INNOVATION

ANECDOTAL EVIDENCE SEEMS to point toward the attempt to over-control organizational behavior through rules and policies as reducing innovative behavior. One often hears the assertion that most of the innovation in business today comes from the small, fast-moving companies, and certainly the less bureaucracy, the more flexibility. But this doesn't seem to explain why most of the innovations still come from the largest organizations. Sure, many of the innovations are commercialized by smaller companies—either because employees leave to start these smaller groups, or the bigger organization simply lets it slip away from them—but a very large portion of today's innovation still happens in large organizations.

This means these organizations need to find better ways to encourage and capitalize on their innovations. In large organizations, the issue of policy proliferation is a valid source of concern. And smaller organizations should resist the temptation to overcontrol in the first instance. Finding the balance of control and flexibility is a moving target, but the closer one can get to the self-organizing, self-managing system, the more innovation can be expected to flourish. We favor approaches that encourage a deeper understanding of the complex interrelated organizational system behavior. Such an improved understanding offers greater promise for the innovative, dynamic organization than does heavy-handed regulation.

SUMMARY

- Policies can discourage innovation when they are excessively rigid and inflexible.

- Management flexibility in policy interpretation and implementation can reduce the rigidity of policy implementation.

- The objective, inasmuch as possible, should be to guide rather than regulate employee behavior. Innovation will benefit.

- Policy is encountered at three levels: (1) the project level, (2) the program level, and (3) the portfolio level.

- Funding policies can either encourage or stifle innovation activities, depending on how funding is implemented. Sometimes the amounts in question are very modest.

- Policies intended to overcontrol employees should be avoided.

NOTE

1. For an in-depth discussion of decision screens, see Roger Bean and Russell Radford, *Powerful Products: Strategic Management of Successful New Product Development* (New York: AMACOM, 2000).

CHAPTER NINE

LEVERAGING LOGIC

A RNAUD DE PONTAC WAS A member of the French merchant class, descended from artisans and on the rise socially. Titles would be forthcoming, but the lasting achievement of the Pontac family, and Arnaud in particular, had little to do with titles, French nobility, or French politics.

The Pontacs were lawyers and landowners. They had been up-wardly mobile for over a hundred years prior to the period described here—1647. By any measure, they were not poor. But the stone-built family chateau, called Haut-Brion, was an hour from the city, situated on a mean patch of gravelly soil where little would grow. Arnaud's country property would in fact grow little but vines, vines that had been producing wine here since the Roman occupation. Grapes grew rather well in Arnaud's modest stretch of rocky terra.

Most of the wine produced here at the time was pretty ordinary and was sold to the Dutch, who were striking tougher and tougher bargains. With the exception of their favorite, sauterne, the Dutch merchants called for bulk wines, undistinguished by area or producer, and as we would say at the onset of the 21st century, price competition for undifferentiated commodity products becomes increasingly fierce. And so it was with wines of 17th-century Bordeaux.

Arnaud de Pontac was no man to stand aside and be driven to penury by the tightfisted Dutch. His property was capable of producing wine well above the average, and he vowed to change his fortune by changing his strategy. Rather than attempt to change the buying habits of the Dutch for the local wine, Pontac turned to London to improve his fortune.

Pontac selected the product of his very best vines to be sold by name, and he called this select produce Haut-Brion, after the family chateau. He produced another, lesser wine from the nearby area of Le Taillan that he sold simply as Pontac. The strategy was highly successful, and the English gentry quickly came to know that wonderful claret could reliably be found in the bottles named Haut-Brion. Samuel Pepys recorded in his diary having an unusually good wine, noting on April 10, 1663, "Drank, as sort of French wine, called Ho Bryan, that hath a good and most particular taste that I ever met with." The first of the renowned French first-growth chateaus of Bordeaux had been born.[1]

Pontac had created the first brand name in the world of wine. His Haut-Brion and Pontac wine "brands" were preferred and yielded premium prices over all other claret. Pontac's innovation was not in technology, production (though he tended to quality), or viniculture. Arnaud de Pontac found his innovation in marketing. He broke out of the mold of bulk production of a commodity-grade product and created increased value by permitting his high quality to be identified by name. He was able to see his situation differently. He was able to think differently. By so doing, he achieved unmatched success.

Today, Chateau Haut-Brion is still among the most prized wines of Bordeaux, and being among the very best, it still commands a very high premium. Arnaud de Pontac started something in 1647 that today we take for granted, but his innovation is remarkable nonetheless.

We don't know precisely how Pontac arrived at his strategy of branding wine for the London market. We do know that today, we can approach opportunities systematically, and in so doing, we can improve our performance immeasurably. There is no reason for the enterprising manager today to routinely resort to trial and error. We have at our disposal highly effective tools we can apply to the challenges of the 21st century. We can leverage our logic.

LOGIC, CRITICAL THINKING, AND THE SCIENTIFIC METHOD

IN ADDITION TO our systems thinking discussion in Chapter 2, we will offer two additional kinds of tools. Their provenance is diverse, and their power is great. The sources are science, which provides us with a proven method for appraising observable phenomena. Critical thinking (logic) provides us with the tools to guide effective thinking, and cybernetics has given us the relatively new field of systems thinking (discussed in Chapter 2). Taken individually, each is worthy of our undivided attention. Taken together with systems thinking, critical thinking and scientific method provide us with a powerhouse of intellectual energy.

In Chapter 2, we strongly advocated the power of systems thinking, in good part because it is circular and interrelated in its approach to explaining complex systems like business organizations. Both the scientific method and critical thinking are linear in nature and approach. *If this, then that.* We're not being inconsistent in our support of all three approaches—systems thinking, scientific method, and critical thinking—to improving our understanding, our discovery processes, and our decision-making abilities. Rather, each tool has different applications. Just as we wouldn't use a screwdriver to drive nails, we benefit from access to multiple tools to help us deal with complex situations and organizations. Every businessperson should add the principles of scientific method and critical thinking to her repertoire of creative and analytical tools. Applications appear daily for those skilled in their use.

THE SCIENTIFIC METHOD

BACK WHEN WE attended high-school science class, the imperious Mr. Blivet extolled the applications and merits of the scientific method. Each of our individual Mr. Blivets worked hard to convince us of the power and validity of the scientific method while we were usually thinking of something else. Since we probably weren't listening, and since each of our Mr. Blivets explained it in a different way, let's turn to the *Columbia Encyclopedia* for a common definition:

> The scientific method has evolved over many centuries and has now come to be described in terms of a well-recognized and well-defined series of steps. First, information or data is gathered by careful observation of the phenomenon being studied. On the basis of that information a preliminary generalization, or hypothesis, is formed, usually by inductive reasoning, and this in turn leads by deductive logic to a number of implications that may be tested by further observations and experiments. . . . If the conclusions drawn from the original hypothesis successfully meet all these tests, the hypothesis becomes accepted as a scientific theory or law; if additional facts are in disagreement with the hypothesis, it may be modified or discarded in favor of a new hypothesis, which is then subjected to further tests. Even an accepted theory may eventually be overthrown if enough contradictory evidence is found, as in the case of Newtonian mechanics, which was shown after more than two centuries of acceptance to be an approximation valid only for speeds much less than that of light.[2]

Figure 9-1 recaps the scientific method. We make an observation, then form a hypothesis on it. Following this, we draw implications from our hypothesis. Finally, we perform experiments to validate the implications.

In other words, if you think you know something, and it's important to be right, get out of your office and go find out! Go to the source to see if your hypothesis is borne out by the evidence. The motto of the Skeptics Society is "Extraordinary claims require extraordinary evidence." A healthy skepticism is both productive and a spur to innovation. It's not difficult to find people (including managers) with opinions about anything and everything. It's harder to find those who regularly go out and test their opinions (hypotheses), if only to openly discuss them with others in possession of firsthand information.

An illustrative use of the scientific method in business is in the development of a market segmentation model. We are strong advo-

FIGURE 9-1. THE SCIENTIFIC METHOD.

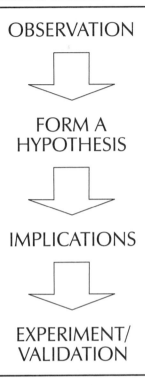

OBSERVATION

FORM A
HYPOTHESIS

IMPLICATIONS

EXPERIMENT/
VALIDATION

cates of segmenting markets to guide strategic and innovative activities, and the method we have found consistently successful is based on scientific method. By assembling a collection of experienced sales, marketing, and customer service representatives, each with personal customer experience in the desired product market, an experienced facilitator can methodically walk the group through a rigorous series of exploratory discussions. Usually conducted over a two-day period, this exercise lets you carefully and methodically assemble and document the hypothesis. This hypothesis (the tentative market segmentation model) is then validated through a sampling of personal interviews with real customers at their offices. This method has proved extremely cost-effective and remarkably effective and accurate, particularly with business-to-business situations where there are multiple layers of decision makers and influencers. It is also relatively easy to update when necessary.

In such situations, the scientific method of first, hypothesis, and then, validation in the field, is also an unusually cost-effective approach to many difficult challenges (like segmenting markets). It works equally well with other complex research problems. Use reasonable care, though. The scientific method does not sanction just any old slapdash hypothesis and validation approach someone might conjure up. But exercised skillfully, it can be much cheaper and in many cases more informative than traditional methods like market surveys.

But regardless of the method one uses, humans still fall prey to error. Possibly the most common errors, and the most costly in both human and material terms, are errors in thinking.

ERRORS IN THINKING

ELVIS IS ALIVE and has been spotted in Austin, Texas. Aliens have landed and kidnapped a couple from Oklahoma, then released them unharmed after three days of intense interrogation. In the 1930s a man developed a special carburetor for automobiles that would guarantee at least 50 miles per gallon from a normal Chevrolet, but the invention was bought by Standard Oil and concealed from the public to preserve profits. People can come to believe some really fantastic stories, totally convinced they represent important and unappreciated truths, and the proponents may be completely sincere. If otherwise reasonable people can tell and believe fantastic stories like these, just imagine how the same errors in thinking that lead to such beliefs can easily cause innumerable errors in common day-to-day business decisions.

People regularly come to believe things that simply are not true. Some of these erroneous beliefs are humorous, such as the folks who believe pyramids sharpen razor blades. Some are sad or even tragic, as with the members of a misguided suicidal religious group who believe they will be transported to another world on a given day by killing themselves. More commonly, though, it's just folks like you and me going through life making common errors in our thinking.

Likewise, every day businesspeople accept beliefs that are not true. They probably make these errors in thinking because they fall victim to one of the mistakes described below. Innovations, by their very nature, are typically new, novel, or unfamiliar. That which is novel may cause people to respond in unusual ways. Some will respond favorably; sometimes they may be distinctly hostile. Getting the most from our innovation efforts and talents demands that we think clearly and process information efficiently and accurately. To consistently think clearly, we can benefit from understanding errors in thinking that surround us in our everyday lives. We can then identify the errors and avoid them with a little study and a little discipline. (The types of errors listed here have been adapted from numerous sources,[3] but the authors have provided the text and examples.)

ERROR NUMBER 1: THE FALLACY OF THE EMOTIONAL APPEAL

Unfortunately, this approach is often used to great effect in the field of politics. It could go like this: If you elect Senator Cheapskate as president, then Social Security will go bankrupt and elderly Americans will go hungry and risk the loss of their homes. When people fail to examine such claims carefully and critically, they can let fear, hatred, or greed overcome their otherwise good sense. They fall victim to the emotional appeal, and emotionally charged words overpower reason.

The error of falling for the emotional appeal is by no means confined to politics. It happens regularly in business, too. It's likely to happen more often in an industry with high barriers to exit because these companies have fewer choices, and hence more basis for fear. "If we don't install this new enterprise software system, we'll be noncompetitive and in three years put out of business by our competitors." That may or may not become reality, but fear is a poor reason to take a large risk. "We'll lose market share if we don't retain that unprofitable line of widgets. We'll really lose out."

Fear, greed, animosity, anger, condescension, pity, hope, passion, flattery, indignation, hate, humor, or any of a cast of other emotional reasons are poor reasoning vehicles. Calmer heads nearly always prevail with better decisions.

ERROR NUMBER 2: THE FALLACY OF COMMON WISDOM

This fallacy, also called *argumentum ad populum,* goes like this: Everybody believes X, so X must be true. By that reasoning, since so many people believe that standing in a draft causes colds, hence, standing in a draft causes the common cold. During the late 1960s, auto executives believed that Americans wanted big cars: "No American wants to drive around in a roller skate." The common wisdom again, unquestioned by auto company executives. The oil crisis of 1973 showed the auto industry, and the common wisdom, to be wrong.

This chapter's opening vignette about Arnaud de Pontac and the rise of Chateau Haut-Brion showed how he innovated and overcame the common wisdom of his day, i.e., that he had to sell bulk wine to the Dutch at low prices. Others overcame common wisdom as well. In the late 15th century, people believed the world was flat, but Columbus believed otherwise and turned out to be right. More recently, Rocky Aoki overcame the common wisdom that Americans were averse to eating unfamiliar "foreign" foods with his Beni Hana Japanese restaurants. It may sometimes be uncomfortable or even unsafe to go against the prevailing ideas of a society, but it may well result in clearer thinking. Just because "everybody believes it" is really no reason at all.

ERROR NUMBER 3: THE FALLACY OF THE IRRELEVANT CONCLUSION

Thousands and thousands of AMC Pacers were sold. So, it was a great little car, right? Soap operas are among the most watched shows on TV. Hence, they must be quality entertainment. Tabloid newspapers are read by millions of people. Thus, tabloid newspapers must be reliable sources of news and information.

In each of these cases, the statement is irrelevant to the conclusion. How about this: "Two of our competitors have introduced a new, low-cost milling machine reported to be made of plastic. We need to introduce a plastic milling machine." The moral of the story: Think for yourself; your competitor may have just made a stupid decision; better not to compound the issue by following blindly. Some competitor actions are totally irrelevant. It is immeasurably better to understand your customers than to follow your competitors in any event.

Early in the 19th century, the Ford Model T was the best-selling car. But this didn't mean people would actually want to buy the car if something better came along. Nor did it mean they would want to buy it if they had enough money to buy something better. Likewise, because more people are flying these days does not mean they appreciate the service provided by most airlines in North America.

ERROR NUMBER 4: BOLD STATEMENTS DO NOT MAKE CLAIMS TRUE

Often this is a version of the "squeaky wheel gets the grease" argument. Those willing to make the boldest, loudest proclamations often receive more credibility than their proposal deserves. "The information revolution will make manufacturing obsolete in the United States. Everyone will be either a knowledge worker or a service worker (flipping hamburgers)." We all know how that one turned out.

Dot-com companies frequently justified losing money on the basis that there were "new rules in a new game." In 2000, the old rules of real assets, real products, and real profits were resurrected. Many of these "new rule" dot-coms folded like a cheap tent. Bold claims do not equate to truth.

Stelco, a Canadian steelmaker, had to decide whether to install large or small basic oxygen furnaces to convert iron into steel. The company's marketers wanted large furnaces, arguing that the market was moving to flat products from shapes. Manufacturing wanted small furnaces, arguing that Stelco's strength was in rolled shaped products, such as I-beams. Manufacturing spoke loudest and longest and won the day. Then the market moved to flat sheet, and Stelco lost leadership to its main competitor.

ERROR NUMBER 5: HISTORY DOES NOT EQUAL CORRECTNESS

"But we've always done it this way. It's what made the company great." Maybe, maybe not, but in either case history does not validate the efficacy of a decision to be made today. Just because it worked last year does not mean it's the best choice today. We are always eager to fit yesterday's answers to today's problems.

The mechanistic view of the world as a machine dates to the 16th and 17th centuries, and the Scientific Revolution recalls the names of Newton, Copernicus, Galileo, Bacon, and Descartes. We believed for 300 years that the way to understand the world was to break it up into pieces and analyze the parts. Only recently has this long-held view been eclipsed by discoveries in physics, biology, psychology, and social sciences that validate the view that the world can only be understood as a whole—that the world is more than the sum of its parts.

ERROR NUMBER 6: THEORY INFLUENCES OBSERVATIONS

Mental models are the prejudices (intellectual and otherwise) we carry around with us. We each form opinions, rules of thumb, and stereotypes because they speed up our ability to respond to commonly encountered situations. Mental models are useful, even necessary, in our everyday lives to allow us to function effectively. But major problems can ensue when our mental models are wrong. When we go to visit a client to gather information for a new product or service, we need to be sure we are not just going to find only what we *want* to find, to see what we want to see.

It is not at all rare for such a well-intended visit to result in the marketing representative finding conclusive evidence that "what is really needed is a lower-cost product." Nor would it be shocking for the engineering representative to come away with the conviction that "what is really needed is a higher-performance application of new technologies." Judge the quality of the tea without all the cream and sugar we commonly bring along with us.

Bombardier Regional Aircraft Division, manufacturer of the Dash 8 regional aircraft, received a complaint from an Austrian customer concerning the difficulty of using the aircraft's air-conditioning system in Alpine regions of Europe. Instead of investigating to find out what the exact problem was, the engineers immediately began a total redesign of the air-conditioning system, and the marketers sent a field service representative to check on the systems in all the airline's aircraft. A project manager who was in Europe on vacation called on the Austrian airline to see exactly what the problem was. It turned out to be quite simple: The air-conditioning system had to be adjusted before the plane could land at airports at different altitudes, and the rotating knob used to make the adjustment had no indicator to show where to set the knob for particular airports. To get around this problem, the crews had been marking the wall with lead pencils to show where to set the knob, but the cleaning crews kept cleaning off the marks. A 50¢ engraved piece of plastic mounted behind the knob was all that was required to satisfy the pilots and the airline. Yet the engineers had first leaped to conclusions based on inaccurate theories.

Error Number 7: The Observer Changes the Observed

Many readers are familiar with the famed Hawthorne Study conducted on factory lighting in the 1930s. It showed, in short, that the group given better lighting increased productivity, but—much to the researchers' surprise—the control group without the improved lighting also improved productivity. This was the most famous example of the finding that the process of being studied actually affects the results of the observation.

One of the revolutionary discoveries of quantum theory has revealed that the behavior of the subject was altered by the act of being observed. Subatomic particles cannot be studied independent of the observer. The very act of observing affects the behavior of the particle. The particle is "real" only in its relation to the observer.

Everyone is familiar with how leading questions can elicit the answer the questioner wants; that is why such questions are not allowed in criminal court proceedings. The bane of focus groups is getting incorrect information because the focus group leader forced the pace.

ERROR NUMBER 8: EQUIPMENT CONSTRUCTS RESULTS

The equipment we use in our research may well determine the results we achieve, and survey questions can be constructed to lead the respondent to answer in a particular way. An entomologist, for example, studying insect life in a stream chooses a net to capture specimens. The net he chooses has 1/4-inch openings. The researcher collects many specimens. After carefully studying the specimens, he concludes that the stream contains no insects smaller than 1/4-inch. The choice of equipment makes a difference.

ERROR NUMBER 9: ANECDOTES DO NOT MAKE A SCIENCE

The anecdotal curse is alive and well in business. Hearsay, the sharing of personal experience, and the telling of a funny story are all part of the normal decision process. But anecdotal examples are not a substitute for real evidence. Anecdotes are seldom quantified or qualified, or even verified, so they often do not mean what they seem to mean. When the consequences of the decision are important and substantial, anecdotal evidence should be suspect every time. When in doubt, go find out.

Businesspeople are particularly vulnerable to the boss's anecdotal evidence. When the boss visits a customer and has an epiphany, it's hard to bring the conversation back to real evidence. No one wants to tell her that her latest brainstorm is not necessarily based on real evidence of an epidemic of customer demand.

ERROR NUMBER 10: SCIENTIFIC LANGUAGE DOES NOT MAKE A SCIENCE

Technical jargon and language does not confer credibility. Beware of the proposal couched in jargon unintelligible to nontechnical folks. Proposals should be written in such a manner as to be intelligible to everyone. When they are not, they should be suspect. Obfuscation is alive and well and served admirably by liberal application of technical jargon.

An article to be published in an academic journal was sent as a courtesy to the business executives whose observations were the basis for the analysis in the article. The article was incomprehensible to them, but they assumed that the results had to be valid, even if they couldn't understand or make intuitive sense of them. It turned out that the results were invalid. The article was published, though, because the reviewing executives could not spot the errors in the paper.

Never be intimidated by jargon. Ask for an explanation in genuine, understandable English. If they can't or won't provide one, send them back until they can. In the long run you won't regret it.

Error Number 11: Burden of Proof

The burden of proof should always rest with the person making the claim. When the engineering manager claims that proceeding with a new product modification will double profitability, it is up to him to prove it to the satisfaction of the decision makers. Conversely, when marketing makes the case that the proposed modification will cripple sales, then the burden lies with them to provide persuasive evidence for their position. Many business decisions are made on the basis of opinion, valid and invalid, but when the consequences are large, evidence is preferable to opinion.

Remember, it should *not* be up to the recipient to prove the proposal wrong. Proving negatives is a waste of time. It should be up to the proponent to make the case conclusively.

In the Stelco steel example noted in Error Number 4, the executive committee did not seriously question the manufacturing people, who had absolutely no proof to offer about future markets. But manufacturing's proposal held sway, and Stelco lost out.

Error Number 12: Rumors Do Not Equal Reality

"ABC Manufacturing is about to introduce a new product that will cause our main line to be obsolete." "I hear Harry Austin is trying to torpedo our project." "Hey, I just heard the new microswitch project is really screwed up. That's what they get for putting Bill Wakefield in charge."

We've all heard rumors, and we all know how they sap morale and productivity in units and companies under pressure. Despite the apparent stupidity of it, we all like to hear what we *want* to hear, and when it's a rumor, we may be tempted not to challenge the rumor if it's what we *want* to hear—often to our own detriment.

ERROR NUMBER 13: UNEXPLAINED IS NOT INEXPLICABLE

This is particularly true in causal modeling, where the model is an imperfect representation of reality. The independent variables "explain" a certain amount about how the dependent variable (sales, say, or productivity) changes with changes in the independent or causal variables. The rest of the effect is "random error," or effect unexplained by the model. This doesn't mean we don't have a good idea what is causing the rest of the effect.

How many times have we heard "God only knows" or "it's just the way it is—there's nothing we can do about it"? There are many mysteries present in our world. Science has explained many and will explain many more. Simply because something is as yet unsolved, in itself, does not mean it is unsolvable—only that it has not been solved . . . yet. Innovators thrive on finding out—explaining the unexplained and showing the way.

ERROR NUMBER 14: FAILURES ARE RATIONALIZED

Business seems highly vulnerable to this error in thinking. Generally, because there is no legal or moral reason to "come clean" with their failures, managers (and employees when they can) generally try to sweep mistakes under the rug. Executives and others, not wanting to be chastised for simply making a mistake, find reasons why the failure "really wasn't a failure."

In the area of product failures, the finger pointing begins soon after the bad news—sometimes before: "Our market analysis was right on the mark, but engineering failed to incorporate the necessary features." "The product was superbly designed, but sales failed to promote it effectively." In business, unlike government and the military, failures are seldom audited. As much as anything, this is a learning failure.

We fail to learn when we fail to be honest. An international paper maker undertook the rebuilding of a large paper machine. The rebuild took longer to accomplish, and achieved lower performance levels, than was envisioned in the proposal. Higher operating costs were explained away by a downturn in the market that reduced paper machine utilization rather dramatically. However, poor management of the rebuild project was the real culprit, as a subsequent and independent audit showed. What lay behind the problem here of rationalizing the blame was scapegoating—having to fix the blame on someone else.

ERROR NUMBER 15: AFTER-THE-FACT REASONING

Probably more business mistakes have been attributable to this error than any other. We gave the sales department a real dressing-down, and widget sales increased 40 percent. Hence, poor widget sales were caused by lack of sales effort. Maybe, maybe not. We turn the temperature up, and productivity increases. Hence, higher temperatures cause increased productivity. We turn the temperature down, and absenteeism decreases. So lower temperatures cause decreased absenteeism. In July maybe, but in January? Maybe sometimes, sort of.

3M allows its people 15 percent of their time to focus on pet projects, and 3M is an innovative company. If we do the same for our people, we too will be more innovative and creative. Perhaps, perhaps not.

ERROR NUMBER 16: COINCIDENCE

Coincidence can be related to other errors in thinking. In the case of our increased widget sales in Error Number 15, maybe a major competitor suffered a labor dispute and couldn't ship product to its regular customers, and our own sales benefited. What if EPA regulations created a need for customers to replace aging widgets with new, more efficient ones? Maybe a pop star was reported using widgets to good effect and swears by them, and this was reported in the press. Coincidence never sleeps.

The Gulf War coincided with GM's opening of a truck plant in Saudi Arabia. Sales locally did not meet GM's forecasts, principally because Saudis weren't able to buy the vehicles because of the war. GM closed the plant and was then pilloried in the business press for yet another bad decision, to build the plant in the first place.

ERROR NUMBER 17: REPRESENTATIVENESS

Events need to be considered in their proper context. When we fail to consider context, we risk letting coincidence be mistaken for profound conclusion. When we fail to note that the phenomena we are discussing are simply representative of normal occurrences in that context, we make an error of representativeness.

Psychics frequently make forecasts widely touted in tabloid newspapers, and there are claims that the psychic has predicted one astounding event or another. Closer examination nearly always reveals that the predictions were really just generalizations completed by coincidence.

ERROR NUMBER 18: THE FALLACY OF THE ARGUMENT FROM IGNORANCE

This error—also called *ad ignorantiam*—is popular in all areas of argument. The proponent makes a claim or proposal, and if you cannot disprove it, then the inability to disprove it is taken as proof that it must be true. "The Easter Bunny exists and deposits Easter Eggs in hidden places on Easter morning." If you cannot prove that the Easter Bunny does not exist, then he must exist. This is absurd. There is no proof that God does not exist; hence, God exists. God may indeed exist, but the proposal is not proven by this form of argument.

When marketing's claim that extending a line will greatly increase sales, it may or may not be true. When the skeptic questions their assertion and is asked to prove that it's not true, this is *ad ignorantiam*. When the skeptic is personally attacked with statements that he has no credentials to question their claim, they add the *ad hominem* dimension (see Error Number 19) to the error.

At one time GM designers believed that assembly workers were idle and didn't want to do a good job. Hence, the designers overdesigned the vehicles in ways like adding six welds where four were completely adequate. When the vehicles couldn't be built in the allowable time, workers had to cut corners to remain on schedule. The result? The corner-cutting reinforced the designers' previous opinion that workers were idle and didn't want to do a good job.

ERROR NUMBER 19: THE DISCREDITING ATTACK

This is also called the *ad hominem* attack. By discrediting or attempting to discredit the claimant, the adversary attempts to discredit the proponent's claim. This is a particularly disagreeable form of argument. George Smith makes a proposal that product A is overengineered and that costs could be reduced substantially by reducing the number of bolts and fasteners in product A without risk of failure. The head of engineering opposes the change to product A, which was originally designed by his department, and he intimates to the decision makers that "George isn't a real engineer, you know. I think his degree is in psychology or something like that." Hence, one is to infer that because George does not have an engineering degree, his recommendation should not be given serious consideration.

ERROR NUMBER 20: THE HASTY GENERALIZATION

This is also known as "jumping to conclusions." More accurately, it is a form of improper inductive reasoning. Reaching conclusions before the evidence warrants it happens every day in every organization. In some cases it's a very expensive way to save time.

This is a classic product design fault: "This is the problem, and this is the solution." Without careful analysis, we don't know what the problem is. Without investigation, we don't know what the plausible solutions are, either. This is particularly true about what customers really want. Getting the answer right is always preferable to getting the wrong answer quick.

ERROR NUMBER 21: OVERRELIANCE ON AUTHORITIES

We all like authorities and look to others for expert advice. We read consumer reports to see what the experts think, and we buy auto magazines to see which new cars get the best ratings. Both sides at a trial have their dueling experts. In short, we often look to others for expert advice. Particularly those of us, according to Dr. Jung, who are, in his term, extroverts.

If Dr. Know-it-all advocates reducing inventories by increasing parking lot space, we think, "Well, it must be right. Dr. Know-it-all is the expert." Let's get that parking lot going so we can get those inventories down. But smart people, even experts, sometimes say stupid things. To say it another way: If it walks like a duck, quacks like a duck, and looks like a duck, it may be an imitation duck.

ERROR NUMBER 22: EITHER-OR

The error of either-or occurs when we create a false dilemma. The proponent seeks to dichotomize the situation into a forced choice. If we don't do X, then we will be forced to do Y. "We will have to double our investment in research or we will certainly face ruin inside of two years." If the proponent is successful in forming the argument in this artificial manner, all other choices are eliminated. Obviously, the proponent is seeking to limit the choice to her favored selection and a clearly undesirable result for her adversary. If we do not artificially limit our choices, we will make better decisions.

An artificial limitation of choices was, in fact, the logic wherein the U.S. government supported the Cuban exiles' invasion of Cuba during the Bay of Pigs. Other choices, obvious now, were available to the government then, but were excluded by the either-or approach. Those favoring invasion artificially structured the argument to "either invade or bad things will happen." There were other choices available, but they were not permitted consideration by those structuring the argument.

ERROR NUMBER 23: CIRCULAR REASONING

Sales increased because we are the best in the business. We are the best in the business because our sales are largest. We are the largest because we are the best. Because we are the best, our products must be the best. Because we make the best products, we will continue to be the best and the biggest. Hence, we must continue to develop the most sophisticated products in our industry and need to increase our research budget drastically. We are the best—thus we are the best. Some would claim Microsoft is an example.

This simply begs the question and creates the fallacy of redundancy. It is a path that takes you nowhere.

ERROR NUMBER 24: *REDUCTIO AD ABSURDUM* AND THE SLIPPERY SLOPE

This error takes the form of carrying the argument to a logical end and thus reducing it to a ridiculous conclusion. Most of us have known folks whose favorite means of putting forth a position involved a leap to an obviously ridiculous conclusion in an effort to discredit a lesser and more reasonable position, as if the extreme position was the natural and necessary result of accepting the lesser position.

For example, Mediterranean farm workers consume above-average quantities of olive oil. Mediterranean farm workers live longer than the average person in the United States. Then, by extending this logic to an extreme, we might conclude that consuming three quarts of olive oil per week will make you live forever. True, olive oil is better for your health than saturated fat, but consuming more and more and more will not extend the benefits indefinitely.

CONCLUSION: AVOID ERRORS IN THINKING TO MAKE BETTER DECISIONS

THE MORE TOOLS we have at our disposal, and the more rigorously we apply them, the better our decisions will be. Innovation suffers from many of the errors discussed here, both on the side of the innovators (in which case management better have a good command of spotting logic errors) and on the part of those approving innovations when they use erroneous logic to shut down innovative thinking. Either situation is costly, and either can be avoided with a better understanding of the tools.

SUMMARY

- The scientific method of observing, hypothesizing, interpreting, and validating has proven itself in the sciences but is seldom applied to business problems.

- The scientific method of segmenting markets is a particularly effective way to understanding customers and a good application of the method.

- Critical thinking skills offer useful tools of reasoning for the businessperson as well as the professor of logic.

NOTES

1. The wine enthusiast can find this story and others equally engaging in Hugh Johnson, *Story of Wine* (London: Mitchell Beazley, 1998).
2. *The Columbia Encyclopedia*, 5th ed. (New York: Columbia University Press, 1993).
3. Two notable sources are Michael Shermer, *Why People Believe Weird Things* (New York: W. H. Freeman, 1997) and Francis Watanabe Dauer, *Critical Thinking* (New York: Barnes & Noble Books, 1989).

CHAPTER TEN

COPING WITH SERENDIPITY

SOME YEARS AGO, IN JAPAN, the then–general manager of new product development with the Polaroid Corporation noticed the popularity of small photo booths, packed with teenagers seeking the small photographs the booths produced. He proposed that Tomey, a Japanese toy manufacturer and Polaroid customer, produce a small pocket camera aimed at the teenage market.

Many Polaroid engineers had strong objections to the project. It was a struggle, developing and introducing the Pocket Camera. Many engineers thought it was beneath them and their exalted image for technical excellence. These engineers doubted that such a low-end product—a low-priced, low-tech camera, with marginal picture quality, and aimed at a new market segment (teenagers)—could succeed, and they feared it would wreck the quality image of Polaroid. After all, they had been beaten up over the poor acceptance of the Swinger, aimed at youngsters in the 1960s, and the ill-fated Captiva, a small camera targeted at upscale customers. The techies had little confidence in the new product calls from the marketing department, disparagingly referring to them as "the marketeers." But over the insistent objections and ridicule of many of the old-line Polaroid factions, the project was pushed forward—to ultimate success in both Japan and the United States.

In fact, the Polaroid Pocket Camera has been touted as the product that almost single-handedly turned around an ailing Polaroid Corporation.[1] In December 1999 it became the No. 1 selling camera. But some question whether Polaroid can repeat the success. Maybe, but if the company is to prosper, it will need a more flexible attitude toward new markets, new segments, and the innovative use of technology.

Despite its success, the Pocket was, after all, little more than a guess gone right. This story is not really an unusual one—the serendipitous discovery of a new product idea. But it is a good indication of a company lacking an adequate understanding of the larger marketplace for its products. Why did it take a chance event on a Tokyo street to lead to a successful product after twenty years of effort?

STUDYING THE ENTIRE MARKET

WE ASSERT THAT it's indeed possible to do much better. Innovation is the child of knowledge—knowledge of the greater marketplace in which a company competes. We applaud Polaroid's success with the Pocket camera, but how does the company intend to repeat the success? Are Polaroid executives planning walks through the streets of other international cities in search of inspiration for the next product?

We hope not. If they're smart, they'll be working on a comprehensive market information system, one that permits them to evaluate all the segments of their marketplace and identify those segments offering the best potential for sales and profits. Apparently, past failures at Polaroid were typified by detailed knowledge of their traditional products and customers, but little knowledge or experience with other segments outside their traditional business. This is a key lesson for all companies: Always study and segment the *entire* market for the product type in question, even though you currently do business in only a limited part of that total product market. You may well choose to remain focused upon only a very narrow segment, but it will be a choice born of the knowledge that it is your best opportunity, not just a matter of chance. It is not just the *next* opportunity.

By way of contrast, Canon intended to design the extremely popular ELPH compact camera to be innovative. Canon's leaders consciously chose the path less traveled. Other manufacturers all took what they thought was a safer and more prudent route of designing their new Advanced Photo System (APS) cameras to look, feel, and operate like the familiar 35mm pocket cameras. Canon, on the other hand, sought to make the most of the new opportunities offered by the new technology by creating a better camera, a smaller camera, and they gave the camera a quality feel in the hand by using a metal rather than plastic case. It would seem that Canon knew something that Polaroid didn't, or maybe the customers for APS cameras were more homogenous. Clearly, they hit the mark.

The results were dramatic. The Cannon ELPH simply ran away with the APS camera market. Canon had done a better job of understanding its customers and had met their needs straight on, without hedging or apology. Canon has recently launched a digital ELPH. To pose the same question we asked above, can Canon's leaders do it again? We bet they can, because while they may take advantage of serendipity, they certainly do not count on it. They try to maintain a repeatable process.

SHIFTING THE BALANCE OF INNOVATION

A CENTRAL PREMISE of this book is the idea that it's possible to focus innovation activity through conscious management. The book aims to demonstrate how an organization might go about managing innovation better, but there remains the issue of what to do about the unplanned, unforeseen, and in some quarters even unwanted innovation. It's an often frustrating fact that the best, most important, most powerful innovation of the decade may well be a surprise—an unexpected windfall that throws all our plans into a cocked hat.

After all the planning, investing, and building around our strategic direction, we find that something indeed better has come along. Our experience is that these really important unexpected innovations do not come along very often. If they do, then you are an exceptionally innovative organization and should be delighted. If you are not delighted, then it would be wise to examine your approach to planning an understanding your marketplace to discover why your processes are constraining your ability to exploit the opportunity of the decade.

Our objective is to effect a major shift from a reactive and frenetic approach to innovation, to one where customers are more consistently and profitably served by conscious application of customer knowledge in ways that improve the customers' experience with your company and your product. We seek to plan more and better innovation. We seek to shift the balance of innovation from mostly unplanned and unexpected to the reverse. We see in Figure 10-1 that as our strategic focus increases, we should see more innovation falling into the "planned" category. This occurs simply because our efforts are more focused on activities that support our plan. But the unexpected still occurs.

We don't expect to always have everything fall neatly into our plan. This chapter is about what we can do with the unexpected ideas. This chapter is about the exceptions.

WHEN THINGS UNEXPECTEDLY GO RIGHT

IT'S EASY TO see why some managers respond with hostility to "new ideas." Managers spend most of their time in the present moment, not

FIGURE 10-1. THE SHIFTING BALANCE OF INNOVATION.

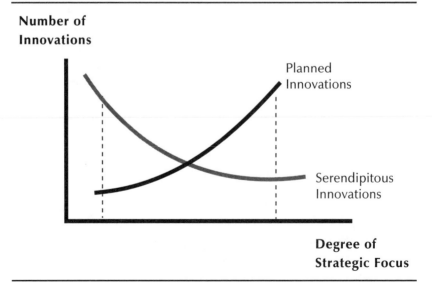

the future, managing now-type things. One manager we know described his work life as a continuous process of "putting the puppies back in the box." So it's not unusual for operations to seem constantly out of whack. Thus, the manager focuses his effort on keeping the train on the tracks, or getting it back on the tracks, when—out of nowhere—Harry Jones Jamison proposes a new, and unsolicited, idea to replace the train. In Steven Covey's vernacular, such a manager is fixated on the "urgent, but not important" (i.e., the mundane task of getting things back on track because they are off *now*).[2] Harry, our unwelcome innovator, is proposing a new idea that, in Covey's terms again, is "important, but not urgent." Thus, the timing of the conversation dooms the idea from the outset. Moral: Urgency usually wins over importance.

At the aggregate organizational level, the situation is often essentially the same: Everyone is working diligently, pursuing the organization's plan of action, and then, Zap! Out of the blue comes a new opportunity or direction idea (or reorganization). There is an old Arabic saying that "the nail that sticks up will get hammered down." Unexpected innovations are frequently the nail that sticks up, and frequently they get hammered down, much to the frustration and disappointment of the innovator. Like Kermit the frog says, "It isn't easy being green." Sometimes the innovator can feel pretty green.

The answer isn't to rail against the frustrated manager. For reasons of nearsightedness, she's just getting today's checklist completed, but bypassing a good and applicable innovation. Anger and contempt might make the unrequited innovator feel better, but it does nothing to fix the problem, which goes much deeper. The problem here is structural, and thus the fix must be structural. The problem is one of inflexibility, not focus. Inflexibility is exacerbated by:

- An excessively internal focus
- Processes that do not support change
- Lack of training to handle change
- Fixation only on the plan, to the exclusion of new information
- Overcommitment of resources
- Absence of a broad customer perspective
- Middle and even senior managers who do not understand that the company *wants and needs* innovation and will give ideas serious consideration

- Failure to delegate the power to innovate to a low enough level

- Rewards, policies, and processes that encourage the status quo

Inflexibility is the eternal enemy of innovation. Innovation is always change, and inflexibility fights change at every turn.

Innovation, by its nature, benefits from the unexpected. Innovation is the process of recognizing the unexpected and applying applications of the unexpected to serve some useful purpose and customer. In addition to the Polaroid example that opened this chapter, the literature is filled with stories of how the unexpected resulted in a powerful discovery.

At 3M, the Post-it Note was the result of a failed adhesive experiment. The glue simply wasn't very sticky and wouldn't permanently bind the objects together. Someone was quick-witted enough to visualize a different use for the "failed" experiment. Why not an adhesive that you *don't want* to stick permanently? The result was a product—notepaper with glue that doesn't stick—that is so universally accepted now that few of us would want to do without it.

The remarkable part of this story is not the discovery of the unsticky glue (the invention). Rather, it is the much more notable flexibility and capability of the organization to capitalize on an unexpected development (the innovation). Truth be known, 3M has organized to capitalize on whatever may come over the transom from their research efforts. Most companies would not attempt to emulate the organization of 3M, but would be well served to consider the 3M mind-set that values the unexpected.

Everyone likes a good story, and a *Wall Street Journal* article that makes a serendipitous discovery sound like a major achievement is fun to read—so long as we don't mistake a good story about a lucky discovery for good innovation management.

MORE THINGS THAT GET IN THE WAY

PROBABLY THE MOST common complaint from innovators is that good ideas don't get a hearing. Nobody seems to care. Or, innovators complain that they don't know how to get an idea to the "right" person. (These are, of course, innovations and creations of the unplanned variety.) Also, contrary to what some managers may think, most of these innovators would be satisfied with a reasonable answer as to whether their idea makes sense or not. They do not necessarily need to have every idea implemented, but just expect a reasonable response to what they feel is a good idea—or what *might* be a good idea. Some managers leap too far ahead, expecting Harry, our innovator, to be angry at having his idea rejected, thus avoiding the perceived confrontation by ignoring it and hoping it will go away. It never does. Ignored, now Harry *is* angry. All he wanted was a simple yes or no and why— and that could have been provided quickly and effortlessly.

Company politics comes up in discussions with innovators. Almost always in the negative, this usually has to do with someone thought to have stepped on someone else's idea as some means of advancing her own personal cause. In organizations that encourage internal competition, this situation can be expected to occur frequently. When people are given reasons to see their work life as "us" versus "them," competition will bring out the worst, even in a saint. Nobody wants to lose, so the enlightened manager never sets up win/lose situations if he can possibly avoid it. Whenever we feel we're at risk of losing something—and it may be trivial—we fight back. Most office politics arise in this way. One could make the case that managing innovation is also about managing internal competition. We may never eliminate internal competition entirely, but less is better.

We've all heard the expression "not created here." The implication is always that if the person or department did not come up with the idea, the person or department won't support it. It implies small-mindedness on the part of those accused of employing "not created here." However, small-mindedness usually has little to do with it. More likely, if one looks closely, there will be a form of internal competitiveness at the root. It may be rooted in a fear of being perceived as unable to run your own shop, or a perception that everyone or every department is supposed to somehow be self-sufficient. Environments that are judgmental and critical, where put-downs are frequently heard, are likely to be fertile territory for "not created here." Fear is a powerful motivator, even when it's really silly little things we're afraid of, like fear another group might have a better idea or fear of being seen as having somehow failed. We are a society where failure is not rewarded. We're not allowed to fail. Ironically, the most prolific innovators usually have a lot of failures and see them as learning opportunities.

It is a lot more effective to encourage openness and cooperation wherein every person can see herself can see themselves as winning and able to enjoy the pleasure of helping another without paying a big price for it. IDEO, the world-renowned product development company, is a master at brainstorming, and it has the results to prove it. One of the reasons brainstorming works so well for them is that they emphasize the energy and power that comes from *building on the ideas of another.* In the rapid-fire format of a brainstorming session, with ideas flying about from all corners, the cooperative energy is very different from the "go around the table and everybody gets two minutes" kind of meeting. The same principle of building on the ideas of others works in less intense situations of everyday work too, but to get there requires a cooperative, not competitive, internal environment.

How the System Handles the Unexpected

ALL THESE ISSUES are elements in the larger system. The systems perspective helps us understand how seemingly unrelated elements can cause mischief in places that are far afield. Flexible systems are not only more forgiving but tend to be much more durable, more resistant to failure.

Figure 10-2 shows another simple systems diagram. The lower circle represents a simple plan, which results in projects, which, in turn, support and influence the goals and strategies. The upper circle represents a feedback loop that illustrates an unexpected discovery feeding into the goals and strategies (the planning process), which if important enough will then change the plan to incorporate the new discovery. Problems arise when this feedback loop is absent. We then hear the complaint "nobody around here seems to care about innovative ideas." The loop, and how well it works, is a key to the systematic approach to managing innovation.

Several Alternative Ways to Capitalize on Unexpected Innovation

WHEN WE JUST can't use the innovation ourselves, using our current organization and resources, we may still be able to avoid tossing it out

FIGURE 10-2. SERENDIPITY AS A FEEDBACK LOOP.

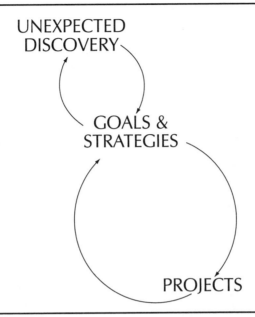

UNEXPECTED
DISCOVERY

GOALS &
STRATEGIES

PROJECTS

or ignoring it. Some of these alternative ways to capitalize on innovations are given below. Choices are listed below and described briefly.

TRYING TO APPLY THE INNOVATION INTERNALLY

This is the first application that comes to mind for most of us and generally is the use intended by the innovator. Ideally, the innovation—if it's a product, for example—would be tested via the new product decision screen (see Chapter 8). If it passes it, then it becomes an approved project and moves on to the next phase of development. But not all ideas or products can be successfully exploited internally. They may simply be shelved, leaving time to take its toll, rendering the idea or product obsolescent.

MAKING AN ACQUISITION

Some innovations are important enough to justify acquiring an existing organization capable of applying and exploiting it. The company that came up with the idea simply buys a capability to make, design, develop, market, or otherwise exploit the opportunity. Many acquisitions are made to actually purchase innovation—to buy the creative power of the company being acquired. Microsoft has acquired many smaller companies for their products and skills. Amazon has done the same.

TURNING TO A GREENFIELD START-UP

It may be more desirable to start from scratch, either because of the nonavailability of suitable acquisition candidates or the cost of acquiring those that are available. The advantages may be greater value, direct experience, conservation of resources, and cultural match. The downside is often the time involved in getting a greenfield start-up going. If time is of the essence, acquisition may prove the superior choice. Establishing brand identity may also be slow or expensive.

FORMING AN ALLIANCE

The topic of strategic alliances has been popular since the 1990s. Some have been spectacular successes, like Microsoft and Intel, Magna and Mercedes in Alabama, and McDonald's Canada and Martin-Brower, to name a few. Through strategic alliances, each party benefits by cooperating with another separate company to achieve something neither can (or chooses) to do alone.

The alliance is usually formal but need not be a contractual agreement in every instance. In some smaller and simpler cases, it might simply be cooperation to get to an agreed destination together, each benefiting along the way.

PURSUING A JOINT VENTURE

Sometimes an organization wishes to pursue an opportunity, often in a different country, that it feels ill-equipped to handle alone. The organization may feel that it vastly increases its chances of success by partnering with an existing player in that field or country. Often, this is a smaller organization that finds it in its own interest to grow with the help of a larger joint venture partner. The venture need not be 50/50, but usually ownership and contribution is somewhere near that point.

Finding a suitable partner may be an obstacle, as the choices may indeed be limited, and a reasonable match of corporate personalities makes the marriage much happier. But the joint venture may be a viable way to exploit innovations outside the expertise of your own organization.

SELLING THE IDEA

You shouldn't overlook the possibility of simply selling the idea to someone who does have the interest and ability to benefit from it. For example, sale of patents and copyrights takes place every day, benefiting both parties. Smaller organizations may find that the patent process is too costly or time-consuming to be practical. In many cases, of course, if there is no patent, there is nothing to sell, so it can be something of a catch-22.

Even larger organizations where patent costs are easily borne find that it's too costly to try to patent every innovation they come up with. They often have a conscious policy regarding how they will handle and apply patent decisions.

SUMMARY

- "Planned innovation" results in more usable innovation than trusting to "chance innovation."

- Serendipitous innovation still occurs in every healthy and dynamic organization. These unexpected innovations may be bigger than those that are planned.

- The goal is to get more useful innovation to the customer by shifting the balance from unplanned to planned.

- Failure to recognize and capitalize on serendipitous innovation can be traced to systemic causes and must be treated at the systems level.

- When an innovation is good but not usable, for whatever reason, there may still be opportunities to profit from the idea through alliances, joint ventures, acquisitions, start-ups, or selling the idea to someone else.

NOTES

1. "On a Roll," *The Wall Street Journal,* May 2, 2000.
2. Stephen Covey, *The 7 Habits of Highly Effective People* (New York: Fireside, 1990).

CHAPTER ELEVEN

MEASURING AND EVALUATING INNOVATIONS

SENIOR EXECUTIVES IN THE FORD Motor Company were ecstatic when the Edsel was unveiled in 1957. The development and launch of the Edsel had been carefully and skillfully managed, and the executives were confident the car would be a success. Yet as we all know, the car that was to be the key to Ford's return to a position of power in world auto markets was an immediate market disaster. In many companies, this would be the prelude to finding scapegoats and cutting off heads. Ford's senior executives did not waste time blaming irrational customers or poor internal performance, however, as these managers were convinced that the Edsel was close to being a perfect car—if the prevailing wisdom in the U.S. auto industry about consumer behavior was correct. So Ford carefully investigated the assumptions it had used about market segments.

What the investigations showed was that the socioeconomic segmentation of the industry (used so effectively by Alfred P. Sloan to market General Motors vehicles some thirty years earlier) was no longer valid. In its place, the researchers found a "lifestyles" form of segmentation, and analysis using the new segmentation method showed that the Edsel's market failure was predictable and inevitable. The new model showed that the Edsel, positioned between the Mercury and the Lincoln, was really in no "position" at all.

The Edsel remains a famous market failure. But the postintroduction evaluation of the Edsel led to two of the auto industry's most successful vehicles, the redesigned Thunderbird and its later sibling, the Mustang. Ford learned from its failure. Many do not.

EVALUATING THE CORPORATE INNOVATION STRATEGY

ALTHOUGH THE EVALUATION of the corporate innovation strategy is not strictly part of the innovation evaluation, the corporate innovation strategy must be reviewed at regular intervals by the senior executive team. If the strategy makes no sense in light of changes in the external and internal environments, then the proposed innovations probably make little or no sense either. As Peter Drucker has noted, there are five basic innovation strategies, which we have condensed to four. You can be:

1. The first to market

2. A rapid follower

3. A niche player, either product or market

4. The one to respond to changing market needs and expectations[1]

Each requires quite different skills and capabilities, and each implies a unique set of measures of success.

FIRST TO MARKET
Being the first to market requires that the innovator aim at dominating the market, either permanently or until a predetermined level

of competitor response has occurred. The innovation needs to be very carefully researched and developed, and the launch must be exploited aggressively. If the innovating company intends to stay in the market, it must invest heavily in order to keep lowering prices and creating greater value in the product. Should the company intend to exit the industry as competitive pressure increases, it must be able to identify the point at which exit is necessary, and it must have the ability to switch resources to the next innovation. Sony's Walkman is an example of this strategy.

RAPID FOLLOWERS

Rapid followers need not necessarily be excellent at product innovation, although it certainly helps. They do need to be good at process innovation, for the rapid follower needs to be able to drive costs down faster than the market leader. The rapid follower also needs to be able to identify significant market needs that the market leader is not satisfying, and must be able to adapt product designs quickly to exploit these opportunities. This strategy requires that the rapid follower capture significant market share from the market leader in a limited time or be forced to exit the market. Xerox lost significant market share in photocopiers when the Japanese manufacturers launched smaller, less expensive machines for smaller business offices.

NICHE PLAYERS

Niche players specialize in developing special products for general markets or products for specialized markets that the major players identify as being uneconomic. This requires the niche player to be able to develop and produce products cost-effectively at low volumes; exploiting economies of scale is not appropriate. Here are some examples. SAAN department stores of Winnipeg, Manitoba specialized in serving smaller, secondary markets in Canada, markets in which larger, national competitors would not place stores. Irwin Seating of Walker, Michigan specializes in producing theater seating and is the global leader in this niche. Barrday of Cambridge, Ontario specializes in weaving specialty industry textiles, among them: the material for ice hockey skates, and filter material for use in ore-extraction industries.

CHANGING CUSTOMER NEEDS AND EXPECTATIONS

Those innovators who focus on changing customer needs and expectations necessarily aim at increasing the value customers receive from the product package. In effect, these innovators expand the customers' notion of what the total product package is. Singapore Airlines has been at the forefront of innovation in service offerings and service performance in air travel for over twenty years. The airline consistently ranks at the top of airline performance surveys by business and tourist air travelers. Manufacturers can also change customers' needs and expectations through service innovations. Japanese automobile manufacturers captured market share in North America in the 1980s in part because their dealers provided service of a higher standard than did the U.S. auto companies' dealers. Toyota now offers customers in Japan the ability to order a customized car and have it delivered within seven days. All these innovators have one thing in common: an ability to identify latent needs that customers do not realize they need and then "delight" the customers by providing the performance or service need.

Identifying an opportunity is one thing. Being able to exploit the opportunity is quite another. As previously stated, a company must have the innovation-exploiting capabilities in place or available *before* the concept is approved. And, as we have also noted, the most critical capability is competent management.

EVALUATING INNOVATIONS

THE EDSEL STORY that opened this chapter has three lessons. First, the clearest (and most important) evaluation of an innovation takes place in the marketplace. Second, innovations need to be evaluated by the marketplace *before* the innovation is launched. And third, careful and objective evaluation of marketplace performance of *all* innovations is critical to the longer-run performance of the company. As Figure 11-1 shows, therefore, evaluation takes place at all stages of the innovation management process, and at every level in the system.

Without evaluation, we are guaranteed failure of both the current innovation and future innovations. Knowing that we have to evaluate innovations is one thing, though—actually practicing effective evaluation is quite another. In this chapter, we focus on the evaluation aspects of managing innovation.

Perhaps the most appropriate place to start is with six basic ques-

FIGURE 11-1. EVALUATION AT ALL STAGES OF THE INNOVATION MANAGEMENT PROCESS.

ACTIVITY	EVALUATION FOCUS
Nurture	Corporate Values Focus Organization Compensation Communication
Develop	Market Segmentation Process Development Resources Recruiting and Developing People Corporate Knowledge Base
Implement/ Commercialize	Operations Experimenting and Prototyping Process Application Technology Application Distribution Suppliers
Exploit	Sales Growth Marketing/Promotion Product Line Extensions Distribution Extensions Financial Return New Capabilities

tions: When? What? Why? How? Who? Where? Providing answers to these questions defines an organization's innovation strategy.

WHEN?

Effective evaluation is conducted regularly. We need to evaluate innovations at all stages of their development and use. Appropriate evaluation, early and often, invariably identifies changes that need to be made before the change becomes strategically, operationally, and financially prohibitive. Ford could have identified the market segmentation problem well before the Edsel got to the marketplace. Evaluating too frequently, though, places a heavy burden on those conducting the evaluations and distracts people being evaluated. It is true that we manage what we measure, but overmeasurement leads inevitably to overmanagement and control, not support and guidance. And if the interval between evaluations is too short, there may be no new usable information obtained, which defeats the purpose of the evaluation in the first place.

All managers should remember that the evaluation process forms part of the adaptive feedback loop in the innovating system. When a manager acts on the results of an evaluation, it is as important as when the evaluation is carried out. As a general rule, the person controlling the process under evaluation should make the first corrective moves. Superiors should not intervene until it is clear that the subordinate does not have either the resources or the capacity to make effective corrections. This is as true of mechanical processes as it is of organizational processes. If, as we suggested in earlier chapters, appropriate policies have been established, reasonable managers ought to make reasonable decisions. After all, the most critical capability is effective management, so all efforts should be made to develop effective managers, not to stifle their development.

WHAT?

Customers don't see all our innovations. Only product and service performance are observable, and then only in the marketplace. Innovations in process technology, organizational innovations, value chain innovations, and innovations in the other categories discussed in Chapter 6 are not directly observed by customers, even if we bring them into our facilities. How should we evaluate innovations before the marketplace sees them—if it sees them at all? Waiting for the marketplace may be too late. This requires us to also understand *what* to evaluate.

From a strategic point of view, it is important that organizations critically evaluate performance of the development process and the system in which it is embedded. Evaluating the innovation itself is generally fairly straightforward. Evaluating the process and systems aspects of the innovation is considerably more difficult. So we have to understand what aspects of the innovation process and system we need to evaluate, as well as when to do this.

WHY?

Evaluating innovations themselves is critically important. If we limit ourselves to this single purpose, though, we probably short-change ourselves and ignore valuable information. Why not use our innovations to critically evaluate the process of innovation itself? And why not use our innovations to evaluate our capacity to innovate? We evaluate at different stages for different reasons, but in effect at all times we are evaluating:

• Our innovation strategy

• The market opportunity

• Our ability to exploit the opportunity

• The opportunity for further innovation

• Trends in market needs and demands

• Our innovation performance to date

HOW?

Given the need to evaluate innovations, we need to think about how to do the evaluation. The most important aspect of this is the measurement system we use. The choice of measurement system and its metrics depends in part upon the purpose for innovating, as discussed in Chapter 5. Using an inappropriate set of measures guarantees that we will focus on the wrong issues. In addition to the metrics we develop, though, we need to understand the processes we will use in evaluating, and the tools to be used for this purpose. Metrics for evaluating innovations themselves should be value-based, the bases being time, cost, quality, and service-centered. Metrics for evaluating strategic issues should be (market) performance-based.

There is another important issue under *how:* How will the evaluations be used? Evaluations should be used to enable the personal and organizational learning process, so that the company becomes better and grows in desired ways. To use the evaluation process to rank people, and to merely punish the guilty and reward the praiseworthy, is shortsighted. As we might imagine, and as we know, the use to which we put evaluations determines how results are reported, and also determines the ways in which the system responds to evaluation. Measurement systems that inculcate fear and finger pointing should have no place in an innovative organization.

WHO?

As in all things, those people with the best knowledge and the greatest ability to effect change—those people *in* the process being evaluated—should be deeply involved in the evaluation. They should not be the only group, though. Higher-level managers should, where possible, also evaluate process performance (from a strategic point of view), as should disinterested auditors (from technical and operational points of view). It is all too easy for groups to subjectively analyze their own performance. And the group may unwittingly create problems through faulty logic or "groupthink." Multiple assessments provide a much greater likelihood of objective evaluation and assessment.

WHERE?

The issue of *where* is more critical in larger, multinational organizations, but it is important in all organizations. Most organizations appear to conduct evaluations where the innovation is being developed. Often, nothing could be less appropriate. Market-focused evaluations should be conducted in critical market locations. Technology evaluations should be conducted where the technologies are being developed. Strategic evaluations should be conducted by the senior executive team. And as we want multiple evaluations anyway, parallel evaluations will likely be conducted in sites removed from the area of interest. The question of *what* is being evaluated at each stage will need to be understood before the *where* can be answered.

These issues have to be resolved no matter what innovation or cluster of innovations we are evaluating. Organizations need to develop a process for developing and using market-focused innovation evaluation protocols.

A FRAMEWORK FOR EVALUATING INNOVATIONS

FIGURE 11-2 IS an outline framework for evaluating innovations. The columns represent the four stages of an innovation's life cycle:

1. Preselection

2. Development

3. Launch

4. In-service

Each row represents a different aspect of the evaluation processes. Let's look at the evaluation that occurs in each of the four stages.

EVALUATION IN THE PRESELECTION STAGE

In the preselection stage, we concentrate almost exclusively on the target innovation. We know, as discussed in Chapter 6, that we will probably need to innovate in other areas to ensure real success. These "support" innovations need to be thought through only to the point that their resource needs and the overall innovation timeline can be reasonably established.

We want to emphasize that concept evaluation is strictly strategic. Because it is strategic, it is a System IV evaluation, conducted by the executive team. Their evaluation is best carried out using a decision screen developed specifically for the company (see Chapter 8).[2] During this stage, senior managers need to emphasize the internal and external environment, asking questions like:

• What market segment do we want to target?

• What do customers in this segment need?

• What new capabilities will we need?

• How long will it take us to gain access to these capabilities?

• What is the market potential for the development we have just made?

FIGURE 11-2. AN OUTLINE FRAMEWORK FOR EVALUATING INNOVATIONS.

	PRESELECTION	DEVELOPMENT	LAUNCH	IN-SERVICE
SYSTEM IV	Strategic Issues • Market • Competition • Capabilities			Portfolios of Products •Develop •Milk •Drop Innovation Process
SYSTEM III		Innovation Innovation Process Innovation Team Support Systems Customer	Innovation Innovation Process Innovation Team Market Risk Management	Customer Service Learning Innovation Process
SYSTEM II		Support Systems Suppliers	Order Processing Distribution Warehousing	Service Maintenance Retirement
SYSTEM I		Innovation Innovation Process	Innovation Innovation Process Market	

- How long will it take to begin influencing the market segment?

- What assumptions about the industry can we exploit for competitive advantage?

Regardless of the source and type of the primary innovation, senior management has to be satisfied that the innovation or the results of the innovation will create significant value for the target market segment. Further, senior managers have to be satisfied that the investment in the innovation will be handsomely returned to the organization. For products, this should be reasonably straightforward, as discussed in Chapter 5. Innovations in the other sectors (as discussed in Chapter 6), however, require more thought.

These latter innovations must unambiguously demonstrate their strategic value, and their impact in the competitive environment or in the marketplace must be clearly stated. Infrastructure innovations, in particular, have to be critically examined to ensure that they satisfy the strategic criterion. Non-product innovations make sense only if they achieve one or more of the following:

- They increase desired value for customers in the target market segments.

- They reduce internal costs, including transaction costs.

- They improve strategic competencies and capabilities.

- They create new barriers for competitors, perhaps creating sustainable competitive advantage.

Sometimes process innovations are made for the wrong reasons. A division of Dominion Bridge (located in Winnipeg, Manitoba) undertook several process innovations in the late 1980s as part of a major quality management program. These innovations were all suggested by workers and came out of discussions among work teams formed for the purpose. In line with the quality philosophy the division had adopted, any innovation was accepted as being valuable. All the innovations suggested focused on improving conditions for the workers, and most made very modest improvements in process quality. The innovations were all implemented, at some cost to the division, only for the division's management to discover once the changes had been made that customers saw no added value for them in the new processes.

Toyota's production system was already mentioned in Chapter 6. The intent of the innovators involved was to develop a production system in which flow through the system would be smooth and predictable. Managers knew that to make this happen, they would need to eliminate all uncertainty in the system, which meant eliminating waste. Waste creates uncertainty, which requires buffers to be placed at strategic intervals. Eliminate the uncertainty, eliminate the buffers— eliminate the buffers, and drive down working capital costs and throughput time in the process. Lower costs translate into a potential selling price advantage. Couple this with a dealer network that customers want to deal with, and vehicles whose maintenance requirements are low, and you create a sustainable competitive advantage.

The developers of the Toyota Production System knew before they began all the years of innovation required to produce the system that the new system would achieve all of the strategic objectives. It *is* possible to identify strategically significant non-product innovations and to understand what needs to be done in order to achieve the potential success. And it is possible to articulate this, and identify the evaluation metrics, before the executive team approves the project.

In a similar vein, the team that transformed Southwest Airlines' strategy from a charter operator to a scheduled airline decided to focus on reducing aircraft station time to ten minutes, as a way of keeping the airline flying. Having achieved this feat, and in order to expand past being an airline with only three aircraft and three destinations, Southwest had to ignore the airline industry's standard "hub-and-spoke" operating philosophy. The company went instead with a series of intersecting "milk runs," with aircraft arrivals and departures at intersecting airports totally independent of the movement of other aircraft. Breaking the industry assumption that the hub-and-spoke system gave the best operating economies meant Southwest could achieve substantially better economies than any other domestic airline.

To make the milk-run system operate, Southwest had to prove another industry assumption incorrect. Most airline executives believed that the low-fare tourist traffic was unprofitable for regular, scheduled airlines and was best left to charter operators. Southwest demonstrated that the low-fare tourist market segment was large and profitable, because these customers were prepared to accept some routing and time inconvenience in exchange for very low fares. Both Toyota and Southwest Airlines demonstrate that breaking industry paradigms with non-product innovations creates sustainable competitive advantage that can be measured conclusively by improved market performance.

When the executive team considers an innovation proposal, the team rarely considers the proposal solely on its own merits. The executive team is rather concerned with the total portfolio of innovation projects into which the proposal will fit, and what the proposal does to the organization's risk profile. Many middle managers seem unaware of the risk management role of the executive team and expect their proposals to stand and fall on their own merits. Executive teams might help themselves and their subordinates by taking the time to spell out their risk management strategy and policies and distribute them throughout the organization at regular intervals.

EVALUATION IN THE DEVELOPMENT STAGE

The development stage starts with the executive team's acceptance of the proposal and the release of resources, and ends with the implementation of the innovation. For a product, this stage ends when production ramps up to target output levels. During the development stage, the emphasis switches to the innovation, the development team and process, and the execution of the innovation by internal and external suppliers. The development stage is a major project in its own right and should take on the characteristics of a project. All development plans should have been presented as part of the project proposal, and both the development team and the innovation should be judged against these plans.

The Focus of Evaluation

What needs to be emphasized here is that we are not simply evaluating the innovation for its own sake during the development stage. What we are really focusing on evaluating are:

- THE INNOVATION STRATEGY AND PROCESS. Are we using an effective and appropriate process?

- THE DEVELOPMENT TEAM. Do we have effective management in place? Are the organizational structures appropriate?

- **SUPPLIERS**. Do we have effective suppliers who form part of an effective extended team?

- **CUSTOMERS**. Do we have effective customers who form part of an effective extended team?

- **PARALLEL POSSIBILITIES**. If we are assessing different approaches to the realization of the innovation, is it clear when we should be shifting resources from one approach to another that is more promising?

- **CAPABILITIES**. Do we have the capabilities or knowledge necessary to execute the project? Are these capabilities being used appropriately? Do we need capabilities or knowledge of which we were not aware at the beginning? Do we have sufficient resources to complete the project as scheduled?

As previously discussed, every process has suppliers and customers. This is true of the development process for innovations of all types, although the suppliers and customers for most types of innovation are inside the organization. Innovations help people in a system improve their performance. If we cannot identify this group of people (customers) for an innovation, then we better not be thinking about investing resources to develop the innovation.

Reviewing Variances from Plan

These are all performance evaluations; we make evaluations based on prior assessments of resource needs and expectations. So one other important subject for review is the effectiveness of the forecasts and plans we make before the project begins. As we are all aware, too many projects that appear to have come off the rails are actually performing respectably. It is the expectations and forecasts of performance that are poor.

Even though evaluating the external environment is not as important as evaluating the areas above, it should still be undertaken on a regular basis. This allows senior management to be assured that the innovation will still meet market needs. Tweaking an innovation early in its development process is easier and less expensive than making major changes just before launch.

Invariably, the project will be judged using time, cost, quality, and performance metrics. Where variances from the plan occur, managers should be at pains to determine whether the initial plan was overly optimistic, or whether development performance is lower than acceptable. This is often hard to determine, and generally the approved plan is deemed to be achievable. Perhaps the only satisfactory way in which to make this equitable is for the people proposing the project to be placed in charge of its development and implementation.

The development plan might itself contain many stages. There may be a need to experiment with alternative methods of achieving a certain outcome or to build prototypes and conduct tests of service innovations before they are ready for a full-scale launch. The development plan must contain the schedule of experiments and prototyping activities, and the objectives of each experiment or prototype, together with the criteria by which the activity will be judged. Failure to establish the evaluation criteria before conducting the experiment can easily result in the standards being set to achieve the outcome desired by the experimenters. But teams need to be ready to encounter surprises and be prepared for changes even at late stages of the development process.

When McDonald's launched its pizza nationwide in Canada, the development plan called for test marketing of the product in Ottawa and Winnipeg. The tests proved the product would be a profitable venture and confirmed general predictions of sales volumes and sales trajectories over the launch period and beyond. One uncomfortable surprise for McDonald's and Martin-Brower, its logistics supplier, was the tendency for restaurant managers to hoard pizza components. This tendency to protect against stocking out was understandable, but hoarding by managers during the national rollout would guarantee shortages of pepperoni and pizza crusts in the second and third weeks of the eight-week launch period. When this hoarding was discovered, the logistics plan was changed to ensure that inventories were centrally managed during the critical period, reverting to restaurant-initiated resupply at the end of the launch period. The positioning of two weeks of anticipated pizza requirements in each restaurant immediately prior to the launch placated restaurant managers and owners, and left sufficient inventory in distribution centers and with suppliers to cover foreseen demand variability across the country's restaurants.

Reviewing Innovation Performance

The last reason for evaluating an innovation during development is to evaluate overall innovation performance to date. We need to evaluate performance for two distinct reasons. First, we need to make choices among alternative approaches to an innovation, and second, we need to learn how to better manage our innovation portfolio and the process of innovation.

The newer and more radical an innovation, the less certain we are about the best approach to take when developing the innovation. This is particularly true of knowledge innovations. Two other constraints on knowledge innovations are also important. If we don't get the knowledge innovation right, we will not get a second chance, and time to market is critical.

It is important therefore to adopt the "rule of three" when dealing with leaps where the objective is known, but the means of achieving the objective are unclear. This rule requires three different approaches to the problem to be undertaken, if possible, which means the resources required for each approach have to be allocated. Each group will start work on their approach to the objective, working independently of the other team or teams. Performance of each approach will be frequently assessed, as we need to identify both the most appropriate approach and low-probability approaches as quickly as possible. People and other resources should be transferred from lesser to more promising approaches as our knowledge of what is going to be most appropriate becomes clearer. Ultimately, all the resources from the less appropriate approaches should be assigned to the most promising approach; it is important for momentum and morale to reinforce success.

Evaluating Teams and Trends

Although the development stage is the most complex of the four stages of an innovation's life cycle, and is the stage that consumes the most resources, evaluation here is reasonably straightforward. The development teams in System I should evaluate themselves and subordinates at frequent intervals. Higher-level managers in System III should also evaluate teams at less frequent intervals, but certainly at milestones and critical points of the development plan. Evaluation should be carried out with a view to improving team performance, not for assigning blame. If team members are looking over their shoulders, focusing on how they will make sure they aren't blamed for anything, their time is being wasted.

Technical evaluation of the innovation itself should take place continually throughout the development process. The technical people involved in the development in System I should conduct the evaluations, but the evaluations need to be audited in System III. The testing protocols and testing timetable should be established before the development stage begins. One of the most critical repetitive technical evaluations concerns market needs and demands related to the innovation. As we know, market needs and demands are a moving target. The longer the time between concept selection and market impact, therefore, the further the market's needs and demands will have moved. It is possible to project where the market will be, given observed trends. However, these trends need to be checked at frequent intervals.

EVALUATION IN THE LAUNCH STAGE

Emphasis in the launch stage focuses on the innovation itself, market response, competitor response, and the development team. We will have projections of impact in the marketplace at various times after launch, and we need to evaluate the actual results to understand why the differences occur and what their implications are. Immediate market feedback allows adjustments to be made and may allow early follow-up on unexpected success. We will also have our first major tests of the innovation in use, in both expected and unexpected use modes.

It is immediate competitor response that is the most difficult to combat unless companies are prepared, as deliberate response requires the investment of capital and other resources in a planned approach to regaining lost ground. When we expect no or muted competitive response, this can be a telling time, because we would have to develop plans to stop our launch being stalled. Palm Corporation responded immediately when Microsoft launched its new handheld device to compete with Palm's own, and as of early 2001, Palm appears to have effectively stalled Microsoft's entry into the handheld market.

If the development team in System III retains responsibility for the innovation after launch and until the project is through the growth stage on its life cycle, then the development team should continue to be evaluated. If the development team has handed the innovation over to others, this is a good time to do a detailed evaluation of the performance of the development team and the development process, and to make adjustments to the process as necessary.

During a product launch, the initial focus in Systems I, II, and III is on the ramp-up to full-scale production, pipeline filling and other distribution activities, distributor training, rollout of the marketing campaigns, and the implementation of support innovations. Following the launch itself, though, the focus in Systems I and III shifts to the marketplace and evaluation of sales penetration. It is at this point that the organization needs to be flexible, for market response is unlikely to be exactly to plan. The flexibility should be built into the risk management plan for the launch, and emergency management plans should be developed for the most likely scenarios and the scenarios with the greatest associated loss severity. If this is not done, what should have been an emergency can easily become a crisis, with attendant business risk.

When McDonald's launched its pizza in Canada, national sales figures were right in line with projections at the end of the second day of sales. Unfortunately, what looked good at a national level looked less rosy at a regional level. Sales in Canada's Maritime Provinces, for example, were considerably below forecast, while in British Columbia sales were running at twice the projected levels. Only a major effort by Martin-Brower to pick up and transport inventories from Eastern Canada to the West, and to divert all shipments from pizza crust suppliers in the United States to British Columbia, saved Vancouver restaurants from not being able to supply their customers. Building flexibility into logistics and transportation plans allowed a crisis to be averted.

Every group involved in the launch should be monitoring and evaluating the detailed technical aspects of implementation, but the development team itself should monitor key performance factors. These factors are the critical items around which the launch risk management plan has been based. Monitoring must be continual, as responses to opportunities and challenges may need to be made quickly.

Organizational innovations pose a particular challenge for evaluation. All infrastructural innovations rely on people for their implementation and effectiveness, and the impact is often difficult to judge early in the process. Attitude surveys may be the most appropriate instrument for gathering data reflecting on acceptance of the innovation, but the surveys should be conducted by skilled researchers and inter-preted by people outside the organization.

Evaluation in the In-Service Stage

In this last stage of the innovation life cycle, emphasis in System IV switches from evaluating the innovation by itself to evaluating the innovation as part of a cluster of innovations. Clustering takes several forms:

- **FAMILY.** This involves evaluating the performance of a family of innovations, with a view to making changes based on market trends.

- **NUCLEUS.** This means evaluating the innovation as the potential seed for a range of specialized innovations in close proximity to the initial innovation. This requires identifying where the better opportunities lie for repositioned innovations.

- **SUCCESS.** This involves clustering innovations that have met expectations separately from those innovations that have exceeded expectations, and from those that have failed to meet expectations. We want to identify underlying patterns and then try to develop an understanding of why the patterns exist. From there, we should be able to develop effective plans for exploiting unexpected advantage and for eliminating or minimizing unexpected disadvantage.

Evaluating the Innovation System

In addition to evaluating the innovations by cluster, we need to evaluate the ongoing business of innovation. This should be a periodic strategic evaluation of the company and its performance against longer-run competitive measures, and will be a System IV responsibility. It is also an evaluation of our performance in our industry, in particular in the segment of the industry in which we have chosen to compete.

In the in-service stage of the innovation life cycle, it is important that we analyze the longer-run market response to the innovation. This is true of all the innovation forms for, as we have noted earlier, there has to be a market justification for every innovation we undertake. For product innovations, we need to analyze market response to identify whether or not our development process was effective. Products that do not create desired value for the target market segment have not been effectively developed, and management has to understand where the problem occurred in order to improve the development process.

Companies also need to analyze market response to determine what further innovation opportunities exist. Sony has demonstrated the effectiveness of exploiting the "space" close to the original innovation with its brilliant management of the Walkman series of portable players. Exploiting the space close to the original product makes sense for a number of reasons:

- Market opportunities are more easily assessed when potential customers have good to very good knowledge of the product.

- The company has in-house or available all or almost all the capabilities required to develop and launch the new innovation, as these capabilities would have been required during the development of the original innovation.

- The experience gained from the first innovation provides more appropriate measures and measurement systems than were used for the original innovation.

- Senior management is better able to make the necessary strategic decisions for the "exploiter" innovations than was possible for the original innovation.

Perhaps the most important reason for reviewing innovations in-service, though, is to review the portfolio of products the organization offers its target market segments. The review at the highest levels of the organization might be conducted only every three years or so, and may focus on only the most significant products. This review can identify products that should be removed from the portfolio, products that need to be repositioned, and areas in which new innovations seem to be needed. Such a review can also explicitly evaluate overall innovation performance, benchmarked against competitors, to identify any major changes that might need to be carried out in the innovation process.

INNOVATIONS IN EVALUATION

MOST MANAGEMENT EVALUATION methods are based on the mechanical model of the world. They evaluate discrete parts, not the whole. This flies in the face of our systems view. Others have recognized this. For example, financial services companies have begun incorporating intangible elements such as service quality into their formerly quantitative, short-term–focused measurement systems.[3] This involves developing a more balanced approach to evaluation and changes in measurement metrics. Many banks now conduct regular surveys of customer satisfaction, and use the results in evaluating branch performance. One health insurer, National Mutual of Canada, now allows corporate customers to claim premium rebates if service performance is deemed to be below expectations. Standard Life, Canada's oldest life insurance company and part of the Standard Life Group of Edinburgh, Scotland, has melded two such approaches, the Balanced Scorecard[4] and a model based on the European Foundation for Quality Management's self-assessment criteria.[5]

The Balanced Scorecard is based on the assumption that focusing on one set of measures causes strategic and operational drift and a loss of relevance and competitiveness. The four clusters or dimensions of the original Balanced Scorecard are financial, customer, internal business processes, and learning and growth. By deciding on what specific drivers of performance are important in moving the organization toward its strategic goals, managers can develop measures that capture performance in each area. Using a balanced set of measures shows when the train starts to drift off the rails, and corrective measures can be applied. The Balanced Scorecard is indeed part of a strategic management system.

We can, and should, use several performance indicators for each dimension. The innovative company might use some of the following indicators:

FINANCIAL DIMENSION
• Return on innovation investment

• Market share

• Cost savings

• Total project cost

CUSTOMER DIMENSION
• Use of lead users in development

• Customer satisfaction

- Customer retention rates

- New customer attraction rates

INTERNAL BUSINESS PROCESSES DIMENSION
- Overall development team performance

- Development cycle time

- Number of prototyping cycles

- Total project personnel hours

LEARNING AND GROWTH DIMENSION
- New skills introduced to the company

- New core technologies developed

- Number of new project team leaders identified

- Average hours of employee training investment

An innovative company can use the Balanced Scorecard to evaluate individual innovations, clusters of innovations, or the complete product portfolio. However, the Balanced Scorecard's measures need to be augmented if the benefits of innovating are to be effectively captured. One way of doing this is to capture what has been called the innovation premium.[6] This allows companies to calculate the financial returns that accrue from creating new value. The innovation premium can then be used as a key financial indicator in the Balanced Scorecard.

The dimensions of the innovation premium relate to the principal stakeholders in the company, and are:

- Owners—The Best Company in which to Invest

- Customers—The Brand to Buy

- Employees—A Great Place to Work

- Partners—Preferred Partner to Have

The innovation premium is important. Using the Balanced Scorecard in concert with the innovation premium is also important, for it is possible to subvert even the innovation premium for short-term gain, and resultant long-term pain. In all our endeavors, we want to ensure that we have a vital and dynamic system. Concentrating on the innovation premium alone might be analogous to a bodybuilder using steroids, with the same sorts of long-term issues for the body corporate.

SUMMARY

- Evaluation of innovations should be market-based where possible. This applies to both product and non-product innovations.

- The level at which evaluation is done moves from strategic at the concept stage through operational and tactical in the development stage, tactical in the launch stage, and back to strategic in the in-service stage of the innovation life cycle.

- While we are always evaluating the innovation, the focus is often on the process represented by the innovation. This is analogous to the use of product samples in statistical process control (SPC) to understand and improve the operating process.

- The corporate innovation strategy itself needs to be evaluated at regular intervals and when marked changes occur in the environments affecting the company. The only test for the corporate innovation strategy is effective support of the corporate strategy.

- The evaluation protocols must be developed as part of the innovation proposal. The protocols should answer the six basic questions: When? What? Why? How? Who? Where?

- Use of the Balanced Scorecard and an understanding of the innovation premium can be helpful in evaluating the innovative company. All the measures should support those used at higher levels in the organization.

NOTES

1. Peter Drucker, *Innovation and Entrepreneurship* (New York: Harper Business, 1993).

2. Roger Bean and Russell Radford, *Powerful Products: Strategic Management of Successful New Product Development* (New York: AMACOM, 2000).

3. "Survey—Mastering Management," *Financial Times,* October 16, 2000.

4. Robert S. Kaplan and David P. Norton, "Using the Balanced Scorecard as a Strategic Management Tool," *Harvard Business Review,* January-February 1996.

5. Caroline Goulian and Alexander Mersereau, "Performance Measurement: Implementing a Corporate Scorecard," *Ivey Business Journal,* September-October 2000.

6. Ronald S. Jonash and Tom Sommerlatte, "The Innovation Premium: Capturing the Value of Creativity," *Prism,* Third Quarter 1999.

PART THREE

LEADING

INNOVATION

CHAPTER TWELVE

DEVELOPING AND IMPLEMENTING MARKET-FOCUSED INNOVATIONS

A S HE STOOD ON THE surface of the Moon after taking his "one small step," Neil Armstrong must have looked at the Earth and thought about the distance in time and space from the place where he had learned he had been accepted to be an astronaut. His training had been long, arduous, and not without risk. That risk had been reduced somewhat by a series of graduated steps in space exploration that had begun with the first suborbital flight and culminated in this first manned space flight to the Moon. And the actual flights were only a small part of the total effort that had been poured into the space program since President John F. Kennedy had issued the challenge in 1961. Here it was, eight years later, and the leadership in the Soviet Union and the Doubting Thomases at home had their answer. The might of the Soviet machine had been bettered, and the United States at last had clear and unambiguous leadership in space for the first time.

Neil Armstrong was one of a handful of visible figures among the supporting cast of hundreds of thousands of people who had all played their part in the most spectacular innovation in the history of humanity: the safe journey of people to the Moon and back. Feats in space still excite us, but nothing grabbed the collective imagination of the world like the first manned lunar landing in 1969. And this was certainly a market-focused innovation, aimed at several markets at home and abroad.

Although few innovations take as long to be realized as the first moon landing, the successful launch of any innovation starts a long time before a product reaches the market for which it is intended. In this chapter, we follow the path of development from idea to physical movement of a product or service to a customer. On the way, we look at some of the issues surrounding development at various stages of the process, always intent on ensuring we give the market what it wants and needs, and what we have promised.

These two clusters of activities in the innovation process—creating/developing and implementing/commercializing—require the greatest amount of time, resources, and management of all four activity clusters in the Innovation Management Model. The risks of omission or commission are also greatest here, so good management of the process is important. Attention to management of the projects—in essence, System I activities—and management of project portfolios—System III activities—is essential if System IV goals are to be met.

The basic lessons apply to market-pull or technology-push innovations, and to product, process, managerial, and/or organizational technologies. And they apply to commercial or noncommercial innovations as well. The race for the moon was not a commercial innovation, even though it was market-focused. Instead, it was designed to energize a nation and a scientific and engineering community stunned by the achievements of the Soviet space program. And it was designed to show the rest of the world that the United States was capable of responding to any challenge quickly, creatively, and effectively.

MARKET-FOCUSED INNOVATIONS

MARKET-FOCUSED INNOVATIONS aim to give customers in the target market greater value than the customers currently realize, at prices customers are prepared to pay. If customers find no value in the innovation or its effects, the innovation will fail. And if the entrepreneurial company cannot realize a fair return for the investment, the innovation will fail. Engineers at Bombardier were ecstatic when they were able to redesign the Global Express corporate jet to provide 11 cubic feet more cabin space—a real and expensive engineering feat. However, when the engineers were asked how much customers might be prepared to pay for the innovation, they were unable to answer. To the engineers, it had been strictly an engineering challenge, and they had given no thought to the economic consequences. As the marketers knew, the answer to the question of how much customers would be willing to pay was "nothing at all." An engineering success was a stillborn innovation.

And innovations need not be embedded in the product or service that the buying public embraces. The buying public may not even be aware of the innovation. For example, thin-strip casting of steel, developed by Nucor, is a process innovation. The just-in-time (JIT) philosophy at the heart of the Toyota Production System is a managerial innovation. "Efficient Consumer Response," developed in part by Procter & Gamble, is an organizational innovation involving all players in the value chain. Changes in the way in which dentists and family doctors organize their practices and interact with their patients are organizational innovations. The paying customer need not be aware of these innovations, yet each of these innovations markedly increased the value to the customer of the actual product purchased or the service sought. In all the cases recounted here, the innovations reduced the price paid by the customer and often improved the product in some observable and appreciated way.

FROM IDEA TO LAUNCH

AS FIGURE 12-1 indicates, the process of launching a market-focused innovation moves through the stages of visualizing the innovation, developing the design envelope, designing the innovation, producing the innovation, and launching the innovation. Not all innovations are launched into a consumer market. Process innovations, for instance, are launched internally, and organizational innovations might only be launched into some members of the value chain.

FIGURE 12-1. THE INNOVATION LAUNCH SEQUENCE.

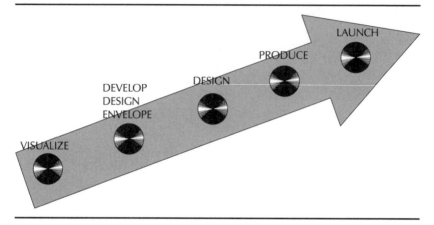

In mapping innovations in various industries by innovation category and year, the Chicago-based Doblin Group uses ten innovation categories. These categories can be placed in one of two groups:

CUSTOMER-TRANSPARENT	CUSTOMER-OBVIOUS
• Business models	• Product performance
• Networking	• Product systems
• Enabling processes	• Service
• Core processes	• Channel
	• Brand
	• Customer experience

The ultimate consumer using the product or service is likely to be aware only of the customer-obvious categories, such things as how the product performs and the service is provided. She is usually not aware of the customer-transparent categories, such things as the processes the company uses.

DEVELOPMENT PROJECTS *ARE* PROJECTS

EVERY INNOVATION THAT passes from concept to market reality and beyond is a project and should be managed as such. We don't want to dwell on the technical aspects of project management (although our experience suggests that training everybody who will be a project manager in project management practices is very valuable). What is important is to think about the organizational implications of projects.

THE PROJECT PROPOSAL

Time spent in preparing the project proposal is seldom if ever wasted. The more exhaustive the proposal (sometimes called the design brief), the better positioned the senior executive team will be to review the proposal and make a decision. This doesn't mean that every *i* can be dotted and every *t* crossed. In fact, at the outset of many commissioned architectural and engineering design projects, neither the flow of the development process nor its outcome can be closely defined. The onus is still on those preparing the proposal to be as detailed as possible, though, even if the detail is only for the first few steps of the development process.

Project timetables and financial projections are important. So, too, are the social implications of the development process and the proposed development system. This involves discussion of how other parties (customers, suppliers, special interest groups) will be involved in the process. Monsanto's development strategy for genetically modified food required the company to move very cautiously. The plan was to encourage regulators from the U.S. Food and Drug Administration and the Department of Agriculture to impose conditions on testing and approval of genetically modified foods, and to work with environmental groups, farmers, and food processors to relieve anxiety about such foods and their effect on humans in the short and longer term. This strategy worked well for several years. Unfortunately, a change in leadership at Monsanto led to a strategy of confrontation rather than one of cooperation. As a result, opposition solidified against Monsanto and set back public acceptance of genetically modified foods at least ten years.

PROJECT ROLLOUT

Few innovating organizations have only one project in progress. Projects therefore need to be managed by the project team, but project timetables must be coordinated with other projects competing for resources. Most organizations therefore need to appoint a senior manager to be in overall supervision of the project portfolio, and they may need other managers and specialists to coordinate the allocation of shared resources across the project portfolio. Projects will therefore be part of System I, with project portfolio managers operating at System III and coordinators of shared resources operating at System II.

It is critically important that the allocation of both dedicated and shared resources to a project be made as early and as logically as possible. This requires the project team to develop timetables and resource needs for each project element as tightly as possible. Given high technical uncertainty, this won't be very tight. However, all projects are designed from the "outside in"; that is, the large elements are defined according to customer priority, and successively smaller elements can then be worked on. Under these circumstances, project resources can be allocated only when needed, as the project focuses on an increasing number of smaller components. Incidentally, this approach to project conduct requires increasing amounts of resources, principally people, but also tends to reduce considerably the total project completion time.

Project managers need to keep in mind at all times the primacy of the customer. Customers should therefore be involved with the project as much and as frequently as appropriate. It is never appropriate to exclude customers from the project completely. After all, we can never be absolutely sure that we have precisely captured the customers' needs, expectations, and priorities. Experience with the product or a prototype may change a customer's requirements, and over the duration of a project, customers' needs may change anyway. And the more likely these changes are to occur, the more frequently should customers be involved in the development project. In the extreme, this means the actual presence of customers on the development team. More likely, it means including customers in determining the detailed product concept, then in looking at and testing prototypes.

GETTING IDEAS FROM THE MARKET

IT IS POSSIBLE to use the marketplace to help define the innovation, but only if the innovation is to be product-based. As 3M has discovered, drawing upon what have been called "lead users"—customers themselves working at the leading edge of technologies, and often innovating in the product area themselves—can dramatically improve the effectiveness of a new product launch.[1] 3M's approach has four phases:

1. Laying the foundation for the innovation by identifying the target market segment

2. Determining the trends in the target market by asking experts in various technologies

3. Identifying the lead users in the target market by networking with market members and, in the process, developing product ideas from discussions with the lead users

4. Developing the breakthroughs by working with lead users, which may involve hosting one or a series of workshops with groups of lead users to determine what breakthroughs are required, and the potential market size for each breakthrough

3M's approach is therefore very focused. It is focused, first, on products used by customers; second, in an attractive market segment; third, by expressed customer need; and fourth, by potential return to 3M. Companies of any size can use this approach but must realize that focus and painstaking research are critical to success.

Almost as an aside, it is ironic in a world where many customers have many alternative products available to them that even large companies have only one buyer of the source of tomorrow's successful products. The board or a subordinate committee vets ideas that bubble up from within the company, and then makes decisions about which ideas will likely win. 3M has been very successful identifying products this way, but the experience of one of Shell's groups suggests that there is at least one alternative. Shell's Exploration and Product Group trained people throughout the group to be innovative. Individuals were asked to submit ideas for innovations to a committee, and a small number of those who submitted ideas were asked to take part in computer-based training in innovation. On completing the training, the group brainstormed about the ideas each had brought forward, and then selected a small number of ideas for further development. The group then developed business plans for each innovation, and the plans were implemented.

The most intriguing aspect of this approach is that the role of the senior executives or the board changes from one of allocating financial resources to one of attracting knowledge resources to the process. Now the process is one of allocating knowledge resources to develop a larger innovation portfolio, and not one of apportioning scarce financial resources in a zero-sum game.

DESIGNING THE INNOVATION

UNLIKE INVENTIONS, MOST innovations are extensions or a next generation of an existing product or process. Even with incremental innovations, though, it is best to gain input from those who will purchase, work with, or influence the purchase and use of the innovation. This becomes more imperative when the innovation is more radical, and is most critical when the buy-in has to come from internal groups who are being subject to change which they have had little say in initiating. Krug Furniture installed a new automated cut-off saw in its components plant in Stratford, Canada. To make the change more effective, Krug rearranged the layout of the shop, but without involving the shop workers in the decision. Although the change made sense from an engineering point of view, from a management perspective it was not totally appropriate and was handled in the wrong way. The long-run result was a process change that did not achieve the goals set—and a more militant workforce.

An interesting example of both ineffective and effective process innovation comes from General Motors' Baltimore assembly plant, where, in the early 1980s, robots were to be introduced on the frame assembly line. The robots were placed in the area where they were to be installed—alongside the workers they were to replace—and remained draped in plastic for several weeks. The morale of the workers whose replacements sat complacently alongside them every day dropped, to nobody's great surprise.

GM decided to move the robots to another plant—a sign that the Baltimore plant had fallen out of favor. In fact, the plant went to a single-shift operation on the car that was being produced, and then went on temporary furlough when nationwide inventory for the vehicle was considered excessive. During the furlough, a group of workers from the front-end assembly area approached management with a request to change the process of assembling the front-end metal components of the vehicle—in other words, to initiate their own innovation. Plant management agreed to this, and the workers radically changed the layout of the process. When assembly of the car started up again, the change was immediately apparent. Before the innovation there was at least one major assembly disaster per shift in front-end assembly, but after the change there were no major assembly disasters over the first eighteen months of operation. The lesson here? Challenging those in the process to design the innovation often results in better innovations than those designed by managers and engineers—and results always in smoother implementation.

Resistance to process and organizational innovation is legendarily strong in government and not-for-profit organizations, where power and influence are often only applied inside the organization. But for-profit corporations have their share of managers who see everything to lose, and nothing to gain, from jumping onto the innovation bandwagon. Northern Telecom (now Nortel Networks) introduced targets for waste and inventory reduction in the late 1980s. At one plant, managers were shown how to reduce inventory quickly through some simple but effective techniques. There was little enthusiasm for the ideas from the logistics managers, who pointed out that they had already met their inventory reduction targets for 1987, and that doing more would gain them no benefits that year and would make it more difficult to make their 1988 targets (which were already known). In this case, changing behaviors and attitudes would have been relatively simple. By making changes to the management evaluation and compensation scheme, Northern Telecom could have achieved its inventory reductions in a much shorter period, possibly even in the first year of the program.

TEAMS: THE DESIGN CONUNDRUM

IT IS NOW almost axiomatic to involve most players in the supply and distribution chains in the design of any new innovation, particularly a large and/or radical innovation. And it makes a great deal of sense to use the best brains and experience around in order to achieve an effective design for the new innovation, no matter what type and form the innovation takes. We certainly endorse the use of teams and a team-based approach to systems design and operation. However, there are a number of issues that the organizers of the design function and the design process must consider before unleashing the teams.

How Big?

The team managing the overall project must be as small as possible, but it must also contain the mix of skills, understanding, and experience necessary to manage the design process. Experts can be co-opted for short periods, but if some attribute is required reasonably frequently, it should be on the team.

How Wide?

The "width" of the design team—the extent of the value chain represented on the senior design team—depends on the critical nature of upstream and downstream chain members in understanding and designing the critical *customer* value-adding aspects of the innovation. Magna International, the automotive parts manufacturer, has been chosen by BMW to assemble BMW's new sports utility vehicle. Magna will be part of the design team, and will play a leading role in the vehicle's development.

How Deep?

The "depth" of the overall design team depends entirely on the complexity of the innovation and the time available for development. Where time is short, more people will need to be involved with smaller pieces of the design puzzle, and the design team will be several layers deep. This is true also of innovation complexity: The more complex the design, measured in terms of the number of designed components, the deeper the design team. One rule of thumb is to look at an exploded parts list for the potential product and allocate design teams for each of the lowest assemblies, with more design teams at each higher point on the build diagram.

What Training?

Most organizations try to train people to be team players. This, however, is not enough, particularly where a mix of personalities exists. For effective teams, a mix of personalities and perspectives is important, for having a whole group of people of the same personality and communication style leads quickly to groupthink and relatively shallow results. In order for teams to function effectively, therefore, it is important for team members to be able to work with each other.

One step in this direction is to test every team member to determine his or her personality type (using the Myers-Briggs Type Indicator or equivalent) or his or her communication style. Knowing your own style or type is not enough, however. The strength in this process is learning how to work with other styles to ensure more effective communication among the team members. The most appropriate means of learning how to communicate effectively is to work at it through a series of exercises designed to reinforce the lessons. Nissan's Design Institute in California has used this process to improve the effectiveness of teamwork.

In doing this, of course, we are not trying to create a placid environment. Creativity requires challenge and conflict; there is a fine line to be walked between purposive and productive personality tension (with personality types grating on each other), and destructive tension. The personality or communications-style testing helps to ensure that the tension helps with creativity. For team leaders, and those entrusted with managing the creative process, finding a team of diverse personalities and integrating them is critical. After all, innovation is unlikely to occur in a team whose members are clones of the leader.

How Many Teams?

Many companies seem to think that the best chance for effective innovation comes from having the greatest number of projects as possible going on at once. No matter what size the organization might be, this is not good policy. A study involving twelve companies found that innovation and development projects were each completed more quickly if there were fewer projects.[2] This was because less strain was placed on critical shared resources. And few teams work truly independently of other teams or other organizational resources.

In fact, judicious investment to relieve pressure on these shared resources is another key to reducing innovation project lead time. In the study, this form of investment reduced disproportionately average time-to-market. Eliminating unnecessary variation in workloads (the duration of each project) at critical points also eliminated distractions and delays, thus freeing up the organizations to focus on the strategically important part of the innovation task: the creative element. The study reported that the average development time was reduced by 30–50 percent when a more process development approach was taken in the innovation projects.

Every manufacturing manager understands the concept of the bottleneck operation—the operation that limits the output of the process. When it is a shared resource that is the bottleneck, queues develop in front of the bottleneck, and all the products in the queue are delayed. Queue length increases, and the completion time of projects becomes less predictable when planned utilization of the resource exceeds approximately 75 percent of its capacity, when the work required to be performed on each task or project is variable, and when the processing capability is itself variable. Innovative companies therefore need to ensure that, as much as possible, the quality of shared knowledge resources is uniform, and the amount of work required of a shared resource by any project at any time is also uniform. This may require one or more projects to divide the work they require of a particular shared resource into two or more uniform "packets." Although the total elapsed time through the bottleneck will increase for a project whose work requirement is bundled into packets (assuming that the packets are interspersed with work required by other projects), the total time required to perform the work on all projects remains the same. And the time at which a project's work is completed by the bottleneck resource becomes more predictable.

All projects will be completed more quickly, of course, if the bottleneck resources are not overloaded. Managers responsible for managing the portfolio of development projects need to closely monitor this threshold level of resource utilization and make senior managers aware of impending critical usage levels. And the senior executive team needs to be aware of the impact of approving more development projects in addition to projects currently in development, especially if one or more are given a "rush" priority.

In some organizations, rush priorities may be common. Where this occurs for good strategic reason, it makes sense to load shared resources well below the 75 percent threshold with normal priority projects, to 60 percent, for example. This will allow rush projects to be scheduled into the bottleneck without creating a capacity crisis. It may also be possible to bring in other resources to handle peaks, in much the same way that temporary workers or subcontracting is used in manufacturing.

One means of increasing the processing capacity of bottlenecks is to reduce the setup time—the time required to change from one task to another. For development projects, the setup time can be reduced appreciably by improving the project documentation. As mentioned in Chapter 11, we manage what we measure, and measuring the time it takes to set up for a project will highlight difficulties created by poor documentation—and create pressure to improve this aspect of project administration. And, as we know, the shorter the time required for development and rollout, the less likely it will be that market needs and expectations have moved appreciably from where they were at the beginning of the development process.

INVOLVING EXTERNAL DEVELOPMENT RESOURCES

IT IS RARE for organizations involved with large development projects to own all the resources they need, or as much of a resource as they require at any time. Under these circumstances—the need for new capabilities or the need for increased capacity—companies have to consider outsourcing or collaboration on a project. The need for external development resources brings with it risks for the project and the company itself. In general, the greater the risks and uncertainties involved with the project, the less able managers are to settle conflicts and coordinate activities. Where these conflicts involve external resources, deciding how to organize the project becomes more critical than usual.

Many organizations are now actively engaged in cross-boundary Internet-based development projects. The question is, when is this appropriate? A recent study suggests the circumstances under which a "virtual" organization may be appropriate, with portions of the project being given over completely to outside groups.[3] Two factors help determine the organizational relationship with external resources: (1) whether the project is independent or systemic, and (2) whether the capabilities needed exist or must be developed.

Independent innovations are innovations or developments that do not rely on other projects for technical or resource inputs, nor do other projects rely on the independent project. Systemic projects are interdependent with other projects, requiring the same technology developments to enhance the innovation, for example, or developing capabilities that can be used on other projects. The second factor is the set of capabilities the organization needs to gain access to, in order to complete the project. These capabilities either exist now or need to be developed.

The study on when a virtual organization is appropriate suggests that such an organization should be considered only when the project is autonomous and the capabilities already exist. Also, the greater the degree of uncertainty with either factor, the more appropriate it is to bring the innovation in-house. We will come back to this point in Chapter 14, but note now that the rush to outsource innovation should be slowed to a deliberate dawdle. Otherwise, it might be a panic sprint to the courthouse.

COST: THE FINAL FRONTIER

IF TARGETED CUSTOMER research is done, it indicates what price range the market will accept, and the proposal will have been based around cost and price assumptions. The project team will therefore have to focus constantly on product cost over the life of the product. Probably the most appropriate tool for this task is target costing. The philosophy behind target costing is simple: Costs are designed into a product, process, or service—they are not built in.

The target-costing process starts with understanding the prioritized needs of customers and purchase decision influencers, and also understanding how current offerings satisfy customer needs and expectations. Until we understand all this, we cannot decide what product to make, what it should do, and where it should be positioned in the market space.

Having decided the market positioning, the development team needs then to develop specifications for the product offering. Two sets of specifications need to be established: technical and strategic specifications. The technical specifications should focus on quality and functionality/performance issues, and the strategic specifications should focus on price, production volume, and timing/time line issues.

The technical specifications will generate an idea of what product cost is likely to be. This is not surprising, as the developers will assume a production process and its attendant economics for producing a product with the required specifications. The technical path will, therefore, produce expected costs and expected product performance. The strategic specifications will produce targets for costs, volumes, and timings, based on competitive considerations. The target costs will be influenced by corporate financial requirements, as well as what the market will pay.

It is unlikely that the initial sets of specifications will generate expected and target costs that are identical, or where expected are lower than target. So the project team will need to revisit the technical specifications, working to challenge assumptions about the process and the product until the expected costs are acceptable. If the target costs cannot be met, the product cannot be launched.

One place to start when thinking about how to reduce costs is to look at the major components of the product and assess the relative value of the component to the market performance of the product. Target costs can then be allocated to components. This is admittedly arbitrary, but it does highlight where cost reductions might be targeted in the future. It is also useful as a check during the development process as costs begin to escalate.

The then–Northern Telecom used target costing at the component level when the Harmony telephone was designed. Armed with the knowledge that costs in the telephone had to be reduced by 50 percent from expected, the development team looked for 50 percent reductions in expected costs from each component in the telephone—without compromising any of the quality or functionality specifications. The team was able to achieve the savings. In order to reduce costs in the transmitter assembly, housed in the telephone's handset, the transmitter team chose a lower-cost microphone than that originally specified, but with greater performance variability among the microphones. To meet specifications, the team had to redesign the transmitter assembly process and include a performance test on each microphone. Including this step, and two more steps as a consequence of the test, increased assembly costs minimally, without changing the transmitter specifications. Without target costing, the challenge would probably not have been made.

BROADENING THE INNOVATION TARGET AREA

IT IS INEVITABLE that development teams will try to limit their focus, and it is generally appropriate. However, as we know, it is not generally possible to launch an effective innovation without innovations being made in other areas. And even if the innovation could be launched and be successful, often innovations in other areas might improve market success. Innovations that reduce roadblocks, and make it easier and more pleasant for customers to do business with you, improve the chances of success of the innovation. So thinking through considerations around the product are as important as thinking through considerations about the product. This is true whether the customer is a consumer or an organization.

By expanding the innovation target area, we might discover new ways of differentiating ourselves from competitors and new sources of competitive advantage. Doing this constantly may give us a source of sustainable competitive advantage—the ability to rapidly develop successful differentiation strategies.[4] Ian MacMillan and Rita McGrath suggest a two-part process for the analysis: (1) mapping the customer chain, and (2) analyzing customers' experiences.

The customer chain is the complete social process of the customers' involvement with the product, process, or service. The stages of the customer experience chain are as follows:

1. Awareness of the product

2. Finding the product

3. Product selection

4. Ordering or purchasing the product

5. Product distribution

6. Product delivery

7. Product installation

8. Paying for the product

9. Storing the product

10. Moving the product

11. Actual product uses and usage

12. Customer queries

13. Product returns and exchanges

14. Product repair and service

15. Product disposal

The social process thus begins with awareness of the product and ends with disposing of the product. Each question needs to be addressed in as much detail as is practicable, given constraints on time, resources, and costs. The richer the detail, the better the information.

Internet retailers have begun to focus on some of these service aspects. Internet furniture retailers, for example, have begun to focus on physical delivery of their products, particularly where assembly of the furniture is required. Apologies and damage control do not generally make an irate customer into a repeat purchaser.

Some of the information may come only from observation. This is particularly true in organizations, where managers may not understand the variety of useful purposes to which a product is put. The ability of people to be creative in making life more pleasant and less arduous cannot be overestimated.

The real key is analysis of the customers' experiences, particularly where it is possible to allocate customers to particular clusters or segments. As with any data, what might be meaningless or misleading at the highest level may be very revealing when segmented. Whether we segment or not, though, the only way we can begin to think about how to change or adapt the services that go with the product is by understanding not only what customers do but why they do what they do with our product, and what else would make it easier for them to deal with us.

EXPERIMENTATION AND PROTOTYPING

MAKING GOOD DECISIONS about experimentation and prototyping can lead to a more successful innovation and get it launched more quickly and at less cost than might otherwise happen.

The greater the uncertainty surrounding the innovation, the more necessary it will be to look at alternatives and to experiment. This should never be haphazard. Experiments should be conducted only on important issues, which means they should address strategic issues— cost, value, and/or timing. Experiments are internally focused. Their results provide information and an understanding of how we should do something. Experiments invariably involve thinking about process options, such as how to integrate new research discoveries into products using current processes, and what new processes to develop to make new products. Prototype development and testing invariably involves thinking about the product, how customers interact with the product, and what features the product ought to have. Prototypes ought to be built early and often, so that we can guarantee building what the customer wants. All of us who have been involved with building a house know that what looks good on paper or as a sketch looks very different during construction or when in use.

There are interactions between experiments and prototypes, of course. Accepted prototypes constrain the process options and often require experiments to be conducted to determine which manufacturing approach is most appropriate. The outcome of an experiment is invariably a new prototype, ready to be assessed for market acceptance and conformance with the cost, value, and timing parameters already established.

Experiments should be conducted in parallel, not sequentially. Time is likely to be a more critical resource than the availability of experimenters and equipment. If you have to, start work on the experiments with skeleton staffs, and start switching resources from less to more attractive approaches as the results come in. Products that launch late but on cost are not as profitable as products that launch on time but over cost. This is particularly true when a competitor gets wind of the product and rushes to follow rapidly.

PREPARING FOR THE PHYSICAL LAUNCH

AFTER ALL THE experimentation and prototyping, after all the market research, focus groups, and observations, after all the processes have been built and all the training carried out, it would be a pity for the product to be a damp squib in a world of firecrackers. So it is incumbent on us to make it impossible for the target customer to do business with us any other way than easily and professionally. If we've thought through all the social issues involving customers and our product, we are well on the way. But that isn't enough.

We have to ensure that we have thought through the logistics issue, particularly for the launch period. Think of the innovation launch in the same way that the planners of D Day thought about the Normandy landings—as a mission that *had* to succeed, for there was no way of recovering quickly from operational failure. Make sure all the links in the chain understand their roles and are capable of fulfilling them.

Make sure you develop a risk management plan and emergency management plans for likely alternative scenarios. As McDonald's and Martin-Brower knew before the launch of their pizza in Canada (discussed in Chapter 11), what happens on average never happens at the average restaurant, so plan on average but manage the particular. The flexibility required to do this will be determined by the plan you develop to manage the risks.

It is generally more appropriate to err on the side of too much rather than too little in strategic reserves, particularly of product inventory. Probably the worst unplanned outcome is a wild success that cannot be exploited because inventories have been exhausted and resupply is not possible, at least quickly. Enthusiasm quickly turns to anger, as some toy maker discovers every year. If the shortage is planned, of course, that is a different story.

Remember, too, that failed innovations have one saving grace: They require no further investment. Successful innovations *always* require further investment, and investment immediately after launch will generally need to be much greater than the income generated from sales. If you cannot reinforce success quickly, the innovation may have a short life. That is the topic of the next chapter.

SUMMARY

- Market-focused innovations should give customers greater value at prices the market will bear. If customers won't buy, the innovation is a failure. Any major innovation, whether product or not, must have a clear market-based rationale.

- The process of launching a market-focused innovation moves through the stages of visualizing the innovation, developing the design envelope, designing the innovation, producing the innovation, and launching the innovation.

- Development projects are first and foremost projects and should be managed as such.

- The better the proposal or design brief, the better the chances of a successful innovation.

- Using lead users can be a very effective means of identifying new innovation possibilities.

- Obtaining buy-in from those with vested interests is important, even with incremental innovation.

- Organizing for development means organizing teams. Having the appropriate number of teams with the right mix of skills, and the appropriate mandate, is essential.

- External resources will most likely be necessary. Outsourcing should be contemplated only when the skills required are available and the innovation is independent.

- Expanding the innovation target area allows us to discover new ways of differentiating ourselves from our competitors. Increasingly, the target area should be expanded to think about service offerings.

- Experimentation and prototyping are powerful processes for producing appropriate innovations. Early and often are the watchwords.

- Approach launches as though failure would be catastrophic. It is.

NOTES

1. Gary Hamel, "Bringing Silicon Valley Inside," *Harvard Business Review,* September–October 1999.
2. Paul S. Adler, Avi Mendelbaum, Vien Nguyen, and Elizabeth Schwerer,

"Getting the Most out of Your Product Development Process," *Harvard Business Review,* March–April 1996.

3. Henry W. Chesborough and David J. Teece, "When Is Virtual Virtuous?" *Harvard Business Review,* January–February 1996.

4. Ian C. MacMillan and Rita Gunther McGrath, "Discovering New Points of Differentiation," *Harvard Business Review,* July–August 1997.

CHAPTER THIRTEEN

EXPLOITING MARKET-FOCUSED INNOVATIONS

IT WAS BLOWING a gale as the ship approached England, but the young man who sat hunched in thought in his cabin scarcely noticed. Four years at sea—all unpaid—on a voyage around the world, he thought, and it hadn't been easy. Several moments of anxiety, even panic, had occurred. All these had been eclipsed, though, by the wonders he had seen and documented. Now he needed to make some sense of them.

As Charles Darwin collected his thoughts and his specimens on his last few days aboard the *Beagle,* he reflected on the sights he had seen on the Galapagos islands off the northwest coast of South America. Most amazing had been the finches, all obviously descended from one family, but each island having one or more distinct variants, adapted to suit a particular environment. What did this mean? How did these variants occur? Thinking that through would take time. What

Darwin realized already was that animals could adapt to a new environment, given time.

We are all aware of Darwin's Theory of Evolution, and the basic argument of survival of the fittest. Companies, too, survive by adapting, and one way of adapting is to produce variants of original products.

When Sony introduced the first Walkman to rapturous acclaim in Japan, nobody was aware that over forty variants of the original product would be produced and purchased in large volumes. Daimler-Chrysler has been able to combine two successful innovations in its recent past—the minivan and retro styling—and produce a hot-selling passenger/cargo carrier, the PT Cruiser. Swatch watches continue to sell in impressive numbers worldwide, years after it was confidently predicted the product would have a short product life.

The fact that a company can complete the first three clusters of innovative activities in the Innovation Management Model ought to mean it can successfully complete the fourth cluster—exploiting the innovation. The examples given above indicate that it can be done, and done consistently. Why, though, are so few companies able to do this on a regular basis? Why is it that a dynamic innovative system can fail at the final hurdle?

WHAT IS EXPLOITATION?

OF COURSE, EXPLOITING innovations doesn't necessarily involve follow-on products, and success need not be measured in market share or financial terms. The focus of exploitation can be one (or a couple) of the means listed in Figure 13-1.

Let's look at these possible focuses.

EXPLOITING MARKETS

Exploiting markets can take one of two forms: (1) expanding current markets, or (2) moving into new markets. One of the most interesting facts of innovative life is that quite often there are uses for an innovative product or process that the innovators did not appreciate. Johnson & Johnson's Baby Shampoo was developed as a nonirritating shampoo for use with the fine hair and sensitive eyes of babies and small children. However, an even larger market was discovered acci-

FIGURE 13-1. POSSIBLE FOCUSES OF EXPLOITATION.

Markets
Current

New

Products
Current

Follow-on

Innovations
New

Competitors

Corporate
Capabilities

Sell innovations

Sell the company

---

dentally when some teenagers began using the shampoo on a daily basis, because the daily use of traditional shampoos damaged hair. Johnson & Johnson was quick to capitalize on the discovery and developed a very successful marketing campaign promoting the daily use of the Baby Shampoo with teenagers.

And innovation is not limited to physical products. Consultants quickly took that ubiquitous management innovation, TQM (total quality management), from the factory floor to the office, from manufacturing to service settings, and from for-profit to not-for-profit and government institutions. Similarly, inventory management processes developed for large job-shop applications were installed in repetitive manufacturing facilities and also used for distribution planning downstream of all manufacturing operations.

One of the oldest forms of market extension is syndication. Practiced first in newspapers as a way of providing news services that local newspapers could not provide, syndication now involves film and television productions. Movies are now expected to generate greater revenues from sales to non-English–speaking countries and from North American video rentals and sales than at the box office. This requires a new player in the value chain, the syndicator. Syndicators buy information from providers and bundle packets together in ways customers might want. Providers usually do not have the ability to reach new markets, and customers do not have the ability to find new sources easily. The most ubiquitous syndicator these days is our local cable company, buying programs and feeds from a variety of sources and putting together a number of alternative programming packages.

The ability to exploit new market opportunities requires companies either to envision the new markets themselves or to listen to interested people and organizations beyond the expected market. Both approaches require open minds and an ability to quickly follow up the perceived opportunity with solid market research. They may also require a willingness to adapt the organization to take advantage of new opportunities that prove to be strategically suitable.

This willingness to adapt or reshape the organization structure may also be important to companies intent on introducing new innovations into, or supporting, their traditional markets. Chrysler reorganized when their minivan became wildly popular in North America in the 1980s, reshaping itself so that one division looked after the passenger vans. Incidentally, the popularity of the minivan was due not only to its design but also to an innovative way of reducing the cost to the customer. Station wagons, built by Chrysler and the other North American manufacturers, were and are classified as automobiles by the federal government, and are required to meet all automobile safety and administrative requirements set by national agencies. Chrysler's innovation was to have the minivan classified as a truck, which allowed the company to build the vehicle without automobile-specific safety features (for example, collision protection in the doors). The lowered manufacturing cost that resulted from the less stringent manufacturing requirements, and the lower taxes on trucks, allowed Chrysler to sell the minivans for thousands of dollars less than the perceived competition. Astute marketing to complement the new vehicle, aimed primarily at households with young families, cemented the minivan as an acceptable second family vehicle.

Chrysler was not the first automobile manufacturer to sell fully enclosed, passenger-carrying trucks in North America. Japanese auto manufacturers were able to convince U.S. regulators to allow their vans (for example, the Toyota Previa) into the United States as trucks. This move allowed the Japanese to bypass the quotas on automobiles they were allowed to bring into the country. Chrysler's management quickly saw the fuller potential of the approval and brilliantly exploited the opportunity.

This was not the only opportunity realized by others, but exploited by Chrysler. Ford engineers suggested that Ford install a driver's-side sliding passenger door on its minivan. Ford's senior management demurred for safety reasons, but Chrysler took the concept and used it to competitive advantage. In 1999, Opel's management (Opel is GM's German subsidiary) suggested to GM's corporate board that a van designed for European driving conditions be built in North America for North American markets. GM's board turned down the suggestion. Daimler-Chrysler, however, took advantage of the opportunity and introduced the PT Cruiser, another successful extension of the minivan line.

So companies intent on exploiting market opportunities must not only be aware of the opportunities. They also must be quick to assess and then act on the opportunities as they appear. Neither Ford nor GM investigated the suggestions that came from within their companies. Had they done so with open minds, it is likely that Ford and GM would have seriously considered the introductions. But there is no guarantee they would have acted on them. Neither Ford nor GM appears positioned to be an innovative company. Both seem content to allow others to introduce new ideas, and then the "Big Two" see what is successful and copy the idea. Given stable markets and accepted ways of operating in their industry, this notion of the big players following the innovation lead of the smaller players might make some sense. This does not seem to be appropriate in the current of the global automobile industry, as the global and North American market shares of both Ford and GM indicate.

EXPLOITING PRODUCTS

A favorite means of exploiting product opportunity is to develop follow-on products. This makes good sense, if the initial product is a success in the marketplace. Given a satisfactory market size and customer base, and postexperience feedback from customers about the first-generation product, the design of the next-generation product ought to be relatively simple. In addition, costs ought to be easier to predict—and control—in subsequent product offerings.

There are, though, a great many follow-on products that fail miserably—too many, in fact. Why do these products fail? We believe there are three basic reasons: (1) the arrogance of pride, (2) a loss of focus, and (3) drift away from the strategic target market segment. Let's examine each of them.

The Arrogance of Pride

Many products fail in the marketplace, as we all know. For each product that fails, at least one senior manager's judgment can be called into question, and a great deal of corporate cash seemingly wasted. It is very easy, and very tempting, for senior management (or anyone with a great deal to lose) to argue that the innovation was appropriate for the marketplace, but poor work in development or marketing, or poor timing into the market, was the reason for the failure. The road to hell is paved with good intentions, it is said. Well, the road back is littered with postlaunch reports and analyses that point out that the failure was inevitable, given suitable scapegoats inside the company and intransigence outside the company.

Under these circumstances, it is a natural human tendency to reinforce failure by trying to force a "new and improved" product on a resisting market, without trying to understand why the innovation failed. That is why Ford's Edsel story is so inspiring. As we said in Chapter 11, Ford acknowledged that it did not do a good enough job of understanding its customers, and it spent a great deal of time revisiting and questioning its assumptions. The result was the successful launch of the four-door Thunderbird, followed by the spectacular Mustang.

The first lesson is: *If at first you don't succeed, accept the fact that the market is telling you something, and find out what the market is really saying.* Pride comes before a fall; humility may come before a windfall.

A Loss of Focus

Confess it: We've all tried using chopsticks at least once. All of us are clumsy at the beginning, and most people give up after their first attempt. Perseverance pays off ultimately, though, and the occasional user can confidently pick up and eat a peanut. Then comes the challenge of picking up two peanuts at once and popping them in your mouth and the realization that very skillful users of chopsticks can pick up and pop *three* peanuts in their mouth at once. Nobody takes lightly the challenge of picking up two, then three, peanuts; even for skilled users, concentration and focus are required. Holding an intense conversation or reading a book at the same time as you attempt to pick up the peanuts is out of the question. Three peanuts seem to be a limit.

The same is true for follow-on products. Managing the overall introduction and follow-through on an initial product is difficult enough. The greater the number of derivatives, new generations, and product extensions that are introduced and maintained in the marketplace concurrently, the easier it is to lose focus on what is critical—identifying and capitalizing on successful products, and capitalizing on synergies that are *proven* to exist. GM launched Saturn as one model of passenger car; as of early 2001, there were at least five variants on the market. Every variant competes against at least one other variant in its own particular market segment. And nobody knows which is the most appropriate variant or the most appropriate strategic target market.

And we've all seen jugglers—and tried to emulate them. Most jugglers use five or six dynamically similar objects (nobody successfully juggles paper plates, eggs, and silk scarves at the same time). So why should we expect companies to successfully manage product variants that have vastly different internal and/or market dynamics from the original product? The answer is, of course, that they can, provided they restructure to keep the different dynamics separate. Not understanding the sometimes subtle dynamic differences can lead to a loss of focus in manufacturing or marketing spheres, with disastrous consequences for the company.

The second lesson is: *Don't assume that manufacturing and marketing can automatically and effectively handle the follow-on products without either restructuring or providing additional resources.* Failure to support the overall performance of the manufacture and marketing of the follow-on products can easily lead to a collapse of a category's profitability.

Drift Away from the Strategic Target Market Segment

Drift is not loss of focus. Rather, it is the incremental, unplanned, and unrecognized movement of the crosshairs of the marketing rifle's sights away from the strategic target. Why does this happen? Perhaps a large potential customer is intrigued by a product and suggests that modification of the product will win its business for the new product, which will take the company into uncharted market waters. Smaller companies are particularly vulnerable to the magnet of the annuity-providing large customer. More often than not, the first successful product succeeded on its own technological merits, not because it was developed strategically.

This is the history of the software industry. Technology-focused software developers produced a product that attracts a following, and were then seduced by dreams of perpetual profits if they only modified the product to suit the professed needs of a large potential customer. Of course, the market the developers strive for doesn't exist, and they lose the original market as well because they cannot support both markets at the same time. So we might call this drift by seduction. The drift to a new promise does not allow the company to observe and chart the drift or trend in the needs and expectations of customers in the original market—and sooner rather than later, the company will lose its market share and its market.

The third lesson is: *Companies that fail to have a strategic imperative behind their innovations can easily drift onto the shoals around the market segment they first serve, then ignore.* If you don't know where you're going, any road will get you there, as the Cheshire cat said to Alice. If you don't know *why* you're going there, though, then why did you set off in the first place?

EXPLOITING INNOVATIONS

Exploiting innovations can take the form of exploiting new innovations and exploiting competitors' innovations.

Exploiting New Innovations

We stressed earlier in this book the need for balanced development of the several capabilities required for being an effectively innovating company. These capabilities are also essential for taking advantage of opportunities that become apparent after the market innovation is launched. In many instances, users of the innovative product, process, or service recognize new opportunities.

The Japanese just-in-time manufacturing philosophy was developed by Toyota as the philosophy within which the Toyota Production System (TPS) was developed. A critical requirement for successful operation of the TPS was certainty of demand, and Toyota was reorganized so that Toyota Motor Manufacturing was separate from and independent of Toyota Motor Company, the marketing arm of the organization. Toyota Motor Manufacturing had only one customer, the marketing arm, which gave organization orders rather than sketchy forecasts to the manufacturing group. Firm orders and a realistic build schedule allowed Toyota Motor Manufacturing to achieve its quality and cost targets.

That Toyota and the other Japanese automobile manufacturers were able to win the marketing wars in the United States and redefine auto quality in the minds of North American consumers is ancient history. However, Toyota quickly realized that a successful marketing campaign and excellent products were not sufficient. Its next innovation was to revolutionize the car dealership in North America, for Toyota discovered that North Americans felt the traditional dealerships were necessary evils, plagued by shady sales practices and low service quality for repairs and maintenance. Toyota helped establish independent dealers and insisted on training all personnel to ensure that every person in the dealership was customer-focused and capable of performing their function. Backed by all the necessary equipment to support the vehicles, Toyota dealerships became the envy of the industry, and themselves became a principal reason for individual consumers becoming first-time customers of Toyota cars.

Honda and Toyota have both been successful with developing new products for new (for them) market segments. Both have successfully launched vehicles for the luxury segment of the global car market (Acura and Lexus, respectively). In both cases, the companies have further reorganized their marketing divisions, with the luxury vehicles being distributed through dealers separate from the mass-market vehicles. However, both Honda and Toyota have resisted reshaping their manufacturing, focusing instead on learning how to manufacture mass-market and luxury vehicles on the same assembly lines.

Exploiting Competitors' Innovations

For many companies, it is exploiting the initial innovations of others that drives competitive success, and there is nothing wrong with being a successful follower or niche market player in an industry. Some companies are even capable of improving a fundamental technology so much that they become market leaders in their industry, forcing the initial innovators and early imitators to follow the new leaders at a distance.

A prime example comes from the steel industry. Continuous casting of slab steel was developed initially in Austria, with early followers coming from Germany and the United States. Japanese manufacturers, though, concentrated on developing the next generation of casters, in concert with Asian steelmakers. As a consequence, the bulk of the world's continuous casting equipment for slabs is now Japanese, with very little from Europe or elsewhere. Nucor, a U.S. steelmaker using electric arc furnaces, has developed the technology to thin-cast steel in sheets only 3 inches thick (compared with the 9-inch thick slab from slab casters). Where this technology finishes up is currently in question, but a likely scenario is, once again, Japanese-controlled.

Early followers need to be able to identify areas of concern with the initial technology and be able to work rapidly to make improvements. These improvements need not be with the physical innovation. As previously stated, the market-focused innovation consists of the total package of physical and nonphysical attributes of the innovation, and any one of these can be found wanting in the initial innovation. Many early followers in fact identify and improve on the intangible offerings in the innovation, especially if they are aware of areas in which the developer of the initial innovation has underdeveloped capabilities. Xerox, for example, developed (and still develops) remarkable innovations at its Palo Alto Research Center (PARC), but it has never developed the capability for successfully transferring PARC innovations into salable products. Many European companies used to have inadequate marketing capabilities, arguing that good engineering would sell itself. A major North American paper products manufacturer used to have excellent product development and marketing capabilities, but it also had poor product manufacturing management and control systems. The list goes on. Identifying weaknesses in market leaders, especially where these companies are product innovators, is one key strategic lever followers can have.

Niche players generally focus on market segments that the market leaders find difficult to profitably exploit. Xerox copiers used not to be installed in small companies because Xerox designed products for what it saw as the only profitable market segment—high-volume paper-consuming companies. Japanese copier manufacturers entered the marketplace and showed Xerox there were other profitable segments. In another example, the Watch Company, a Vancouver, British Columbia–based watch retailer, successfully exploits a market segment left untouched by other watch retailers. The company operates franchises that sell watches and batteries from carts in shopping malls. All watches are sold at the same low price, which includes a second battery. The company is highly profitable, and nobody appears interested in competing with it.

However, niche markets are apt to be absorbed into the larger marketplace, and this is particularly true as the technology revolution gathers steam. Innovations in manufacturing technology make it feasible for mass-market producers to now cost-effectively manufacture products for niche market segments. Until these companies have complementary capabilities reasonably well developed, though, the threat they pose to niche marketers remains a distant prospect.

Exploiting on the Corporate Level

There are three possibilities here: (1) exploiting new capabilities, (2) selling off the innovations, and (3) selling off the company.

Exploiting New Capabilities

Companies organize around products, markets, processes, technologies, region, or stage in the product life cycle. It is natural for companies to then think about exploiting what they organize about. But few companies think about exploiting capabilities, and they miss opportunities for exploitation in a number of areas at once.

It has been suggested that capabilities consist of four elements:

1. Knowledge and skills

2. Managerial systems

3. Physical systems

4. Values[1]

More important than these essential elements, though, is a fundamental *understanding* of some basic process or activity.

Daewoo Shipbuilding and Heavy Machinery builds ships, including some of the world's largest crude oil tankers. The company builds these vessels in much less time than its competitors, at lower cost, on time, and to the highest technical performance levels. Daewoo has excellent managerial systems, and its scheduling system is impressive. It also has impressive physical systems, including the world's heaviest capacity gantry crane and huge dry docks. Labor relations are the best in the industry in Korea and among the best globally.

None of these attributes, though, explains Daewoo's performance. The key is that Daewoo *understands* the arc welding of large pieces—not just how to weld two pieces of metal together, but how to do it perfectly, consistently, cleanly, and on time. Even that is not enough. Daewoo engineers, scientists, and designers know how large pieces of steel act, change shape, distort, and change their crystalline structure when they are welded. It is this fundamental understanding of how the metal acts that allows Daewoo's designers to predict exactly how a welded structure will act, and precisely what changes in shape will occur as a result of the welding.

This understanding allowed Daewoo to fundamentally change the process by which large ships are built. Propeller shafts are inserted into the vessel after the vessel has been built; other shipbuilders must place the propeller shafts in their bearings not long after the hull has been laid. Daewoo is also able to build the vessel as very large modules and then put the modules together like a large, expensive, and impressive Lego set. There is no need for "just in case" welding or extra internal bracing; this gives weight and volume savings and increases the vessel's cargo-carrying capacity.

Understanding welding thus allowed Daewoo to make improvements in three aspects of shipbuilding. It also allows Daewoo to design and build other large structures in which accuracy in welding allows changes to be made in the construction process. Until someone else gains Daewoo's understanding (which will take a long time to develop), Daewoo stands to reap the benefits.

Selling Off the Innovation

Most companies that innovate want to retain the product and grow with it. Sometimes, though, the innovation doesn't fit with where the company wants to go, or the costs of getting there may be too onerous. Selling off the innovation might then make sense, and companies should always be open to the thought that they might make more from getting out of an innovation early rather than staying in. This is particularly true if the company is good at working in the early stages of an innovation, but is not particularly good at managing the rapid growth stage of the product life cycle.

It doesn't take long to find a company that is good at taking someone else's development and growing it to maturity, especially in a global economy. Fewer companies are capable of innovating effectively than are capable of solid stewardship. And it is generally a seller's market. Not for ideas—for proven innovations.

The issue is whether to sell the innovation or license it. Licensing can be attractive, but the conditions have to be appropriate. In all likelihood, the decision is up to you and your lawyers, but there are a few rules of rules of thumb. If you are the small potato, sell; arguments over licenses are generally won by the person with the greatest financial muscle. This holds true in thinking about joint ventures.

Sell as well if the person interested in the innovation resides in and wants the innovation for a country in which you wouldn't want to set up shop in the first place. And get the money up front, in U.S. dollars, and into your bank before anything is handed over. If you won't get a fair hearing from local courts, why do you think a licensee would play by the rules?

Finally, sell if counterfeiting is a local pastime. Rampant counterfeiting is a good indicator of local business and legal practice.

Selling Off the Company

One way to exploit an innovation is to sell the company. This has been a pattern in the software industry for years, and there is lots of evidence that many dot-coms were set up simply to be sold. That they were purchased doesn't say a lot for the buyers, but many companies know they are "one-trick ponies." If you are small, have had one excellent idea that has been brought to market, and don't have a clue about why the process worked and where the next idea is going to come from, sell. Be aware, of course, that the purchaser probably thinks there is something else coming out of the company. The purchaser is also buying particular people. If you know you aren't that person, polish your resume. And sell before the real knowledge assets in your company find out that the company is likely to be sold to some large organization with lots of funds and a dearth of ideas. If key people leave before the deal is signed, it will likely fall through. Then you will be worse off than when you started.

WHAT DOES IT TAKE
TO EXPLOIT SUCCESS?

WE DISCUSSED DEVELOPING the capability to innovate in Chapter 6. In order to innovate, we have to develop or have access to a wide range of different capabilities. While we tend to think of these capabilities being required for developing and producing the innovation, if we don't develop the capabilities necessary to exploit the innovation, then our system will fail. It will fail in the short run because we don't generate revenues from the innovation, and losing money jeopardizes the company's future. But we compromise the company's future also by not being able to find out from the market what it likes and doesn't like about our innovations so that we can modify our offerings as tastes change. So we need to think about what it takes to exploit success—what capabilities we need to develop.

FINANCIAL RESOURCES

First and foremost we need resources, particularly financial resources. We mentioned in Chapter 12 that a successful innovation requires more investment almost immediately, because the cash required to meet a growing market demand will rarely be generated by sales. If we are going to exploit the innovation by developing follow-on products or derivatives, each will need to be treated as a new innovation project. This requires the whole process to be gone through again, with its attendant cost and other resource implications.

Bonne Bell of Lakewood, Ohio, the manufacturer of Lip Smackers, in 1996 hired retired workers to staff an entire production department. Using older, slower equipment than was being used in other departments, the company found that retired workers (some as old as ninety) could perform more than adequately. In order to exploit the underutilized capacity of the senior workforce, Bonne Bell is looking to physically expand the senior department in 2001 and to purchase newer and faster equipment that will keep up with the workforce. A company looking to exploit even a comparatively modest innovation requires access to cash.

DISTRIBUTION CAPABILITY

Especially straight after the launch, a company should have access to distribution capacity and inventories to be able to exploit a runaway success. Having good order-taking capabilities is also crucial; if we've got it and can move it, it doesn't matter if customers can't order it. The successful Internet marketing companies witnessed demand growth and demand spikes many times greater than anticipated. The rule of thumb now is to be able to provide 1,000 times the order-taking and distribution capability than is seen as the optimistic demand scenario.

MANAGEMENT CAPABILITY

Any business that has only one product and then wants to develop derivative products finds itself in a new game. That game is managing not just one innovation but a portfolio of innovation projects. These new management challenges will be greatest at Systems III and IV in the Innovation Management Model. System IV managers need to deal with a much more complex strategic environment and now have to think about more complex internal and external conditions as they make decisions about future product offerings. System III managers now start managing development portfolios and make resource allocation decisions across an increasingly diverse range of products.

This increase in the complexity of innovation management often requires a new breed of manager being brought into the company. Often, the threat of challenge to the corporate culture is enough to make good people leave, so the decision to invest in new management should not be taken lightly.

Given follow-on products, there will also be a need to be able to produce and market products at different stages of the product life cycle. This will likely require a more complex organization, but it certainly places different pressures on managers. Managers trying to manage products in both growth and maturity stages of the product life cycle are likely not to manage either well. More managers may be the order of the day.

ORGANIZATION STRUCTURE

Growth brings with it the need for a change in organization structure, and new challenges. When the company has more than one site, it is reasonable to ask what the role of each site is in the innovation process. The focus around which the corporation organizes its operations helps dictate that decision. Equally important, though, is the charter given to each operating entity. The charter determines both the structural and infrastructural characteristics of the operating entity, and this in turn limits what the entity can reasonably do.

This raises the question: Is it possible to move projects around multisite organizations? The answer is yes, and we can use information technologies now to distribute the project team across the organization. This works well when the innovation is "virtual." As soon as physical elements start to appear, however, the bulk of the project team needs to be near the innovation. Even with new information technologies, it is not possible to capture all the information and knowledge required for furthering the innovation if the innovation is moved without the key people in attendance.

Given different charters for different operating entities, it is reasonable that the physical entity would move within the organization. This is particularly true of complex products, such as automobiles. The project team management should move with the project. An important issue is what happens to the project team when the project has been launched. Most of the people involved in the project will go back to their "homes" within the organization and be given new tasks. Scientists and engineers in the R&D department, for example, may be working on more than one project at any time; they will take up where they left off. Reallocating members of the project management team can be more tricky. In some instances, it may be appropriate to have the project team leader take over management of the product at launch and remain with the product for several years after launch. This is appropriate where the product is an expensive one sold in large volumes. Automobiles are a good example. Honda, for instance, has used this practice successfully with its new car launches.

In Chapter 7 we discussed Elliott Jaques's principle of accountability time horizons as the key to requisite organization design. As long as we keep this in mind as we develop new organizations, we should have few problems with the design. Staffing and implementing are, of course, different issues, but they are minor in the long run compared to having a poor design with its attendant pathologies.

TIME

The innovation process is deliberate and is very hard work. This holds true for new ideas as well as derivatives. Although we can expect to reduce the elapsed time to develop a derivative product, the greater the difference between the original innovation and the planned derivative, the longer we should expect the derivative development to take. Rushing a derivative to market can, therefore, be harmful to corporate health.

"Everybody" knows that being first to market is risky. We are all cautioned against using "bleeding edge" technology and against creating markets for others to usurp. What we are told is that rapid followers reap the greatest rewards. But we aren't told that *rapid* is relative; in some industries, the current market leader didn't enter the industry until over twenty years after a significant innovation occurred. So a mad rush by the market leader and really close followers to get new and improved models into the market might be missing the point. It is better to take the time and position the derivative product accurately, rather than confuse the marketplace.

MARKET AND COMPETITOR INTELLIGENCE

If we don't know why an innovation is a success, then we had better not try to exploit the success. So we had better gather very good market intelligence, and about more than unit and dollar sales. We need to know who is buying, who is using, why the product was purchased, and exactly how the product is being used. This can be a daunting task, but it must be done. Most products, after all, are "experience" goods—that is, we need to experience them to understand if we are comfortable with them, and by using them we learn what they can really do and what they can't do.

We can always try to ask users about the products, and we will get a lot of thoughtful answers. Unfortunately, the answers won't be reliable or particularly useful, because users generally forget the small things that irritate them—which are often where the next innovation takes place. It is best to follow people around who are using the product. Only then can the real interactions be observed.

Doing this for competitors' innovations is just as important as doing it for our own. We ought to be able to learn at least as much as the developer from observing users actually using the innovation, and we'll learn even more if we find out *why* the user does certain things. Understanding the user's relationship with the innovation is fundamental to making meaningful derivatives.

Competitor intelligence is important: We have to know who our competitors are and what their strengths and weaknesses are. But there are three things to keep in mind. First, if we understand ourselves, we know a good deal about our competitors. Second, the competition that will blow us out of the water probably isn't on the horizon yet, so we should look farther than today's competitors. Third, if we have two dollars for intelligence gathering, we will always be better advised to invest it in understanding customers, not competitors. The only value in understanding competitors is in gathering another understanding of customers.

A SERVICE AND VALUE FOCUS

We haven't differentiated in this book between product and service innovations. An innovation is an innovation, so to speak. But we do need to acknowledge a trend that occurs with most major innovations, be they industrial or consumer market-focused. To do this, we need to think about exactly what a product *is.* Figure 13-2 illustrates the three-part concept of a product.

The central portion is the core product (or service). It is what everybody in the industry and the marketplace recognizes as being the essential elements of the product, and which no developer challenges without difficulty. No aircraft manufacturer would dream of building a jet aircraft without having a pressurized cabin, for example. Everybody knows what the basic elements are, and nobody competes on the basis of supplying the basics. Competition takes place in the other two sets of elements.

FIGURE 13-2. THE THREE-PART CONCEPT OF A PRODUCT.

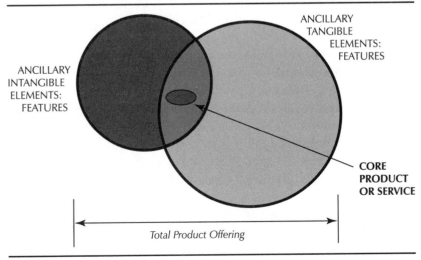

One of these two sets is all the ancillary tangible elements of the product, those pieces of hardware (and associated software) necessary to make the product perform as required by the marketplace. We make choices about what tangible elements we add, and we differentiate ourselves from our competitors by the choices we make. The other set is all the ancillary intangible elements around the product. Again, we differentiate ourselves from our competitors by the choices we make.

Early in the life cycle of the innovation, the core product is extremely small. We only need to think of the amazing horseless carriages that were in vogue in the late 19th century and compare that wide range of designs to the limited variability among mass-market cars today. As the product matures, its core product grows larger as our consensus on what is part of the car increases. Air bags, seat belts, antilock braking systems—which automaker today places full-page ads in the newspaper extolling the virtue of any of these products? In general, early derivative innovations focus on tangible elements, offering choices that the market either accepts or rejects. Those competitors who read the market incorrectly exit the market.

As the dominant design becomes increasingly established, the focus starts shifting to the intangible elements. In the auto industry, developments such as purchase financing, warranties, service and repair facilities, emergency roadside service, and the like have become common. It is in meeting customers' expectations about how they interact with their car and its manufacturer over the vehicle's whole life that the automakers face their greatest challenge, and it is in intangibles—services—that innovations will take place.

This appears to be true for all industries and all major innovations. Thinking early about the ancillary services that will make it easier for customers to purchase, own, and use a product will likely reap big rewards to the service innovator. Having a service focus, or a focus on services, is therefore an important precondition for being able to exploit an innovation.

And it is in service innovation that sustainable competitive advantage can be found. Japanese automakers have changed the face of the North American automobile markets through their attention to vehicle serviceability and vehicle servicing. Singapore Airlines has had a service quality advantage over all other airlines for over twenty years—and counting. Unconditional service guarantees are powerful signals of quality in insurance, pest control, and courier services. It is no coincidence that the guarantees are offered only by the market segment leaders.

How do we find out what service needs the marketplace has? We can ask customers, and we should. We can observe them using the product or service, and we should do that, too. But most important of all, we should involve the customers and users in experiments. Why so? Well, as it turns out (to nobody's great surprise), people can tell us only about what they know, and they can demonstrate only what they can do. They cannot tell us really what is missing from a product or service, and they can't tell us what they would do if we added a thringle widget to the thingummy. We have to devise experiments to test how users feel about new services. Then, if the results are overwhelmingly in favor of the new services, we have to figure out how to integrate them effectively into our service performance.

Yes, it is difficult, and yes, it can be done. Singapore Airlines does it, and Saturn does it. Yes, adding new services costs money. But adding extra services that the marketplace values reaps bigger rewards than it costs. Service innovations generally take less time and money to develop and implement than do product innovations. And service innovations are not copied by competitors nearly as quickly as product innovations. Why not? We think it is because the service innovators really focus on adding value to the customers. Everyone else sees the innovation as unjustifiable expense, not as an opportunity.

As of early 2001, the world's airlines are rapidly consolidating. Times are tough, and airlines are cutting routes, cutting people, squeezing suppliers, and reducing passenger services and service levels. What better time to make a mark by actually improving service in a way that passengers value? Which is why Singapore Airlines is working even harder now to decide what the next service innovation should be.

In all of this, don't forget one critical class of customer: internal customers. If the innovation is to be introduced internally, the internal customers need to be convinced that the innovation is in their interests. Sometimes we don't recognize certain internal groups as customers but, as long as the innovation affects them in some way, they are customers. Treat them as such, sell them on the benefits of the innovation to them, and the chances of successful implementation and exploitation increase tremendously.

SUMMARY

- Exploiting innovation takes a number of forms and is not limited to selling products. Sometimes we might want to exploit the innovation by selling the innovation itself or possibly some or all of the company.

- Financial resources are essential if we are going to exploit success. Successful innovations always require more investment than failed innovations.

- Exploitation generally requires a good distribution system, backed up by good order-taking capability.

- New management capabilities may be required. This is most likely for a small business that experiences great success. New managers may put pressure on the corporate culture and may force out good people. Be prepared.

- The organization structure may need to change. Provided we keep in mind the principles of design mentioned in Chapter 7 and develop hierarchies based on accountability time horizons, this should not be a major issue.

- It takes time to exploit an innovation, and it is hard work. Rushing derivatives to market is risky.

- We need good market and competitor intelligence. Given stretched resources, gain market intelligence ahead of competitor intelligence.

- We must have a service and value focus, and we must give customers what they want—and let them know what we have. This is particularly true for internal customers, the people who will kill an innovation if they aren't sold on its benefit to them.

NOTE

1. Dorothy Leonard-Barton, "How to Integrate Work *and* Deepen Expertise," *Harvard Business Review*, September–October 1994.

CHAPTER FOURTEEN

BRIDGING THE GAP BETWEEN THE OLD AND THE NEW ECONOMIES

HE COULDN'T UNDERSTAND IT. HERE he was, stumbling along in what was both a familiar and an unknown world, with all the familiar landmarks changed. Worse, he felt—and looked—old and tired. Only this morning he had been in the prime of his life. This afternoon he was out of his element. He hadn't changed—the world had changed.

When Rip van Winkle woke up just over two hundred years ago from his twenty-year sleep, his world *had* changed. Just imagine him having to understand the changes that have taken place in the business environment since 1980—in just over twenty years! Even managers who have been navigating the changing waters over this period face challenges. If innovation is all about preparing the company to take advantage of future business opportunities and challenges, how do companies manage innovation in a dramatically changing world?

These challenges form three clusters. First, what business models seem appropriate in the new economy? Second, how should companies organize to innovate and take advantage of new opportunities? Third, and perhaps most important, what new challenges will confront the successful innovator? If we can determine what the new environment will be, we can then develop strategies for bridging the gap between yesterday and today.

WHAT BUSINESS MODEL?

THERE ISN'T A whole lot new under the sun, at least as far as social organizations are concerned. As Henry Mintzberg has said, companies are about four things: finding, keeping, transforming, and distributing.[1] This hasn't changed from the first corporate venture. Sure, the world has become progressively more complex, we have new technologies that have destroyed industries and created others, and we have instantaneous access to breaking information from across the globe. But the basic business model of people organized to create value— at personal risk and for their own gain—has not changed.

What has changed over the years is more the philosophy of business. Now we are more concerned about conserving limited resources and about sustainability. We are more concerned about the longer-term viability of the communities in which our businesses operate, and about ensuring that our suppliers and customers are successful. We are concerned about our employees being successful. So how we think about doing business has changed dramatically in the past 200 years.

Customers' needs haven't changed a whole lot in that time, but customers' expectations about how they will be treated and what comes in the increasingly complex bundle of attributes we call a product have changed rather fundamentally. The marketing movement of the 1920s recognized that customers had product choices to make, and if we wanted to sell something in a competitive market, we'd better be able to differentiate our product enough that a group of people would prefer our product to that of our competitors.

The mass-marketing model worked when we didn't have the ability to communicate our message very well, and while customers couldn't communicate with us very well, either. Getting good feedback from the marketplace took so long that companies *had* to put new products out into the marketplace in volume and trust they would be purchased. Few people thought that the mass-market model of econo-mies of scale and limited choice made much sense, but it was the only effective means of servicing markets available.

Well, now we have the capability of servicing very small market segments and at the same time economically produce very small batches of product. But that isn't enough. What we have to do now is meet the expectations of customers. This is very much the age of the individual in the organization and in any society. And the golden rule has been replaced by the platinum rule: Treat individuals as *they* want to be treated, not as *we* want to be treated. This throws a new curveball in the business game. In addition to wanting better innovations and wanting them more quickly, customers now want individual treatment. They want businesses to say "I see you," and they want businesses to mean it.

So the basic assumption underlying the generic business model has gone from *the manufacturer rules* through *the customer rules* to *the individual customer rules*. Now companies have to deal with meeting and managing expectations at the level of the individual.

The new information technologies help us do this. We can gather tremendous amounts of data that we can then drill down through to give us insights almost to the level of the individual consumer. And we can link organizations and individuals, or organizations and organiza-tions, at the click of a button. Because we can do this quickly, expecta-tions are that we will do this quickly. Of course, our notions of lines of communication and linearity in distribution are now completely irrele-vant when we think about transferring information and knowledge.

Just as we have pools of customers and pools of suppliers with whom we can deal instantly over the Internet, now we have pools of knowledge that we can access in the same way. So along with the busi-ness-to-consumer and business-to-business hub systems for commer-cial communication, we also have the creativity-to-business hub, through which ideas for development can flow.

The new model of instantaneous access to information and the implication of instantaneous satisfaction of demand together pose a real challenge for developing new innovations. Companies have to be increasingly innovative and flexible enough to satisfy very small market segments if they are to survive in the future. What can they do? How should they organize?

Organizing for E-Innovation

THERE HAS BEEN a lot of discussion about whether or not traditional businesses—the brick-and-mortar companies—should keep their Internet operations separate from their traditional operations. While this might not appear to have much of an impact on the company's innovation, the reality might be very different. Separating the two distribution methods might give greater focus to each and might give more flexibility and access to venture funding to the Internet operations. It also gives rise to a completely different culture, a culture in which the company never sees the product or the recipient of the service. The Internet doesn't merely give rise to a new distribution avenue, one with ostensibly lower costs of acquisition and servicing than the traditional model. Innovation in one side of the business is therefore extremely unlikely to flow to the other system.

What we might finish up with, then, are two different innovations in response to a single customer need or expectation. Both might be appropriate, but they both might be suboptimal. If the common challenge had been looked at with both distribution systems in mind, it might have been possible to develop an even better innovation that satisfied both pieces—and that cost less to develop and launch and would sell in greater volumes than either of the single-channel solutions.

Outsourcing Innovation

STRATEGIC MANAGEMENT OF outsourcing is perhaps the most powerful tool of management, and outsourcing of innovation is its frontier.[2] Outsourcing is attractive for a number of reasons. Suppliers automatically increase the innovation potential of a company, they often have talents that we don't, and they help us manage risk by accepting some of the development risk. And they have knowledge we don't have.

One organization cannot possibly hope to keep track of the new information currently being generated. In the pharmaceutical industry, for instance, it is thought that independent biotechnology research adds 100 gigabytes per day to the databases of the National Institutes of Health genetic sequence database.

How, then, should businesses organize their innovation search and development to take advantage of the flood? One way is to outsource those parts of the innovation process we either can't do well or that are not core to the company's strategy. We won't dwell on the various ways we might think of outsourcing or the parts that can be outsourced. The issue for us is how to manage outsourced innovation.

MANAGING OUTSOURCED INNOVATION

There are a few general principles for managing outsourced innovation. Perhaps the most basic is that we expect the innovations we outsource to have a finite life. But we should expect the value to us to be temporary and plan for it. That means we need a process that allows us to observe and monitor many types of innovation at the same time, and then decide which innovation "wave" we want to follow. And we also need a process that allows us to change direction when the wave begins to change. This is synonymous with fishing in a stream with many active pools, deciding which pool is providing the greatest activity, deciding how to approach the fish, deciding which fish to release and which to keep, and deciding when to leave the pool and move on. It is similar to the Pacific islanders who navigate in unknown waters, sensing where new islands are only by the complex interplay between winds, currents, and tides—reflected in wave patterns. How do we set about following the wave, catching the fish, and sailing into the unknown?

Committing to Exciting Goals

An exciting vision and exciting goals are essential for energizing people internally and externally to work together. What may be exciting to one group might not be exciting to another, so it is important that both parties share similar cultures and senses of purpose. Both groups have to realize that the relationship is temporary in nature and limited in scope. It is not a courtship. Both groups have to jointly develop the vision and goals and be viscerally committed to them. Otherwise, it is very unlikely that useful innovation will occur.

Ensuring that Partners Benefit

Synergies must exist, and these synergies must benefit both parties. The outsourcing organization must be able to add value for the innovating organization, which means being able to provide significant value to customers in a significant market the innovating company could not otherwise access. As a rule, the outsourcing organization has to possess, and use, a competitive advantage built on strategic core competencies.

Developing Internal Experts

As with other forms of knowledge gathering, companies find gate-keepers—now called knowledge brokers—useful as a means of identifying and making known both best-of-breed internal innovations and external innovation capabilities that are of strategic interest to the company. These knowledge brokers are especially important to senior managers, for without them the likelihood of replacing obsolescent or obsolete processes before the system fails is much reduced. Remember: Systems that don't change are already dead. However, developing masters of innovation knowledge will help transform the innovation system from an active to a hyperactive system. And where opportunities are transitory, hyperactivity is important.

Developing Effective, Interactive Models

Without open, interactive software models, it is unlikely that development will occur either quickly or particularly effectively. How the model is structured is not as important as the fact that everybody using the model must understand the model and be able to use it The model therefore should have unambiguous interface, goal, and performance criteria. This will allow experiments to be conducted and alternative prototypes to be built in parallel, speeding up the development process.

Establishing Exponential Performance Targets

One way to make the exciting goals concrete is to establish performance targets significantly higher than trends would indicate. This requires developers to find new ways of attacking the problem. The payoff is in the marketplace, where customers will be willing to shift from one supplier to another for significantly greater value. Canon set that challenge for its developers—the challenge of building a camera using the APS photographic system that was no bigger than a cigarette packet. The result was the Ixus/ELPH camera, a clear market leader.

Concentrating on the Destination, Not the Journey

Riding herd on an outsourced innovator is like having a dog and barking yourself. The interactive software contains the critical aspects of the design envelope and the performance criteria for the innovator's systems, so if the model is appropriate, why not let people get on with it? The risks inherent in relying on one innovator for a particular innovation can be overcome by having an ongoing competition among several alternative suppliers. And if competitors can be encouraged to collaborate, it is likely that the interaction will produce synergies that the customer organization can readily exploit.

Sharing Gains

One way to gain collaboration is to share gains above targets with suppliers, even those whose designs were not accepted. If this expectation is established at the outset, it may lead to better than anticipated performance levels or lower costs that may then translate into better than anticipated market performance.

Managing the Information Interchange

In the Innovation Management Model (Figure 3-1), information interchange occurs in Systems I, III, and IV, as Figure 14-1 shows. Contact is first made at System IV, where strategic goals and challenges are reviewed and set. The second contact point is in System III, where

FIGURE 14-1. INFORMATION INTERCHANGE IN OUTSOURCING.

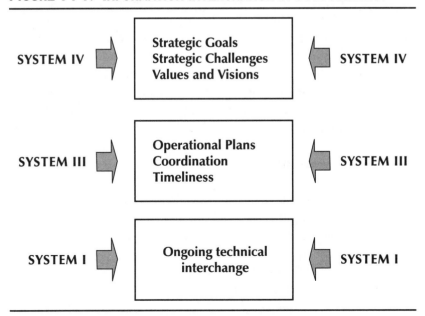

development team leaders from both or all organizations meet to develop operational and coordination plans and time lines. The third contact is in System I, with continuous interchange between lower-level teams and individuals actually working on the project. Managers have to ensure that tacit knowledge developed in one organization and needed by the other is effectively transferred, at the appropriate time. This is the point, incidentally, at which the cultures touch constantly. If the values and vision shared at the top of the organization are not shared at the bottom of either organization, innovation will wither and die.

Developing Incentives and Open Communications

We manage what we measure—trite but true. But we also get what we encourage, and if the incentives encourage behavior other than what we want, we'd better change the incentives. Rewarding stewardship does not encourage people to seek challenges, so if we want to encourage innovation, we have to encourage risk taking and accept the occasional failure. And information has to be available to everyone in order for the innovation team to have the best chance of success.

IDEO, the Palo Alto, California–based design group, goes one step further. Although the contact point for a client is in one of the group's scattered offices, all new projects are posted electronically company-wide. Any person is able to post her thoughts on issues surrounding the project on the project bulletin board and bill her time to the project. Clients are warned that this practice will happen and that they should be prepared for a large bill for the first month's activities. The challenge for the project team is to parse the information and use what is relevant—a more rewarding challenge than having to try to find information by itself.[3]

Accepting Guided Anarchy

The continuing development of the Linux operating system is one of independent developers improving the system as they see fit. We don't advocate going this far for commercial innovators, but there are elements of the process that fit with our model of outsourcing. Letting it be known that we want products or services with certain characteristics, and that we will treat innovators fairly, is one way of encouraging small innovators to work toward our goals. Helping provide or locate resources may encourage more innovators to us. Companies like

Microsoft and Apple have used this approach to encourage software developers. If we decide that we don't want the innovation, the developers can feel free to take it elsewhere.

Using Innovation Incubators[4]

We've all seen business incubators. Usually, they are government-financed centers that provide space, some funding, and some basic services to small start-ups that have an acceptable business plan. Unfortunately, these incubators don't encourage innovation, nor do they coordinate innovation. This shouldn't be surprising, for everything is against them from the start. It is a myth that small companies are particularly innovative; in fact, the majority are not innovative at all. Nor are small businesses the source of new jobs: The rate of closure of small businesses isn't too much different from the rate of formation of new businesses measured over a period of a few years. So independent businesses in small business incubators can't expect much.

So we need a new model of incubator, and we have one. It is called the networked incubator,[5] and it differs from the traditional incubator in a number of ways.

1. NETWORKED INCUBATORS NEED NOT BE STAND-ALONES. For example, Ford and Lucent have incubators. Ford's incubator, ConsumerConnect, focuses on speeding up the process of creating and developing Internet businesses. Meanwhile, Lucent's New Business Group funds and incubates ventures that commercialize Bell Lab's technologies.

2. NETWORKED INCUBATORS ARE FOR-PROFIT ORGANIZATIONS. This means it is in the incubator's interests that innovations be successfully commercialized. To foster this, incubators allow the small innovators to retain majority ownership in their businesses, unlike venture capital firms that typically take ownership. They also ensure that the innovators are relieved of the bureaucratic and organizational drudgery and impediments that can get in the way of the risky challenge the innovators will be pursuing.

3. NETWORKED INCUBATORS RELIEVE START-UPS OF THE OPPORTUNITY COST OF SEARCHING FOR FUNDS BY PROVIDING ACCESS TO FUNDS THEMSELVES. The incubators

provide funds from top-tier sources at competitive rates. Anyone who has done the rounds of banks looking for a sympathetic ear and an open hand knows how long this search can take.

4. NETWORKED INCUBATORS PROVIDE ACCESS TO A NETWORK OF COMPANIES. This can be critically important, for gaining access to development resources and distribution can be the difference between success and failure of the venture. In a sense, networked incubators can play a role in mediating the outsourcing search of a customer and the developer search of an innovator.

5. NETWORKED INCUBATORS CAN PROVIDE COACHING AND MENTORING. They can also provide access to legal services, important to many inventors and innovators. The cost of patenting an invention is very high, and many smaller innovators reluctantly accept the risks they run by not patenting because they cannot afford the cost of the patent application process.

6. NETWORKED INCUBATORS CAN HELP WITH RECRUITING, PARTICULARLY IF THE SMALL BUSINESSES ARE ALL BASED AROUND SIMILAR TECHNOLOGIES. This latter characteristic underlies the success of the networked incubator. The incubator has the opportunity to select each of the innovative small businesses. Ensuring that all the businesses have the same cultures and operate in the same general technology field makes it easier to operate the incubator and to cultivate the necessary networks of resource suppliers and customers.

7. NETWORKED INCUBATORS CAN WORK QUICKLY, EVEN STARTING "COMPANIES" OF THEIR OWN. For instance, Idealab! companies were often started using the incubator's funds. Most were experimental Web sites, opened to see if people would visit and buy the product or service. Given sufficient interest, the incubator would establish the company.

Incubators run risks, of course, principally because they choose to put most of their eggs in one basket. Idealab!, the first networked incubator to be launched (in 1996), has since failed because it ran out of cash before any of its small businesses began returning a profit or could be sold. But that doesn't invalidate the concept. The jury is still out.

SYNDICATING INNOVATIONS

In Chapter 13, we looked at the syndication of media products—films and television products in particular. These products, along with newspaper columns, are information products. The Internet, being a pure information medium, makes it intriguing to think of syndicating physical products as well. How might we do that?

It is now possible for people in all corners of the world to gain access to the Internet. E-retailers therefore compete against each other for all the customers in cyberspace, but choose the geographic limits they impose on themselves. There is no reason the developer of an innovation shouldn't offer the product to a number of e-retailers, who would bundle the innovation with others that they want to sell. This absolves the developer of any marketing responsibilities. If the developer ships the product directly to the customer, it also absolves the e-retailer of any warehousing and shipping responsibilities.

Some companies have been producing house labels for years, such as Sears and Kenmore. Now, though, the e-retailer is simply selling information, bundled with other products for a specific market segment. The developer is being exposed to a great number of different market segments by being aligned with several e-retailers, each of whom focuses on a particular segment. Making the developer/distributor invisible to the customer requires the developer to have access to detailed distribution capability.

CHALLENGES FOR
INNOVATIVE ORGANIZATIONS

GIVEN THE CHANGES that information technologies have wrought, it shouldn't be surprising that there are more pressures on innovators now than there were twenty years ago. These pressures can be grouped into three clusters, as Figure 14-2 shows:

1. Managing knowledge

2. Managing material resources

3. Maintaining control

FIGURE 14-2. THE CHALLENGE FOR INNOVATIVE ORGANIZATIONS.

MANAGING KNOWLEDGE

Locating Knowledge
Spreading Knowledge
Making Transitions

MANAGING MATERIAL RESOURCES

Outsourcing Manufacturing
Managing Distribution
Managing IT Infrastructure

MAINTAINING CONTROL

Control of the Innovation
Control of the Company
Control of Innovation Projects
Control of the Brand

MANAGING KNOWLEDGE

We need to manage knowledge for several reasons. First, knowledge is a perishable commodity, and its half-life seems to be getting shorter. Second, knowledge comes in two basic forms: (1) embodied knowledge, which is the knowledge captured in equipment, books, and increasingly in software, and (2) disembodied knowledge, which is the knowledge in the heads of the people in the organization. This latter knowledge can either be codified (captured as a written procedure) or tacit (residing solely in people's heads). What we need to do in the new economy is ensure that information becomes usable knowledge, and that usable knowledge becomes effective understanding as quickly as possible and is disseminated as quickly as possible to the places where it will have best effect. Turning knowledge into understanding is the slowest activity in the loop, so organizing for effective learning is crucial.

Locating Knowledge

Traditionally, managers have thought of people in R&D and engineering as creative knowledge workers, and workers in operating departments as needing to have predictable jobs. This thinking has to change, and everyone in the organization has to be expected to have something to offer in the way of useful and usable knowledge. If they don't, we haven't lost anything. But if they do, while we've already lost something, we can make up for it.

To find all the useful knowledge, we have to locate the company's best practices—all of them. This is a very difficult task. There are differences between the procedure as laid out in the manual, and differences between what people think they do and what they actually do. The more complex the systems with which people work, the more likely there are to be problems that require new fixes. In addition to watching what people do and determining what actually is best practice, we have to find out why people do what they do and how they manage exceptions. Both "normal" best practice and "exception" best practice capture knowledge that should be spread around the organization. More important, though, is capturing the understanding about why the best practices were needed. Aping others without understanding why change is important is unlikely to result in new embedded practice.

Spreading Knowledge

People working in small groups automatically distribute knowledge. They also generate new knowledge and deeper understanding by challenging each other. It is as true in R&D as it is on the shop floor and in after-sales service. The key issue is how to capture and disseminate the knowledge in a way that allows all receivers to recognize the information as credible.

Building a gigantic database and loading everything into the database—standard practice in many companies—is precisely the wrong answer. What seems to be most appropriate are databases that contain specific classes of knowledge—service and repair, sales and marketing, purchasing and vendor management, R&D, and so on. In addition, a peer group should vet the knowledge in these databases. The scientific community has had peer-reviewed publications for countless years. Extending the process to all classes of knowledge workers (and that's everybody) makes sense. Now some Web sites seem to be accepting the challenge, with articles posted by anybody who wants to post some knowledge and given "value scores" by readers. Those writers who consistently score highly have their writings placed in very accessible places on these Web sites. The more useful the knowledge is deemed to be, therefore, the easier it is to access.

Making Transitions

Spreading best practice is essential, but sometimes it is not enough. When a business wants to make a substantial internal innovation, many different classes of knowledge are required. Xerox faced this challenge in late 1994 when the company wanted to move from proprietary information technology infrastructures to an industry standard. Instead of using either a highly centralized or a highly decentralized approach to initiating and managing the change, Xerox chose a third path. This was an alliance of specialists from corporate headquarters and the business units to share knowledge from different parts of the organization and to create deeper knowledge and understanding of the whole system.[6] This deeper and more robust understanding allowed teams in the business units and in corporate headquarters to more effectively and more quickly develop procedures for making the changeover, and making the change more effective than might possibly have been the case. This approach has great merit and should be more broadly applicable. It is similar to the approach used at Daewoo Shipbuilding and Heavy Machinery to develop and deepen its understanding of welding.

MANAGING MATERIAL RESOURCES

Three things are involved here: (1) outsourcing manufacturing, (2) managing distribution, and (3) managing IT intrastructure.

Outsourcing Manufacturing

Many companies are now intent on getting out of manufacturing. Manufacturing will always be important, as will agriculture and high-contact services, but many e-commerce companies seem content to act more as distributors or final assemblers than their counterparts in traditional businesses in the same industry. This approach isn't new—just ask the companies that manufacture products for Sears under the Kenmore label. But what *is* new is that some manufacturers are now essentially selling production capacity to anyone who wants it. And the approach has its advantages, at least to the seller.

Manufacturing for many clients makes sense in volatile businesses. While the demand for individual products is very unpredictable, the overall demand is much more stable. The key for the manufacturer is to be able to switch very rapidly from product to product. (Celestica Inc. of Toronto, for instance, says it can handle "thousands of new products per month.") For an innovator who wants to get a new product into the market, or who needs extra manufacturing capacity to take advantage of a new launch success, identifying manufacturing sources capable of rapid flexibility is critical.

Managing Distribution

Many of the companies engaged in e-commerce, particularly business-to-consumer (B2C), never see what they sell. All they handle is information. Most of the senior and middle managers in a traditional business rarely see the company's products or the people who purchase the company's services. These managers deal solely with information about products or customers most of the time. In B2C companies, this separation from products and customers extends to the entire organization. This is as true of Internet universities as it is of furniture sellers. Third parties handle the physical distribution, and the receipt and warehousing of the company's products is also at a distance.

This places the B2C company in the hands of those people handling the distribution. This isn't much of an issue for many purchases, but it can be troublesome for larger items that require some assembly. For example, trucking companies delivering furniture and other durables for e-retailers find their drivers besieged and begged to assemble the furniture, to take away the packaging materials and the furniture that is no longer required, and to position the furniture to the satisfaction of the purchaser. Deliveries are also expected to occur on time. This requires buffers built into driving lead times to accommodate highly variable physical handling issues when delivering to a particular customer. The customer counts any failure in the distribution system as a failure of the e-retailer. Selection of these links is critical, and the criteria that customers use for selection are increasing by the day.

Managing IT Infrastructure

We have referred above to the need to have access to sufficient manufacturing sources to take advantage of a highly successful launch. With shortening product life cycles, it is important to be able to ramp up for manufacturing very quickly. But we also have to have the order-taking capacity to handle the demand. The experience with e-retailers is that popular products generate "hits" on the Web site in huge numbers in a very short time. This means that e-retailers, or anybody offering an Internet sales function, have to have a large surplus of handling capacity.

MAINTAINING CONTROL

Working in the chaotic field of innovation that exists around the cluster of industries and technologies that defines the "knowledge" sector creates challenges for innovative companies. There are no greater challenges than the control challenges. Four categories of control challenges exist: (1) control of the innovation, (2) control of the company, (3) control of innovation projects, and (4) control of the brand.

Control of the Innovation

Given the pressures to outsource more, to develop innovation alliances, and to decide quickly how to take advantage of successful innovations, smaller innovating companies face the risk of losing control of the innovation to competitors or to the dominant player in the industry's value chain. This is particularly true where the company's ability to develop the innovation is so limited that the development path will be lengthy, allowing larger competitors to outpace the innovator to the marketplace.

Many innovators resolve this by ceding control early and selling the rights to the innovation to a larger company. Others, though, try a different approach, using relationship marketing to help establish a branding position that becomes impregnable. Dolby Laboratories achieved this with its specialist audio technologies. It is virtually impossible to see a movie or buy a piece of audio equipment that does not have the Dolby imprimatur on it somewhere. The strategy has been so successful that Dolby now sells other technologies, including those developed by other companies, to its customers. This approach is now being used by NXT, a Cambridge, England–based developer of slim-line loudspeakers. Using this approach requires an ability to lead the market, which, for fledgling concerns, is very difficult. Forming an alliance with a potential customer is probably the most appropriate form of protection.

Control of the Company

Innovative companies need to remain in a position of "unstable balance," teetering on the edge of tipping out of control. One thing they cannot run foul of, though, is their fiduciary duty to their owners and lenders. The closer innovative companies get (deliberately) to being out of control, the greater the care they need to take of their financial management, particularly their cash flow. As with any business, a lack of cash and an inability to raise more means an end to the business as we know it. Recent research shows that large innovative companies are using the finance function more and more to support business decisions. And this is not just because of their information systems. Companies seem to be responding by moving more and more of their finance function back in-house, creating control rooms that oversee e-engineered transaction processes. Control applies not just to cash. It also applies to controlling the physical innovation process, particularly when an innovation project should be folded.

Control of Innovation Projects

In some companies, projects that should be beaten to death with a heavy stick keep on surviving. These projects devour resources, particularly management and creative resources, as people develop new and creative ways to keep the sick patient alive. What these companies are disobeying is the "Law of the Rathole": knowing when to quit.[7] The law is important because resources are scarce and the opportunities to squander them numerous. There are five rules of thumb for limiting the loss created by a turkey:

1. DON'T MARRY A TECHNOLOGY. The world may prefer the old. Leading edge is bleeding edge.

2. MONITOR THE DEVELOPERS. Don't allow development to occur in a black box.

3. **CREATE RIVAL RATHOLES.** Try three approaches to the challenge and, if none shows signs of working, can the project.

4. **SPREAD THE RISK.** Use alliances and lay off the risk where applicable or where necessary.

5. **MANAGE EXPECTATIONS.** Don't make grandiose claims at the beginning, as there is only so much humble pie that people will be prepared to eat.

Firm and early decisions to abandon projects also send important signals throughout the company and the industry. Clear messages like this can send a chill through competitors and make it possible to gain competitive advantage.

Companies that are able to stay in control in turbulent times will survive as others lose their cash flow—and their heads. The demise of so many dot-com businesses was not only the result of the lack of an effective product and business model. It was also the result of unrealistic and unwise pursuit of hedonistic pleasure—not the pursuit of innovation excellence. In the final analysis, personal control by those at the head of small innovating concerns is perhaps the most critical control that must be exercised.

Control of the Brand

Successful innovative companies often develop successful brand identities. This shouldn't be surprising, for if we have done everything right, every employee, every department, and every process in the organization is engaged and aligned with the values of the brand.[8] Successful small companies become acquisition targets for larger companies, and companies with well-established brands need to ensure that the brand experience and the corporate values stay intact. The potential purchaser should also ensure that this happens. If they don't, people will leave the organization, and the purchaser will have squandered its own opportunity. And customers will desert the brand.

When Unilever purchased Ben and Jerry's Ice Cream, both parties recognized the need to protect the brand and worked hard to ensure that every Ben and Jerry's employee was comfortable with the sale and the conditions surrounding it. In early 2001, McDonald's purchased Pret A Manger, an English coffee-and-sandwich chain that has an established brand image. Customers have demanded that McDonald's leave the chain alone and its supply and distribution chain intact—a promise McDonald's has made. To meddle invites retaliation from employees and customers. The challenge for McDonald's is to learn from Pret A Manger and to capture the better parts of Pret A Manger's innovation management system and install them in the McDonald's system—and vice versa.

SUMMARY

- Companies still perform only a maximum of four functions: find, keep, transform, or distribute.

- More and more, what is being transformed, processed, and distributed is information.

- Customers' expectations of how they are treated and what services they require are increasing.

- Companies should apply the platinum rule: Treat customers as each customer wants to be treated.

- Companies that separate their traditional business and their e-business gain focus, but they run the risk of suboptimized innovation.

- In managing outsourcing, companies need to:
  Commit to exciting goals.
  Ensure that partners benefit.
  Develop internal experts.
  Develop effective, interactive models.
  Establish exponential performance targets.
  Concentrate on the destination, not the journey.
  Share gains.
  Manage the information interchange.
  Develop incentives and open communications.
  Accept guided anarchy.

- Networked incubators, with access to finance and customers, are the most effective form of business incubators for innovative companies.

- The three major groups of challenges for innovators are managing knowledge, managing material resources, and maintaining control.

- In managing knowledge, managers need to be concerned with locating knowledge, spreading knowledge, and making transitions.

- In managing material resources, managers need to consider outsourcing manufacturing, managing distribution, and managing IT infrastructure.

- In maintaining control, managers need to control the innovation, control the company, and control innovation projects.

- Innovative businesses often develop clear brand identities. Managers selling or buying companies with clear brand identities should protect the brands. If they don't, employees and customers will desert the brand.

- Remember the "Law of the Rathole": Know when to quit.

NOTES

1. Henry Mintzberg and Ludo van der Heyden, "Re-Viewing the Organization," *Ivey Business Journal*, September–October 2000.

2. James Brian Quinn, "Outsourcing Innovation: The New Engine of Growth," *Sloan Management Review*, Summer 2000.

3. Tom Kelley with Jonathan Littman, *The Art of Innovation* (New York: Currency Doubleday, 2001).

4. For a comprehensive survey of incubators, see Morten T. Hansen, Nitin Nohria, and Jeffrey A. Berger, *The State of the Incubator Marketspace* (Boston: Harvard Business School, June 2000).

5. Morten T. Hansen, "Networked Incubators: Hothouses of the New Economy," *Harvard Business Review*, September–October 2000.

6. John Storck and Patricia A. Hill, "Knowledge Diffusion through 'Strategic Communities,' " *Sloan Management Review*, Winter 2000.

7. G. Pascal Zachary, "The Law of the Rathole," *Technology Review*, May–June 1999.

8. Shaun Smith, "Experiencing the Brand—Branding the Experience," *FTDynamo Forum*, January 30, 2001.

CONCLUSION

CHAPTER FIFTEEN

TOWARD THE FUTURE

WE HAVE SEEN THE ENEMY, and it is us. The wild and sometimes euphoric ride on the dot-com bandwagon has ended, but the new economy hasn't gone away. In fact, the rise and fall of the dot-coms emphasizes that effective management of innovation is becoming *more* essential as we embark on the next chapter of our unfolding economic development. Why the dot-com phenomenon occurred is important to future innovators, for the conditions under which the dot-com companies exploded—and imploded—will exist in the future. In addition to understanding the dot-com phenomenon, however, we need to think about the process of innovation itself and how it will change.

The basic Innovation Management Model we set out in Chapter 3, and on which our whole discussion has been based, will not change. This is not a brash statement. The scientific method of experimentation and discovery has not changed since its exposition in the 19th century, nor will it change. What keeps on changing is the environment in which discovery and innovation occurs. And this environment influences the organization and social process of discovery and innovation. Thinking about the social aspects of organizing for and managing innovation in the near future is the focus of this last chapter.

BREAKING PARADIGMS

NEWTON'S THEORY OF matter and motion provided the basis for speculation and discovery in physics for 200 years. The theory was so powerful that observations at odds with prediction were routinely enfolded into the body of orthodox knowledge through masterful mathematical manipulation. When Einstein published his special theory of relativity in 1905, physicists immediately saw that Newtonian physics was a subset of relativity or quantum physics. Further, many of the anomalies shoehorned into the Newtonian theory could be easily explained in Einstein's theory. What this shows is that scientific revolutions do not destroy the basic theory that went before. Rather, they enfold earlier science in a more fundamental understanding of the structure and dynamic of nature. The indicators that a new, revolutionary look at nature is required are the increasing discrepancies reported between theory and nature, and the frank questioning about the basis of the accepted model of nature.

The same ought to be true of social science knowledge. If it is true, then we are on the cusp of a social scientific revolution. Commentators daily question the manner in which groups organize, from countries to companies. Advances in technology call into question the organization of industrial society and the manner in which economies and economic activity are regulated. Dot-com companies are hailed as the precursors of a new economy and a new form of social organization. Perhaps they are, and perhaps the commentators are correct. But where is basic social scientific knowledge headed?

For that, we need to turn to economics. There have been two trends in economic thought over the years since Smith, Ricardo, Malthus, and the other early economists wrote about social organization and social contracts. The first has been to higher and higher levels of mathematical abstraction, as economists have tried to include in orthodox theory an increasing number of anomalies in social interaction. This might be a good indicator that a new theory is about to be published. The second trend is a trend by both micro and macroeconomists to understand and devise theories about the smallest indivisible element of economic activity: the human. If there *is* a new economic theory, it will likely be centered on the human, and it will likely focus on knowledge capital and individual choice as the basis of wealth creation and accumulation.

A New Economic Theory

If a new, knowledge-based economic theory is developed and becomes universally accepted, its social impact will be breathtaking. The whole basis on which assets are valued will change, and this change will call into question all aspects of social organization. Different measures of wealth and importance will inevitably mean changes in the ways in which individuals and organizations think about maximizing wealth and prestige.

We can't pinpoint accurately what the new theory will be or when it will be widely accepted. But we do know what will happen on the way to the new theory being fully implemented. We have only to look at what is happening with global warming.

It is now generally agreed that there is a trend to a warmer ambient air temperature worldwide. What the long-run increase will be, and how long it will take to arrive at a new steady state, is not known. But all commentators agree that it will not be a smooth, gradual transition. The transition will be marked by major fluctuations in temperature and climate until the new steady state is reached. As Californians have discovered, the increased variability and unpredictability of climate change can have a significant impact on relative supply and demand of power, and thus on power prices.

We have lived through the wild ride of the dot-com era. The wild ride was contributed to in large part by the monies that were pulled out of the Asian economies, and which needed somewhere to go. Greed did the rest. That money is still about and is looking for another home. Institutional investors move huge amounts of money around daily, looking for marginal improvements in portfolio value. In the mid-1980s, the greatest number of shares traded on the New York Stock Exchange was around 200 million. In early 2001, the typical day's trading volume on the NYSE is around 2 billion shares. The volatility in share prices creates uncertainty. This uncertainty creates the environment for the next bubble—and the next set of opportunities.

Information transaction costs will play a major role in the new economic theory. For example, changes in the basic costs of information processing, storage, and distribution have already removed constraints on where and how individuals work. And changes in information transaction costs have created industries (software, mobile telecommunications) and transformed business activities (inventory management, advertising, financial asset and credit creation and management). We have already seen one effect of the new information economics: the dot-com phenomenon. This perturbation will not be the last in the transition to an economy based on a new economic theory. It does highlight two important factors for managers of innovation to consider.

The first thing for managers of innovation to think about in the transition economy is that there will be ample opportunity to innovate effectively and profitably in the transition. Opportunities will, though, be transitory, and will need to be exploited quickly. The second factor is one we mentioned earlier: that the basic model of innovation will not change, and all stages through the model will need to be well managed. These factors taken together indicate that innovators will need to identify opportunities early and be organized to rapidly exploit the opportunity effectively. Awareness of the environment, preferably an ability to identify and use precursors of latent demand, will be critical. So will an organization capable of developing, evaluating, launching, and exploiting multiple approaches to a market need.

UNDERSTANDING THE WHITE SPACE

IN THE PERIOD between the publication of Newton's and Einstein's theories, scientists and others began filling in the "white space"—the detailed knowledge that could be obtained by more precise measurement or the development of more elaborate models of how things happen. This is traditional scientific advance—learning more and more about a continually narrowing field of endeavor. Leonardo da Vinci, the archetypical Renaissance man, created a great deal of white space for others to exploit. Were he to try today to work across so many fields instead of filling in the white space, he might be regarded as a dilettante, not a genius. Such is life.

For businesses, there is money to be made by exploiting the commercial white space—the market or product space around new products. We have discussed follow-on products as a powerful means of exploiting fundamentally new products. The more quickly we follow a new product, the more likely we are to profit from the turbulence in the market. The earlier we are in, though, the less certain we are about what customer needs and expectations really are. To us, managing that conundrum is simple: Concentrate on finding out what customers really want by watching them experience prototypes or products at every stage of the customer experience process described in Chapter 12. The dot-coms did not do a good job in general of doing this, and many failures could be predicted. Nothing can be expected to work if we don't understand customers, and understand them quickly.

When the next revolution arrives—and it will—the initial flurry of activity to get ideas into the marketplace will be followed by the rapid entry of many of the start-ups. That will be the time for everybody to use the Innovation Management Model and begin exploiting the new white space. It isn't rocket science: Just look at where the successes are, decide which is the most commercially attractive that you can exploit, get to understand quickly what customers need and expect, and set to work meeting those needs and expectations. And don't forget that satisfying every customer's service needs and expectations should be a principal objective.

SERVICE INNOVATION

IN THE TRANSITION economy, we already know where some opportunities for innovation will occur. That is because there will be a need for essential service functions to be performed. These functions have been performed from the beginnings of social civilization; think of waste disposal, care of the sick and infirm, burial of the dead, and comfort of the bereaved. The rag and bone man, the knacker, the tinker, the peddler, the undertaker, and the priest are all alive and well in our society. Most of them are in industries that are not glamorous or esteemed, but all are quietly profitable. And all need to transform themselves to take advantage of whatever the next bubble will be.

Nobody should ever forget that the real winners from the Yukon gold rush of the 1880s were the logistics operators and the merchants selling essential and/or desirable commodities to the communities of miners. Nobody should forget that the disposal companies and liquidators are among the winners of the dot-com experience. Nobody should forget, either, that it was unbridled greed that created the feeding frenzy in both instances and consumed most of the moths that ventured to the flame. There will likely be more money to be made supplying essential logistics to the players in the next bubble than there will be made by the average player.

SOCIAL INNOVATION

GIVEN THAT INNOVATING organizations will need to be very nimble, how will they organize for speedy innovation? Perhaps we can look for analogies in other areas to see what lessons we can learn. There are at least two analogies from which we can learn, the first in nature and the second in sports.

Have you ever observed a large school of small fish swimming in the ocean? Clustered together for the survival of the school, the fish all swim in one direction, then suddenly change direction. All the fish seem to move in unison, yet each fish has to move separately. If attacked by a shark, the school transforms itself so that the shark passes through the school without placing many fish in danger. The school then regroups, only to transform itself again at the next passage of the shark. Individual actions within a social context allow the organization to transform itself at will. The actions of the individuals define the actions of the group.

For our sports analogy, we look to basketball. Basketball is a transition game, played on a small surface by five players on each team. The innovation of the shot clock forced a transformation in the game, with more shots being taken at goal and more chances of a turnover occurring during play. The turnovers create the transition, and how each team handles the transition from offense to defense (and vice versa) usually decides close games.

The first key to the transition game is very good basic individual skills, skills that need to be constantly practiced if they are to remain finely honed. The second key is speed—speed to recognize cues that indicate where and when a turnover might occur, speed down the court, and speed of the ball to the point of attack. Each of the players has to be able to recognize what is developing, and each player has to recognize his potential role in the transition, where he should be to play his part, and when he has to be there. All this requires good mental preparation, relaxed confidence in the abilities of all players on the team, and endless hours of practice and discussion. The third key to the transition game is teamwork. What looks like improvisation on the court is the result of a great deal of repetitious training under gamelike conditions.

In addition, it is important that the team and its individual members take chances if they are to succeed. Mistakes are a natural consequence of taking chances, but good teams forget mistakes instantly as they regroup to move back again. Their emphasis is on getting the ball and winning, and not on preventing the opposition from winning by denying them the ball. Every team in the NBA is opportunistic and creative.

If we put these analogies together, we have an organization in which effective operation in transition requires:

- A good understanding and awareness of the environment

- Instantaneous communications

- Good policies that allow individuals to make decisions that are in the organization's best interests, as well as those of the individual

- A recognition of the unique value and contribution of each individual

- Good basic skills

- An ability to identify opportunity, and the confidence to act on it

- An ability to reshape the organization quickly, and as necessary

- A focus on developing individual and team capabilities "off-line"

- A willingness to take a chance and fail

- An ability to forget failure and recover from it, yet learn from it off-line

These characteristics are some of the characteristics the innovating company will require in the transition economy. They will remain critical characteristics of innovating companies.

We suggested in Chapter 7 that it is the exclusive responsibility of the executive team to provide an internal environment in which innovation can flourish. The characteristics outlined here are elements that the executive team can influence or provide. There are other elements, though, of the basketball team that wins very frequently, and these characteristics ought to be striven for by the organization that wants to ensure its innovative activities are effective. These characteristics of the superior basketball team are:

- "Franchise" players—the distinctive competencies of the team

- An ability to reshape the team's strategy quickly, given the nature of the competitive dynamic at different times in a game

- An excellent support organization that keeps the team playing at high levels of performance at all times

- A belief that the team will win, despite the situation in the game

TECHNOLOGICAL INNOVATION

TECHNOLOGY CONTINUES TO transform social interaction and the interaction of businesses with each other and with customers. The Internet is the last in the line of major technological innovations in the 20th century, and it will continue to help shape industries and competition in the 21st century.

As we know, the Internet has transformed the manner in which information and knowledge is stored, manipulated, distributed, and displayed. Individuals and organizations are now able to obtain vast quantities of information from cyberspace, some of it useful. The Internet begat the dot-com companies and the e-commerce revolution. What changes, though, has the Internet wrought, and what changes are likely in the future?

The Internet allows distributed creativity and problem solving/information sharing to be conducted at much greater speeds than was previously possible. IDEO takes advantage of this when it invites interested people in all its offices to think about issues on current projects, no matter which office is in contact with the client. There is no reason why a company interested in innovation should not broadcast a request for interested people to participate in the information sharing, and pay for the advice they receive. As a general principle, it is easier to sort and use information than it is to generate the information in the first place.

Business-to-business exchanges have begun to change the way in which large companies or industry associations do business with suppliers. Suppliers are now able to bid on contracts worldwide and with companies with which they have had no previous experience. It is possible that experience with B2B exchanges will turn manufacturing suppliers into contract suppliers of manufacturing capacity. This is not a new practice; textile mills in Italy, for example, regularly contract operating capacity, then make what the customer decides is required.

Should this practice spread to other industries, it is likely that approaches to business development and business practices in supplier industries will have to change. Companies that develop more appropriate costing bases, for example, and that become adept at quickly developing processes for manufacturing what the contract customer wants, will become suppliers of preference. It is axiomatic that when price is the only ostensible criterion for winning a contract, and when there is little to choose among competing suppliers, that price will *never* be the order-winning criterion.

The invention of movable type and the subsequent innovation of the printing press transformed the way in which information and knowledge was stored and transmitted. The learning revolution that resulted transformed Europe, creating the modern university and the demand for literacy. The transistor and the microprocessor and the subsequent innovation of the Internet have transformed information processing and distribution again, with comparable resulting innovations and transformations in how we learn and socialize in learning. What about innovations in other fields?

SCIENTIFIC INNOVATION

LET'S LOOK AT three different topics under the heading of "scientific innovation": the Stirling engine of the 19th century, genetic engineering, and subatomic physics. Each of these is dramatically different. The first is a physical product, the second is a complex set of processes, and the third innovation lies in the search for the "missing" subatomic particles. But each provides us with a way to better understand the social and technical process of innovation, and the changes that will take place in that process as scientific innovations drive further social change. Let's look at these innovations in order, starting with the oldest.

THE STIRLING ENGINE

Have you ever heard of the Stirling engine? The Stirling engine, invented by Robert Stirling in 1896, is a device that in essence runs on the difference in heat levels between the outside and inside of the engine. Once started, using conventional fuels, the machine will run essentially on air. The only difficulty is that the engine has never been commercialized, although its principles of operation have been known for many years. That is, it hasn't been commercialized until now. Dean Kamen has recently taken out patents that appear workable. If they are, then it is possible that small, highly portable electricity generators will be available that can be installed anywhere at reasonable cost. Some enthusiasts predict that the workable Stirling engine will be at the heart of a true Enernet, a globally distributed energy network that will work without the need for mass electricity distribution systems.

If you haven't heard of Dean Kamen, he is the New Hampshire–based physicist who has almost single-handedly created the recent upsurge in interest in physics education in high school and college students, through activities such as the national high school robot challenge. He is also the inventor of "Ginger," the mystery invention that will revolutionize cities, according to those who have seen the invention. Kamen is to product engineering what IDEO is to product design.

The impact of this development on organizations would be at least as earth-shattering as the development of the Internet. Elements of organizations could be located wherever management desired. Cost structures would be changed. Reliance on poor electricity infrastructures in the developing (and developed) world would be a thing of the past. Just as the steam engine was required to launch the Industrial Revolution, and the computer was required to launch the Information Revolution, the Stirling engine may be the precursor of the next technological and social revolution.

Will there be an inevitable impact of these revolutions on the innovation process? We suspect so, principally because of the loosening of constraints on organizational design and location. Increasing flexibility may allow us to think in terms of building appropriate organizations out of a number of discrete and different cells, each cell being a separate work group. Both the change in structure and the manner in which the structure is formed suggests a new organizational dynamic, one of temporary interdependence. Thinking through what this means for the social process of innovation will be important for senior executives.

So it is not the Stirling engine itself, rather the implications of its use and possibilities that concern us. This is true also of genetic engineering, the currently controversial field in medical and agricultural research and development. We look briefly at the insights we might get from this field next.

GENETIC ENGINEERING

We are all aware of Dolly, the cloned sheep. We've all heard a lot about genetically modified food. We've been introduced to gene splicing in an array of animals and organisms. How about "genetic engineering" of businesses? It shouldn't be far-fetched, at least not if we believe companies are dynamic systems. The more we learn about innovation and how to manage it, the more effective we might be in deciding what piece of the system to tweak to improve our innovation potential and practice. The large pharmaceutical companies have enjoyed success from bringing small biotechnology companies into their orbit, thus increasing both the rate of discovery and the rate of development of new chemical entities. Why shouldn't this be possible for other companies? Mind you, what should be the purpose of these genetic implants?

We believe the principal purpose should be to catalyze the corporate culture and to develop a new corporate culture focused on innovation. It is not enough to have elements that can innovate: The whole organization must learn to fish, not be fed fish on occasions. Observing the large pharmaceutical companies encourages and frustrates us at the same time. We are encouraged by the self-realization that the companies are not as innovative as they need to be. We are frustrated because the "quick fix" of buying biotech companies and holding them at arm's length won't help develop a corporationwide innovation culture. Quite the reverse, in fact. Just as the human body fights to reject strange bacteria, so the pharmaceutical companies might find their own people fighting to reject the biotech companies. The reason is simple. Wouldn't most people be threatened by something new that looked like it was becoming the darling of the boss?

What these genetic implants look like we can't say. What we can say is that managers should be encouraged to start thinking about them. We can offer a couple of thoughts. First, there is probably a minimum critical mass for the implant, at least three people in even small organizations. This has been the experience in companies such as Zytec, the Eden Prarie, Minnesota–based manufacturer of power supplies for computers. Bringing in one change agent was not sufficient; two more were necessary before even a sustained effort in changes in quality management practice was possible. Even then, change agent burnout resulted in rapid turnover of agents. The larger the organization, the larger the size of the genetic implant. And it might be more appropriate to implant cells at various locations of the body corporate to increase the visibility and availability of the change agents.

Second, in order to reduce the likelihood of rejection, it might be most appropriate to take current or past employees, and develop them into effective change agents. People with credibility among peers and subordinates may make the best change agents. In any event, converting people with high credibility early in the process is important to the longer-term success of the change effort.

SUBATOMIC PHYSICS

Space isn't empty. It is filled with elemental subatomic particles, called Higg's bosons, that have finite energy and no mass. Only nobody has yet proved the existence of the particles. But they will, for all it takes is the right equipment to do so. The Higg's boson itself doesn't interest us, except that it looks like being a key piece of a grand unifying theory of life, the universe, and everything. What is interesting, though, about the Higg's boson is that it acts to slow down matter that passes around it. The greater the energy of the matter, the more it is slowed down. This sounds very much like new ideas in an organization. The more radical or far-reaching the idea, the more people try to slow it down. This isn't meant to be a glib statement. It is a reflection of the fact that there are basic principles that operate in all systems in the universe, *and businesses are systems that obey basic systems princi-*

ples. Understanding the most basic element in a system is what it will take to understand the system itself. Understanding the individual in the corporation and the individual customer is becoming more vital every day.

We believe that the Enernet (energy network), genetic engineering and the implanting of small bits into large bodies, and the focus on understanding the most fundamental particles in the universe all focus on the small and its impact on the larger system. We further believe that these analogies will help us further develop our theory of the organization in general, and of managing innovation in particular.

CONCLUSION: INNOVATION AS THE LIFE FORCE OF THE ORGANIZATION

WE HOLD THIS truth to be self-evident: that innovation is the life force of a living, adapting organization. It is true of biological systems, and it is true of business systems. Everywhere we look, in all fields of endeavor, we see a focus on the smallest particles. This focus is driving our understanding of the bigger picture and is opening valuable avenues for future endeavor. Focusing on the individual in the marketplace and inside the corporation will pay dividends to innovating companies.

This will be important because we see developments that will further fragment companies and make smaller and smaller subunits practicable. These subunits will be able to be located wherever people want. The only limitations will be the location of markets and the location of resources, and most pieces of a large organization aren't affected by either. The Internet proves that; ask any e-retailer.

We are probably close to another revolution. There are too many inconsistencies with economic theory to think otherwise. When the new theory is widely accepted, the whole nature of costs and social interaction will change—and so will competition and whole industries. When this happens, companies will have to be very nimble and will have to be adept at making—and managing—transitions. The school of fish and basketball analogies presented here will help guide the development of innovative organizations in the age of transition.

Let's play ball!

BIBLIOGRAPHY

Abernathy, William J., Kim B. Clark, and Alan M. Kantrow. *Industrial Renaissance.* New York: Basic Books, 1983.

Adler, Paul S., Avi Mendelbaum, Vien Nguyen, and Elizabeth Schwerer. "Getting the Most out of Your Product Development Process." *Harvard Business Review,* March–April 1996.

Bacon, Frank R., and Thomas W. Butler. *Planned Innovation.* New York: Free Press, 1998.

Barzun, Jacques. *From Dawn to Decadence.* New York: HarperCollins, 2000.

Bean, Roger, and Russell Radford. *Powerful Products: Strategic Management of Successful New Product Development.* New York: AMACOM, 2000.

Bowen, H. Kent, Kim B. Clark, Charles A. Holloway, and Steven C. Wheelwright. *The Perpetual Enterprise Machine.* New York: Oxford University Press, 1994.

Burns, Tom, and G. M. Stalker. *The Management of Innovation.* London: Tavistock Publications, 1963.

Capra, Fritjof. *The Tao of Physics.* Boston: Shambhala Publications, 1999.

Capra, Fritjof. *The Web of Life.* New York: Anchor Books, 1997.

Checkland, Peter, and Jim Scholes. *Soft Systems Methodology in Action.* Chinchester: Wiley, 1992.

Chesborough, Henry W., and David J. Teece. "When Is Virtual Virtuous?" *Harvard Business Review,* January-February 1996.

Dauer, Francis Watanabe. *Critical Thinking.* Cambridge: Cambridge University Press, 1989.

Drucker, Peter. *Innovation and Entrepreneurship.* New York: Harper Business, 1993.

Freeman, Christopher. *The Economics of Industrial Innovation* (2nd ed.). Cambridge, Mass.: MIT Press, 1982.

Girifalco, Louis A. *Dynamics of Technological Change.* New York: Van Nostrand Reinhold, 1991.

Gold, Bela, Gerhard Rosegger, and Myles G. Boylan, Jr. *Evaluating Technological Innovations.* Lexington, Mass.: Lexington Books, 1980.

Goulian, Caroline, and Alexander Mersereau. "Performance Measurement:

Implementing a Corporate Scorecard." *Ivey Business Journal,* September-October 2000.

Gunn, Thomas G. *Manufacturing for Competitive Advantage.* Cambridge, Mass.: Ballinger, 1987.

Hansen, Morten T., Nitin Nohria, and Jeffrey A. Berger. *The State of the Incubator Marketspace.* Boston: Harvard Business School, 2000.

Jaques, Elliott. *Requisite Organization.* Arlington, Va.: Cason Hall, 1989.

Jonash, Ronald S., and Tom Sommerlatte. "The Innovation Premium: Capturing the Value of Creativity." *Prism,* Third Quarter, 1999.

Kanter, Rosabeth Moss, John Kao, and Fred Wiersma. *Innovation.* New York: Harper Business, 1997.

Kaplan, Robert S., and David P. Norton. "Using the Balanced Scorecard as a Strategic Management Tool." *Harvard Business Review,* January–February 1996.

Kelley, Tom, with Jonathan Littman. *The Art of Innovation.* New York: Currency Doubleday, 2001.

Kohn, Alfie. *Punished by Rewards.* New York: Houghton Mifflin, 1993.

Landes, David S. *The Unbound Prometheus.* Cambridge: Cambridge University Press, 1969.

Landes, David S. *The Wealth and Poverty of Nations.* New York: W. W. Norton, 1999.

Leonard-Barton, Dorothy. *Wellsprings of Knowledge: Building and Sustaining the Sources of Innovation.* Boston: Harvard Business School Press, 1995.

MacMillan, Ian C., and Rita Gunther McGrath. "Discovering New Points of Differentiation." *Harvard Business Review,* July–August 1997.

McMahon, Ed. *Bricks to Clicks.* New York: Stoddart Publishing, 2000.

Mensch, Gerhard. *Stalemate in Technology.* Cambridge, Mass.: Ballinger, 1979.

Mintzberg, Henry. *Mintzberg on Management.* New York: Free Press, 1989.

Mintzberg, Henry, and Ludo van der Heyden. "Re-Viewing the Organization." *Ivey Business Journal,* September–October 2000.

Nonaka, Ikujiro, and Hirotaka Takeuchi. *The Knowledge-Creating Company.* Oxford: Oxford University Press, 1995.

Nord, Walter R., and Sharon Tucker. *Implementing Routine and Radical Innovations.* Lexington, Mass.: Lexington Books, 1987.

O'Connor, Joseph, and Ian McDermott. *The Art of Systems Thinking.* London: Thorsons, 1997.

Pine, B. Joseph II. *Mass Customization.* Boston: Harvard Business School Press, 1993.

Quinn, James Brian. *Intelligent Enterprise.* New York: Free Press, 1992.

Quinn, James Brian. "Outsourcing Innovation: The New Engine of Growth." *Sloan Management Review,* Summer 2000.

Robinson, Alan G. *Corporate Creativity.* San Francisco: Barrett-Koehler, 1997.

Rosenbloom, Richard S. *Research on Technological Innovation, Management and Policy.* Greenwich, Conn.: JAI Press, 1983.

Senge, Peter M. *The Fifth Discipline.* New York, Currency Doubleday, 1994.

Simon, Hermann. *Hidden Champions.* Boston: Harvard Business School Press, 1996.

Smith, Shaun. "Experiencing the Brand—Branding the Experience." *FTDynamo Forum,* January 30, 2001.

Stephanou, S. E., and F. Spiegl. *The Manufacturing Challenge.* New York: Van Nostrand Reinhold, 1992.

Storck, John, and Patricia A. Hill. "Knowledge Diffusion through 'Strategic Communities.' " *Sloan Management Review,* Winter 2000.

Suri, Rajan. *Quick Response Manufacturing.* Portland, Ore.: Productivity Press, 1998.

Tushman, Michael L., and William L. Moore. *Readings in the Management of Innovation.* Boston: Pitman Publishing, 1982.

Wheelwright, Steven C., and Kim B. Clark. *Revolutionizing Product Development.* New York: Free Press, 1992.

Williams, Trevor I. *A Short History of Twentieth Century Technology.* Oxford: Clarendon Press, 1982.

Zachary, G. Pascal. "The Law of the Rathole." *Technology Review,* May–June 1999.

INDEX